ADVENTURES
IN THE
WILDERNESS

The Reverend W. H. H. Murray in 1871

EDITOR'S FOREWORD

For five or more millennia of human history man has moved across the face of a wild earth, civilizing it, filling it with his works and his kind, and—on the way—gaining from it both sustenance and pleasure. In July of 1969 man went yet another step further, beyond earth itself, and took "a giant leap for mankind" upon that ultimate wilderness called the moon. A hundred years to the month prior to the moon-walk, a lesser exploration was taking place in northern New York's Adirondack region as hundreds of people milled about in search of accommodations, guides, and boats while trying to avoid as best they could the onslaught of black flies, mosquitoes, and rain which characterized that summer in the north country.

The earlier event was not without its imaginative flavor and implications, but fundamentally it was but another confirmation of the process of physical discovery that had been taking place for thousands of years. Its particular significance within this more or less conventional context, however, was that it represented a fairly original chapter in the story of man's search for a second frontier—an outdoor recreation and vacation frontier. Whatever the fine points, one thing is certain, and that is that a major inspiration for this particular move upon this particular patch of terrestrial geography was the publication in the spring of 1869 of a little book called *Adventures in the Wilderness* by a Boston clergyman named William Henry Harrison Murray. Because what Murray helped to bring about continues to characterize Adirondack life today, and because it is still possible for a person to capture for himself much of that kind of experience which Murray encountered and wrote about, it is only proper that a bit more than a century after the fact the Adirondack Museum brings out his little book again.

5

The republication of *Adventures in the Wilderness* also constitutes a partial fulfillment of obligation to an "artifact" of Adirondack history which, by its very nature, eludes the necessarily finite media of the ordinary museum. By "artifact" we mean not the book itself but rather what that book is largely about—the wilderness and more precisely the Adirondack Wilderness. Museums have to deal with such things as will fit into illuminated glass cases or into galleries, but wilderness, practically by definition, carries with it a romance approaching infinity.

The wilderness, in the Adirondacks at least, lies beyond the Adirondack Museum campus, most of it in the form of constitutionally protected "wild forest lands" of the State Forest Preserve. A living and dynamic example of the American land more or less as it once was, these wild lands in fact demand that anyone who would experience them take the plunge, enter into them, move through them, and live for a time within them on basic terms. To effect such an involvement, then, perhaps even a museum can help by bringing out again a little classic which in its own time brought others into intimate contact with the wilderness.

Even after a hundred years, Murray remains a delightful guide—not simply because there remains, thanks to various measures of conservation and preservation, a wilderness to be experienced, but because Murray was a good writer, because he was generally straightforward and managed to avoid the pitfalls of purple prose, because even his romanticism is offset by genuine humor, and because as an observer he was honest enough to see and appreciate both the pleasant and not-so-pleasant aspects of wilderness experience. There is fiction in Murray to be sure, but there is at the same time a great deal of truth. His book is not all balmy nights and invigorating air and beautiful views and physical delight. There are also storms and bugs and impenetrable tangle and moments of exhaustion. Murray also had a feeling for people, for his guide John Plumley particularly, coupled with the ability to stand back and regard himself with amused tolerance from time to time. The things he wrote about, the present-day camper can still find in the woods if he cares to give it a try, and if he can stand being with himself for the several days needful for a real wilderness trip.

In offering Murray again as our guide to the wilderness, we are fortunate in having Warder Cadbury to lead us through yet other tangles. Murray's own life, his role in the American outdoor recreation movement, and some of the problems of Adirondack wilderness history are among Cadbury's subjects, and certainly no one knows the ups and downs, the ins and outs, of the Murray story and its sources as well as he. In his Introduction the reader should find an invaluable dividend.

A particularly important component of this edition is the complete text of a newspaper article written by Murray about six months after the original publication of his book and following the period of controversy which swirled about him and the Adirondacks that summer of 1869. The "Reply to His Calumniators," hidden from students of Adirondack history far too long already, bears several implications of relevance to Adirondack problems today, and should help dispel a few dubious biographical and historiographical cliches which have arisen in the past century about Murray and the Adirondacks.

There are, we hope, other dividends to be found in this edition of Murray. Besides the book itself, which is reproduced *in toto* from the original—photographically enlarged somewhat in case anyone might wish to read some of the stories aloud by the light of an Adirondack campfire—all the original illustrations are reproduced and even the related advertisements which appeared in the back of the book. In addition, nineteen illustrations have been drawn from the collections of the Adirondack Museum to further enhance the Introduction. Both the Museum and Mr. Cadbury are particularly indebted to a daughter of Murray, Mrs. Ruby M. Orcutt, for providing much in the way of both illustrative and biographical source material.

There are two things which this edition of *Adventures* does not attempt to deal with and very probably would not anyway even if the answers were readily forthcoming. Little attempt has been made to identify or expand upon people mentioned in

Murray's text. It is enough to say that John Plumley was a real man. No attempt whatsoever has been made to identify places such as "The Nameless Creek" or "Phantom Falls." About the latter we would only say, first, *don't* try running Raquette Falls or Buttermilk Falls on the Raquette River in a canoe or anything else thinking one or the other may be Phantom Falls. Murray and John may have made it, but neither you nor I will succeed. Second, if you still insist on knowing if there is any such place as Phantom Falls, you will have to ask Murray himself. *His* answer you will find in *Adventures in the Wilderness*, on page 167.

Blue Mountain Lake, New York
May, 1970

WILLIAM K. VERNER
Curator of Research
The Adirondack Museum

CONTENTS

INTRODUCTION

On or about April Fool's Day, 1869, a little volume concerning the Adirondack region of northern New York first appeared in the bookstores. The book, written by a Boston clergyman named William Henry Harrison Murray and called *Adventures in the Wilderness; or, Camp-Life in the Adirondacks,* almost instantly became both a best-seller and the center of a storm of controversy. In the long run, the book exerted a lasting influence upon outdoor recreation in America, and it left an indelible mark upon the history of the Adirondacks.

Of the initial public reaction to his book, Murray later wrote:

The great, ignorant, stay-at-home, egotistic world laughed and jeered and tried to roar the book down. They called it a fraud and a hoax. The pictorials of the day blazoned their broadsides with caricatures of "Murray and his fools." Innumerable articles were written to the press, and editorials published, denying that there was any such extent of woods in the State, any such number of lakes, any such phenomenal connection of waterways, any such possibilities of pleasure and health as the little book portrayed. . . . But the facts of geography and the truth of nature were in it, and it successfully breasted the current of adverse criticism and hostile comment, of innuendo and jeer, and carried the fame of the [Adirondack] woods over the continent.[1]

"Adirondack" Murray (as posterity came to know him) wrote many other books in the years following the publication of *Adventures in the Wilderness.* They covered everything from the raising of horses, through sentimental fiction, collections of sermons, tales of Texas, the Far West, Canada, and Lake Champlain, to a tract on *How I Am Educating My*

1. W. H. H. Murray, *Lake Champlain and Its Shores* (Boston, 1890), p. 118. Cited hereafter as *Lake Champlain.*

11

Daughters done in his last years, but none of them attained the lasting appeal and exercised the historical influence of this, his first book. For one thing, *Adventures* has simplicity and clarity of expression which have guaranteed the ready accessibility of its subject to over three generations of readers. The subject itself—man and the wilderness—has retained its fascination over the years as well and has proven itself an enduring component of the American cultural heritage. Finally, it appeared at a time when America was undergoing a critical shift from a civilization dominated by agriculture to one characterized by industrialization and urbanization. *Adventures* enunciated views which proved valid to the needs of this new culture. The urban man came not only to enjoy outdoor recreation but to find it increasingly necessary for his well-being. For these reasons, *Adventures in the Wilderness* is something more than the mere antiquarian curiosity it might on first glance appear to be and stands deserving of the tribute of a contemporary of Murray's, the distinguished orator Wendell Phillips, who observed that it has "kindled a thousand camp fires and taught a thousand pens how to write of nature." [2]

Style, substance, and historical importance aside, however, *Adventures in the Wilderness* is an intriguing expression of an uncommon personality. Murray's own strong and special sensitivities, his profoundly democratic inclinations, and his desire and capacity to translate personal enthusiasms into what has virtually become public property are engaging characteristics of the book. These are not easily ignored even a hundred and one years after the fact, and they suggest that only by understanding something of the man can the book itself be fully comprehended.

2. Quoted in Murray, "Reminiscences of My Literary and Outdoor Life," *The Independent* (New York), LVII (1904), p. 278. Cited hereafter as "Reminiscences."

"FULL OF LIFE AND HORSE"

Growing up as a farm boy, Murray was proud of his humble beginnings. "There has never been a rich rascal in our family," he once said, "nor did I come of literary stock. No college-bred dunce had ever handicapped us with his incapable respectability." [3]

He was born at Guilford, Connecticut on April 26, 1840. His ancestors were among the first settlers of the town two hundred years before, and Murray nurtured a great affection for the old family homestead. His father was a man of great physical energy, a skilled carpenter in the shipbuilding yards of Long Island Sound, a good storyteller but improvident. Murray's mother, a former school-teacher, was of a bookish turn and something of a mystic. The son's character turned out to be a composite of these often conflicting traits in the parents.

A love of nature and an aptitude for the rifle and rod came naturally to Murray as he roamed the woods and meadows around the farm. He was also both prankish and studious. It is

3. Quoted in unidentified newspaper clipping in Murray papers, Adirondack Museum MS 69–13; cited hereafter as MS 69–13. Biographical data on Murray in this section is drawn freely from such standard sources as: Harry V. Radford, *Adirondack Murray: A Biographical Appreciation* (New York, 1905); Alfred Lee Donaldson, *A History of the Adirondacks* (2 vols.: New York, 1921), I, pp. 190–201; and William Chapman White, *Adirondack Country* (New York, 1954), pp. 112–20. Additional biographical material is scattered throughout Murray's own writings, including the paper which he edited, *The Golden Rule*, and most of these are cited elsewhere in this introduction. Other sources include: William B. Murray, *Descendents of Jonathan Murray of East Guilford, Connecticut* (Peoria, Ill., n.d.); Francis Atwater, *Memoirs of Francis Atwater* (Meriden, Conn., 1922), pp. 53–54; and "The Murray Memorial," *Good Will Record* (Hinckley, Me.), XXXIII (October, 1920), p. 10. Newspaper pieces on Murray, copies of which are in MS 69–13, include: *Warren Herald* (Massachusetts), February 4, 1898; *Shore Line Times* (Guilford, Conn.), March 3 and 10, 1904, February 19 and October 29, 1931, and November 24, 1932; *Springfield Republican* (Massachusetts), March 4, 1904; and the *New Haven Register*, June 26, 1904. Mrs. Ruby M. Orcutt and Mrs. Maud M. Young, daughters of W. H. H. Murray, have provided valuable help.

not surprising that he once enlivened things at the small district school by putting a small charge of gunpowder in the pot-bellied stove. It was unusual for such a lad to develop a taste for Latin and literature, to become a voracious reader, and to dream of going to college. What seems to have fired his ambition was some slight impediment in his speech and a sensitivity to ridicule. "I had taken hold of the hope of Knowledge with a good grip," he once said, "and I held on. I had no help, no encouragement. My father opposed me in my efforts, and my mother said nothing. But I persevered." [4]

To better prepare himself for a professional career—perhaps in law—he transferred to the newly established private Institute in the village of Guilford. To pay his tuition, he worked on neighbors' farms, where his great strength and energy enabled him to accomplish more in a day than could most men. He was not discouraged by having to walk four miles each way morning and night, carrying his shoes under his arm to economize. His new classmates found him full of enthusiasm, handsome, and a natural leader. Together they organized a debating society, so successfully in fact that the rival adult organization was forced to disband for lack of audiences. Murray found he could conquer his stammer, and he gained further self-confidence from the knowledge that he was the most popular boy in his class, captain of the football team, and organizer of excursions into the woods to hunt squirrels.

In 1858 Murray entered Yale College with $4.68 in his pocket and two small carpetbags in hand. One of them held his few books, and the other contained clothes made by his mother and sisters. On his arrival in New Haven he found himself a member of the largest freshman class in the history of the college, and he promptly planned the abolition of the custom of hazing at the hands of the sophomores—who were now considerably outnumbered. President Woolsey approved of Murray's goal, although he very probably did not know the details of his plan, and the freshmen proceeded to arm themselves with pistols loaded with blanks and establish themselves

4. Unidentified newspaper clipping, MS 69–13.

behind barricaded doors. When the enemy attacked, Murray's forces managed to either drive or frighten them away, with no one being seriously hurt. The following year, when it became their turn to haze the incoming class, Murray again called a special meeting of his fellows and in an impassioned speech persuaded his classmates not to persecute the new students. He recommended to the faculty immediate expulsion for any individual attempting such a thing. Here was a young man with little respect for traditions that had outlived whatever usefulness they may have once enjoyed.

Murray's graduation from Yale in 1862 was followed by his marriage to Isadora Hull of East River, Connecticut. She shared her husband's love of the outdoor life, and she helped him through his studies at East Windsor Theological Seminary and through a brief stint as a pastor's assistant in New York City by teaching school. This short period of apprenticeship completed, the young couple settled into the parsonage of the little Congregational Church at Washington, Connecticut, early in 1864, and here Murray had an experience that was portentous of things to come later in his career.

One afternoon, while out gunning in the hills surrounding the village, he became so engrossed in the pursuit of game that he lost track of time and forgot that he had a service scheduled for that evening. When he did remember it he rushed back to town, skipped supper, and went straight into church, hanging his bag of game over the back of a convenient chair. He leaned his gun against the wall and mounted the pulpit still dressed in his shooting jacket and his velveteen hunting breeches. At the close of his sermon he apologized for having been late and for keeping his congregation waiting, explaining what had delayed him. His parishioners were not amused, however. Field sports were still looked upon in that New England community as an improper recreation for a respectable person, especially for a minister.

Murray's first pastorate revealed his talents for leadership— he revitalized a decaying church, increased its membership, and raised its intellectual and spiritual aspirations—but it ended in less than a year. In his farewell sermon, spoken with

Murray with his famous Lewis of Troy double
muzzle-loading rifle, "Never Fail."

"a calmness and reservation which some older than I would do well to imitate," Murray darkly referred to "a local disturbance," and to "certain coarse and indelicate reports upon which a few minds, craving for such garbage, have been accustomed to fatten." [5]

Whatever the local disturbance and the indelicate reports may have been—and they are a closed book to us today—there is little doubt but that many of Murray's listeners knew exactly what he was referring to. He accepted an attractive invitation from a church in Greenwich, leaving behind him a divided congregation, part of it still loyal and affectionate but part of it glad to see him go.

The following two years of the mid-1860's were apparently less troublesome. He delivered a eulogy on the assassinated President Lincoln which his friends found so moving and eloquent they had it printed,[6] and, perhaps thinking of his father's difficulties, he threw himself into a strong public defense of temperance. When the proprietors of a new steamboat line which ran between Greenwich and New York attempted to justify the installation of a bar by noting that it was located "out of sight, way down below," Murray retorted publicly that this was "the exact location of hell." [7]

In the fall of 1866, Murray left Greenwich to accept a call to Meriden, Connecticut. The move was engineered by a young lawyer in Meriden named Orville H. Platt, who had been born in nearby Washington. Platt, who later served for twenty-six years as U.S. Senator from Connecticut, shared with Murray a love for the outdoor life, and it may well have been he who introduced Murray not only to Meriden but to the Adirondacks. Whatever the details, it was about this time that Murray began his regular summer vacations in the Adirondacks, and it

5. Murray, *Sermon Preached at Washington, Connecticut, November 20, 1864* (New York, 1865), p. 18.

6. Murray, *Address Delivered on the Sabbath Following the Assassination of President Lincoln, in the Second Congregational Church, Greenwich, Conn.* (New York, 1865).

7. Quoted in the *New York Sun*, November 25, 1917. Murray's concern about temperance is developed in his *Prohibition vs. License: A Review of Ex-Gov. Andrew's Argument for License* (New York, 1867).

was not long before Murray's own accounts of these excursions began to appear in a local Meriden newspaper. When these stories became *Adventures in the Wilderness,* Murray gratefully dedicated the book to Platt.[8]

Murray did well in Meriden. He and his wife found themselves settled in a comfortable parsonage, with a salary of $3,000 a year and the knowledge that they were now in a larger and more sophisticated town. To be sure, some of his more strait-laced parishioners were disturbed to read both his sermons and his fishing stories in the same weekly newspaper, and more than one eyebrow was raised when Murray bought a fast-stepping horse and in sleighing time raced up and down the main street. But before such vices could arouse any substantial opposition, his virtues had earned him wide attention in New England. In the fall of 1868, Murray found himself invited to yet another church, this time the historic and prestigious pulpit of Park Street Church in Boston.

With its beautiful spire that still dominates the Common in the heart of the city at what was known as "Brimstone Corner," Park Street Church was the undisputed leader of evangelical Congregationalism in New England. William Lloyd Garrison made his first public address against slavery at the church, and the patriotic hymn, *America,* was first sung there.[9] In taking up his new assignment, Murray was accepting a distinct honor for a man not yet thirty, and he responded to the challenge with his characteristic and uncommon energy. He managed at the same time to find opportunity for extraclerical pursuits, and, within six months of his arrival in Boston, *Adventures in the Wilderness* was published. To the professional honor which had been accorded him in his being invited to Park Street Church, Murray could now lay claim to a certain extraprofessional notoriety.

Though his deacons at Park Street fretted privately over the

8. For more on Platt, see Louis A. Coolidge, *An Old-Fashioned Senator: Orville H. Platt of Connecticut* (New York, 1910).

9. A history of Park Street Church is H. Crosby Englizian, *Brimstone Corner* (Chicago, 1968). The pastorate of Murray, "The Great Innovator," is covered on pp. 164–77.

sensation his first book created, they could only have been pleased when four volumes of sermons soon followed.[10] However questionable his secular interests, the fact remained that Murray was a preacher of extraordinary ability and power, with the unfailing merit of being understood by all classes of hearers and readers. In the fall of 1871, a popular weekly magazine gave this account of the man and his manner:

From a point of dangerous weakness in numbers and spiritual force, his church has been lifted to a level of universal observation. For a stranger not to go Sunday morning to Park-street Church to hear its preacher . . . is to have missed one of Boston's "institutions." . . . Mr. Murray's influence, in its reach, its vitality, and its edifying power is beyond calculation.

There is always a desire to "account" for such a man, as Carlyle has said. . . . [Murray's own explanation was that it was simply due to] "The exceeding courtesy of Boston, and my ability to do hard work." That he works hard all can believe when they see the amount and quality of the workmanship he turns out, but *how* hard he works none but his most intimate friends know. . . .

A visitor at the Adirondacks this summer happened, of course, like every one else, to be talking about "Mr. Murray." And one of the party asked a strapping young guide if "Mr. Murray was lazy." "Lazy!" he exclaimed as he rested on his oars for a moment. "I wish the man who thinks so could help Murray pack in logs for his camp-fire some night, or pull a boat beside him for fifteen miles up the Racquette current, and keep his stroke, as I have done. He is about the only man I ever guided in these woods that I wished *was* lazy!"

. . . He once playfully remarked to some friends, that he knew but three things: Old School Theology, Adirondacks, and the Horse. It must be admitted that he knows these well.[11]

As for the horse—with a good salary, the fees from a series of popular lectures on the Adirondacks, and royalties on the continuing sales of his books—Murray was becoming wealthy

10. Murray, *Music Hall Sermons* (Boston, 1870); *Park Street Pulpit: Sermons* [First Series] (Boston, 1871); Second Series (Boston, 1872); and *Words Fitly Spoken* (Boston, 1872). The volume published in 1871 will be cited hereafter as *Sermons* (1871).

11. "Rev. W. H. H. Murray," *Every Saturday*, II (1871), p. 521. The form *Racquette*, now usually *Raquette*, was common in the nineteenth century.

enough to practice the dictum of another Boston clergyman, Theodore Parker, that the outside of a horse is good for the inside of a man. In 1870, Murray purchased the old family homestead at Guilford, and two years later he bought two adjoining farms. Here he began to develop what became one of the largest and best stock farms in New England, devoted to the improved breeding of horses. Over the next few years he invested much of his time and energy and over fifty thousand dollars in this hobby.

In the fall of 1873 he published a large book, *The Perfect Horse*, which he dedicated to President Grant. To ward off criticism from any who might feel "surprise that one in my profession should devote his leisure to such a purpose," [12] Murray prudently solicited an introduction to his book from Henry Ward Beecher, the only clergyman in the country whose fame and stature then exceeded his own. Beecher came to Murray's aid by writing that "many men think horse-culture a theme unbecoming a moral teacher. Not long ago, many people thought that good folks ought not to own good horses; that a fast horse was a sign of a fast man . . . , while the righteous were doomed to amble through life on dull, fat family-horses, fit only for a plough or a funeral." What, then, could be more proper than for a clergyman to offer advice and information in a field "which has too long already been left to men who look upon the horse as an instrument chiefly of gambling gains, or of mere physical pleasure." [13]

Murray's passion for horses combined with the pressures of his pastoral duties brought him into closer contact with his old friends of college days, the Cook family of Ticonderoga, New York. William Cook, the father, raised thoroughbreds on his farm near Lake Champlain. Joseph Cook, his son, had been a classmate of Murray's at Yale. He had been recommended by Murray to fill the pulpit at Meriden as his replacement in 1868, but Joseph turned the job down, being unwilling to leave the cosmopolitan culture of Boston, where he had settled. On occasion, he was a guest preacher at Park Street

12. Murray, *The Perfect Horse* (Boston, 1873), p. vi.
13. *Ibid.*, pp. ix–xi.

Church at Murray's invitation. Many years later, after this very slow start, Joseph Cook eventually achieved worldwide fame as a brilliant platform lecturer. Some of these connections between father, son, and Murray are revealed in correspondence between William and Joseph Cook in the early 1870's. For instance, a week before Christmas, 1873, Joseph reported to his father:

I have seen Mr. Murray, took dinner with him at the Parker House by his invitation, & afterwards conversed with him three hours in his study. My impressions are that his heart is sound; & that, in spite of a constant whizzing of criticisms & attacks from cultured sources in Boston, his general hold upon the middle class of culture here has strengthened in the last two years.[14]

The following spring, the elderly William Cook wrote to his son with casual indifference to the niceties of spelling:

On Monday . . . Rev. Mr. Murry and othher gentleman from Boston were here with Mr. Harris, to look over the Horses. . . . I Sold Murry the colt that was in the team that carried you to the Lake for $400. He took him away with him. Is to Send check on reaching Boston. Murries wifes Sister was with him here. Murry says that he is going to get you to run his church for Six months So that he can get a little rest. He Seems full of life and Horse. Look well to your own interest for the future. Be careful what baits you bight at.[15]

By that same spring of 1874, long-simmering tensions between Murray and the more conservative elements of his Park Street congregation were approaching a showdown. The conflict, however, was not about theological matters or even the propriety of the pastor's extracurricular activities. Murray was not an iconoclast by temperament, and did not advocate any basic departure from the old faith. The real controversy concerned the proper role of a large metropolitan church. For five years Murray had been urging a wider ministry to the poor and an active and humanitarian program to meet the needs of

14. Frederick G. Bascom, ed., *Letters of a Ticonderoga Farmer: Selections from the Correspondence of William H. Cook and His Wife and Their Son, 1851–1885* (Ithaca, N.Y., 1946), p. 100. Cited hereafter as Cook, *Letters.*
15. *Ibid.*, p. 101.

a changing urban society. This plea for a more relevant church program was greeted by the more aristocratic and sedate elements with stiffening resistance. And when Murray suggested that such reforms as he had in mind would require the assistance of a ministerial colleague, this too fell on some deaf ears. To be sure, Murray had other motives for wanting an associate who could take care of some administrative details and pastoral duties. He was discovering a growing dislike for the limitations the ministry imposed upon his personal freedom, and he had a growing desire to become more active in the horse business, even proposing a partnership with the older Cook. Furthermore, he was bone tired.

When it became clear that private negotiations with church officials would get him nowhere, Murray decided to take his case directly to the congregation. To them, and to the general public, he announced on March 8, 1874, a long list of proposals, concluding with his wish for an assistant to help him. He even offered to surrender his own annual salary until the treasury could afford two pastors. On March 26, Joseph Cook reported to his father:

After the newspaper gale produced by the criticisms made on Murray in his church, I saw him & Deacon Farnsworth separately. Murray was evidently annoyed, but in good spirits; and the Deacon said that he had received any number of letters endorsing his remarks as printed in the newspapers. There are two parties in the church & Murray thinks his side is much the stronger. I hope the difficulties will be settled; but I should not be surprised if Park St. had another pastor in the course of two or three years. Probably Murray has been careless; he has visited little; his farm and his lectures take time his people ought to have; but his sermons everyone seems to consider excellent. . . .

He knows very well that I think he makes too much of horses. Heaven to me will be perfect, even if it does not contain a racecourse.[16]

At a special church meeting in April a majority voted in favor of Murray's proposals, and a committee was appointed to

16. *Ibid.*, p. 103. Murray's notion of forming a partnership with William Cook is mentioned on p. 102.

find an associate minister. But a minority report strongly suggested that if less time were spent in other activities, Murray could adequately fulfill his functions as both preacher and pastor without overtaxing his strength. This strong hint was ignored, however, for in June William Cook reported from Ticonderoga to his son of another horse-buying visit from Murray and a friend:

I studied them close and the most remarcable thing that I found out was that they Seemed determined to Smoke all the tobacco that they could Smoke out of cob pipes which was constantly in their hand or mouth. If God be God, Serve him. If Baal, Serve him. No emalgrimation of the two. I fear that Murray is growing quite as fast in the Horse Spirit as in the Spirit of Christ.[17]

With his horse-trading done, Murray went on to his old campground at Raquette Lake for what turned out to be his last vacation there. On his return to Boston in the fall of 1874, it was evident that matters with his congregation had not improved over the summer months. The promise of pastoral assistance had not materialized, and Murray resigned.

In his farewell sermon, preached in November, Murray emphasized the superiority of practical Christianity over theorizing theology as he had often done in the past. For the next few months Murray supported himself with his public lectures and, no doubt, with some more horse-trading. The summer of 1875 found him exploring new ground in the Adirondacks, camping with a large group of friends at Cranberry Lake in the region's northwest.[18]

Murray's absence from the pulpit lasted less than a year. In the fall of 1875 he organized his own New England Church as an independent Congregational assembly. Many of his supporters at Park Street defected to join him in this new venture, which quickly prospered. The main attraction was still his ever-popular preaching, but there was also an excellent choir

17. *Ibid.*, p. 106.
18. The 1875 vacation is discussed by an author signing himself "Now and Then" in "A Trip to Cranberry Lake," *Forest and Stream*, VI (1876), p. 50. See also, letter to the editor by W. J. Griffen, Sr., in *North Country Life*, XII (Summer, 1958), p. 52.

as well as frequent social and literary meetings where Murray often gave readings from his Adirondack stories. At the same time, Murray established his own weekly newspaper which he called *The Golden Rule* and which printed not only his sermons but agricultural and domestic columns as well. When Murray returned to the Adirondacks in the summer of 1876, again in the northern part of the region, he kept his subscribers amused with still more tales of life in the woods.[19]

Murray's new excursion into journalism provided yet another outlet for his energies. Challenged by a discussion he had with Ralph Waldo Emerson during an author's luncheon hosted by their mutual publisher, James T. Fields, Murray decided to try his hand at all-male fiction. Emerson held that a really good story must make the reader both laugh and cry, and this implied a heroine as a necessary part of the formula. Murray thought otherwise, and to test his position—and with the encouragement of Fields—he created the figure of old John Norton, the trapper, "a personage unique in his quaint, droll humor, simplicity of character, and the attributes of a grand manhood developed amid the solitudes of nature." [20] Two John Norton stories then appeared serially in *The Golden Rule* during the fall and winter of 1876–77, and enthusiastic reader response both increased the paper's circulation and prompted Murray to have the tales published in book form in 1877.[21]

Both the success and the style of the John Norton stories were unfortunate, from posterity's point of view. Their popu-

19. Murray's *The Golden Rule* commenced publication on October 6, 1875, but Murray sold out his interest in June, 1879. The following "Letters from Mr. Murray" appeared between July 12 and September 6, 1876: "Trouting in the Adirondacks," "Adirondack Outfit," "Adirondack Letter No. 2," "Crossing a Carry in the Dark," "Climbing Whiteface," and "Adirondack Letter No. 5." A related piece, "Camping Out," appeared on June 27, 1877.

20. *The Golden Rule* (November 4, 1876), p. 8. Murray's exposition of his personal literary philosophy and the story about Emerson appear in the introduction to his *Mamelons and Ungava* (Boston, 1890), pp. v–xx.

21. Murray, *Adirondack Tales* (Boston, 1877); this book also contains some of the 1876 articles about the Adirondacks cited in note 19. "The Story the Keg Told Me" originally appeared serially in *The Golden Rule* between September 27 and November 8, 1876, "The Man Who Didn't Know Much" between November 15, 1876 and May 23, 1877.

Artist's conception of John Norton, hero of *Adirondack Tales*.

larity encouraged Murray to abandon earlier plans to do a series on such Adirondack subjects as "The Legend of Follans-
bee's Pond," "The Hermit of Long Lake," and "The Legends of
Cold River." [22] Instead, in concentrating upon portraying an
innocent in the Garden before the Fall, Murray mired himself
in a kind of nostalgia and sentimentality already overworked
by Cooper, Emerson, and Whitman. Where John Norton
strains our credibility and cloys our taste today, the unwritten
series on Adirondack history and folklore would probably still
be of interest.

Meanwhile, the entire summer of 1877 was spent at his farm
in Guilford living in the house where he was born. In all, Murray now owned three houses, nine barns, nearly a dozen dogs,
and some sixty horses. One horse, a stallion which once attracted an offer of $20,000, he called "Adirondacks." The farm
itself, equipped with all the latest machinery to enhance its ef-
ficiency, was run solely to feed the horses bred and breeding
upon it, while Murray meanwhile busied himself at his literary
pursuits. Composing as he dictated slowly to a secretary
perched before a typewriter, Murray spun out further tales of
John Norton. These duly appeared in *The Golden Rule* the following winter.[23]

In May of 1878 it was announced that Murray had been
granted a year's leave of absence from his New England
Church. He would continue to send stories to his paper and
raise funds for the church, but, after a brief sojourn in the Adirondacks and a lengthier vacation trip to Canada, he seems to
have been busiest with horse matters. He became interested in
improving the design of carriages and in devising a more comfortable, durable, and economical wagon. Purchasing certain
patent rights, he began to borrow capital to manufacture and
sell what was advertised as "The Murray Buckboard." [24] By

22. *The Golden Rule* (September 6, 1876), p. 4.
23. See *The Golden Rule* between November 28, 1877 and June 5, 1878.
These stories were subsequently included in Murray's collected works, again
called *Adirondack Tales* (5 vols.: Springfield, Mass., 1897–98).
24. See "Verbatim Report of Mr. Murray's Explanation of the Boston Buckboard, often called the 'Murray Wagon,' before a company of Gentlemen appointed to enquire into its merits," *The Boston Buckboard Company's Cata-*

October, *The Golden Rule* noted that in just three weeks some 292 orders had been received. It seemed that Murray's powers with both investors and potential customers was about to pay off, and it was being said that he could make a stone squirt lemonade. In fact, however, Murray was spreading his assets and energies too thinly. Difficulties started to descend upon the business and, to compound his troubles, just before Thanksgiving that year Murray seriously injured a hand in a duck-hunting accident.

The "Murray Wagon," Heavy Gem, with Top. From the catalog of the Boston Buckboard Company, published in Chicago about 1879.

The bubble broke completely in the late summer of 1879. The astonished citizens of Boston read in their papers a letter to the general public from Murray, announcing his retirement from the ministry and his departure from the city. "Leaving my property wholly to my creditors," he said, "and with my health seriously threatened, I turn from a manner of life I have ever disliked. . . . A life in which I can have no peace, no friends, no quiet; in which I can show no courtesies and do no

logue (Chicago, [c. 1879]), pp. 1–6. The Adirondack Museum has a copy of this pamphlet.

charities unless at the risk of being vilely lied about and slandered is one I refuse longer to live." [25]

To some, Murray's action no doubt seemed an act of cowardice or dishonor, but the reasons that compelled this dramatic disappearance from public life have all the ingredients of tragedy. Through no intentional fault of his own, the buckboard business had faltered. With no cash on hand to meet loans coming due, Murray could not face supervising the sale of his beloved farm at Guilford to satisfy his creditors; that, he said to his loyal friends, would be like attending his own funeral. Worst of all, his marriage was breaking up. A clean break with the past was the least painful alternative.

The reasons for the dissolution of Murray's marriage are lost to us today. Mrs. Murray went her own way—to medical school in New York, and then to Vienna where she earned a diploma in the practice of surgery, the first such ever granted in Europe to an American woman. In 1886, the formalities of the divorce were completed.

For Murray himself, these same years were a time of travel, of working with his hands, and a search for privacy to recoup his shattered spirit. His activities during this period are obscure, but the few we know of are characteristically varied. In 1882, the *Boston Herald* reported:

He left the city upon a legitimate and honorable business mission, and, failing in this, through no fault of his own, he declined to return for reasons which, however absurd and unsatisfactory, were at least frankly stated in his famous letter to the public. In his own time and way Mr. Murray came back, and delivered three public addresses with all his old-time eloquence and power. Since that time he has resided in Texas as openly and independently as he ever lived here, and has sent to the *Herald* over his own name, a series of the most valuable and interesting letters ever written from

25. Reprinted in the *New-York Daily Tribune*, September 5, 1879. The full text of Murray's announcement has thus far only been found in an undated clipping, probably from an Albany, N.Y., paper, in a Verplanck Colvin scrapbook at the Adirondack Museum, MS 70–5. A sympathetic editorial on Murray's difficulties was reprinted in the *Boston Herald*, September 17, 1879, from *The Golden Rule*.

that state. . . . It is not to the credit of our human nature that so many people are ready to hit a man when they think he is down.[26]

A visitor to Texas encountered Murray at his ranch in this period and reported:

The proprietor . . . came out dressed in baggy, brown pantaloons, bed-ticking suspenders, and a Yankee chip [hat] that turned up behind like Joshua Whitcomb's. He was a very handsome man— tall, muscular, with a manly brow; features fit for a model, and a rich, full voice, which spoke pure English. I thought at once, "What a handsome man! How did you come down here on a ranch?" "My two men are sick, and I'm working like a slave my- self," he said. "Yesterday I dug out that irrigation ditch, and I've drawn . . . manure this spring myself, and spread it on the land, too." [27]

While in Texas, Murray extended his business into lumber- ing, and again he failed. Following this, he managed to travel a good deal, nevertheless, and he saw most of the states of the Union and even visited England and the Continent. Eventu- ally he settled in Montreal, and in a dark and narrow side street operated a little restaurant which specialized in oysters. A visitor thus described the scene:

Standing behind the counter in this place and quietly and unobtru- sively serving its customers, was a large man with a mane of iron- gray hair and a drooping iron-gray moustache. His massive frame denoted great physical strength but carried also the suggestion of waning vitality—a weariness that appeared also in his voice, which was like the soft deep tones of an organ floating out at dusk from the shadowy depths of an old cathedral. . . . Above the en- trance door, there was a sign bearing in faded yellow letters visible against a dingy black background the brief inscription, "Murray's." [28]

26. Clipping from the *Boston Herald*, dated only May, 1882, in MS 69–13. The letters from Texas have not been located, but Murray's *The Busted Ex- Texan* (Boston, 1889) is based on his experiences during this period.

27. Torn and unidentified clipping, dated in pencil June, 1881, pasted onto a page in a copy of *The Perfect Horse* at the Adirondack Museum.

28. Alfred C. Tate, *Edison's Open Door* (New York, 1938), pp. 102–103.

Canada was good to Murray, nonetheless. He explored the wild country around the Saguenay River, studied Indian lore, and continued writing. He even made a guest appearance with Buffalo Bill's Wild West Show in Montreal, and this may have set him to thinking about resuming his own career as a public entertainer and speaker.[29]

In September, 1886, Murray married Frances Rivers of Montreal, and the couple moved down across the border and settled at Burlington, Vermont, for a time. Here Murray became active in a newly founded yacht club, and he did a book on the history and attractions of the Lake Champlain valley.[30] He began to lecture again on a variety of topics, but most often he read from his Adirondack stories. The tale "How John Norton the Trapper Kept His Christmas" entertained more than five hundred audiences, earning him from $100 to $500 an evening plus the proceeds of the sale of paperback copies of the story which were sold at the door.[31] And then, about 1890, a friend from Guilford contacted Murray and informed him that the old homestead was up for sale. Murray jumped at the chance, bought the property, and moved back with his wife to the house where he was born.

In quiet and contentment, he spent the remaining years of his life in writing, in republishing his earlier works, and in edu-

29. In Canada during this period, Murray was photographed with Sitting Bull, and when the Indian leader was murdered by American troops some years later Murray wrote a vigorous condemnation of the action which appeared in the *New York World* under a December 20, 1890, dateline. See also: Elmo Scott Watson, "The Photographs of Sitting Bull," *The Westerner's Brand Book*, VI (1949), p. 48 and Louis Pfaller, " 'Enemies in '76, Friends in '85'—Sitting Bull and Buffalo Bill," *Prologue*, I (1969), pp. 17–31. Books by Murray from this period include: *The Doom of Mamelons, with a Description of the Lake St. John and Saguenay Region* (Quebec, 1888); *The Doom of Mamelons* (Philadelphia, 1888); *Daylight Land* (Boston, 1888); and *Mamelons and Ungava* (Boston, 1889).

30. *Lake Champlain*. See also J. Armory Knox, *A Devil of a Trip, or the Log of the Yacht* Champlain (New York, 1888).

31. "How John Norton Kept His Christmas" originally appeared in a special Christmas supplement to *Harper's Weekly*, XXVII (1883), pp. 825–32, with illustrations by A. B. Frost including the magazine's cover, p. 809. A paperback edition of the tale was issued by the Murray Lyceum Bureau in 1885.

ADIRONDACK MURRAY

OPERA HOUSE,
PALMER, MASS.,

Friday Evening, Nov. 5th, 1897

Mr. W. H. H. Murray will read that sweet story of

The Dear Old Trapper, John Norton, and How He Kept His Christmas.

Professional elocutionists, literary critics, and the people, are in full agreement touching the "sweetness and light" of this little tale of wood life and the woods, and the lovableness of him whom so many call

"Dear Old John Norton."

This story has been read FIVE HUNDRED AND THIRTY-FIVE TIMES IN NEW ENGLAND ALONE.

No bit of writing has ever been received by Lyceum audiences with greater favor.

If you have heard it I known you will hear it again. If you have not heard it come and hear from Mr. Murray's own lips this, his masterpiece.

TICKETS, 50 AND 35 CENTS.
ON SALE AT ALLEN'S DRUG STORE.
SECURE YOUR SEATS EARLY.

Mail orders to C. E. Fish and Telephone orders to the Palmer Journal office will receive prompt attention.

C. B. Fiske & Co., Printers, Palmer.

cating his four little girls.[32] Murray died on March 3, 1904, a month before his sixty-fifth birthday, and was buried under a great buttonwood tree which still stands in the side yard at the homestead.

THE BOOK THAT LAUNCHED A THOUSAND GUIDE-BOATS [33]

The variety and vitality that characterized Murray's life as a whole are reflected in his adventures in the Adirondacks and in his book about them. The date of his first visit to the region is not clear; the book suggests 1864. What is clear are the names of Murray, Orville Platt, and their wives under the date of September 3, 1866, in the register of the old Raquette Lake House.[34]

On the way into the woods that year, Murray and his party passed through the village of Long Lake. There they engaged John Plumley (or *Plumbley*, as Murray spelled it) and pushed on to Raquette Lake. On Constable Point—now Antler's Point —they found a sandy beach, a clear spring, and, probably, an empty and inviting shanty.

The shanty may have been the one occupied in earlier summers by the celebrated artist Arthur Fitzwilliam Tait and his

32. In addition to the collected works cited in note 23, Murray wrote during this period *The Old Apple Tree's Easter* (Hartford, 1900) and *How I Am Educating My Daughters* (Guilford, 1902).

33. This is a paraphrase of a title, itself a paraphrase of a well known line, used over an excerpt by Murray in Paul Jamieson, ed., *The Adirondack Reader* (New York, 1964).

34. Typescript, "Names from Old Raquette Lake Register," Snyder Papers, Adirondack Museum MS 65–26, Box 8, Folder 4; the register covers the period from August 4, 1857 through September 14, 1873. The complicated question of Murray's early Adirondack trips can be explored in this and in the following sources: Donaldson, I, *op. cit.*, pp. 193 and 199; Radford, *op. cit.*, p. 69; Charles A. Wardner, "Footsteps on Adirondack Trails," Chapter 15, p. 2, and "Sunset on Adirondack Trails," p. 113 (both of these have been copied onto Adirondack Museum microfilm 4.31); and in testimony by Murray taken down at his home on January 15, 1904, and included in State of New York, Supreme Court, Appellate Division, Third Department, *The People of the State of New York, Plaintiff-Respondent, Against Jennie II. Ladew and Joseph L. Ladew, Defendents-Appellants* (Walton, N.Y., 1920), pp. 456–64.

A Good Time Coming. Oil painting, dated 1862, by Arthur Fitzwilliam Tait, in the Adirondack Museum collection.

friends. In 1862, Tait had done a painting of a group of sportsmen at Constable Point which was published subsequently by
Currier & Ives as a large lithograph entitled "Camping in the
Woods—'A Good Time Coming.'" It may be that Murray and
his party settled themselves into this very shanty, for that same
summer of 1866 one of Tait's friends wrote a letter which said
that he "found such a mob of people (men, women & boys) on
Raquette, that I do [did] not go to Constable Point, and indeed did not get into the south part of the lake at all, or even
up East Inlet. One day (last Sunday) there were eighteen persons on Constable Point, and a minister among them per-
formed church. Think of this and shudder." [35]

For the next eight summers, Murray and his friends were
regular campers at Raquette Lake, but probably in 1869—
perhaps to escape the crowds generated by the publication of
Adventures as much as to avoid the insects—they set up camp
on Osprey Island. Here at "Terrace Lodge," as they called it,
they enjoyed themselves and several people who dropped in
on them have left accounts of what they saw.

Charles Hallock, the sportswriter, was especially struck by
Murray's "comely wife . . . attired in a Tam O'Shanter cap
and a mountain suit of red and crimson plaid. How jaunty she
looked! . . . They kept open house in those days, with the
latch string out, and a halo of welcome was luminous about
the rustic roof." [36]

Another writer, H. Perry Smith, described Murray's camp as
built upon "an abrupt bluff on the water side, surmounted by
a green plateau on which was [sic] pitched his tents. These
numbered, that season, six or eight, and as they stood basking
in the sun, backed by the thick foliage of the woodland, and
surrounded by the gay party, their appearance was picturesque in the extreme. Add to this a crooked path down to the
lake, a dozen boats of as many colors, guides in and about
them dressed in colored shirts, and it made up a scene from

35. Letter from Josiah Blackwell Blossom to James Blackwell Blossom, August 8, 1866, in A. F. Tait Papers, Adirondack Museum MS 65–29.

36. Charles Hallock, "Adirondack Memories," *Forest and Stream*, XXXVII
(1891), p. 103.

fairy land." [37] Murray himself he found "a very courteous and sociable gentleman, and perfectly aglow with enthusiasm over the wilderness and its attendant sports." Murray's wife, "the Lady of the Lake," he found no less charming.

For a while, Osprey Island came to be known as "Murray's Island," but the name did not stick. By 1894 one writer bemoaned the lack of a place anywhere in the Adirondacks which "commemorates the name of him who opened the eyes of the world to this Grand Sanitarium and Pleasure Ground!" [38]

Raquette Lake and Murray's Island. Wood engraving after an unknown artist by M. Bradley Co., published in *The Modern Babes in the Wood* in 1872.

When in camp, the Murrays often had guests, as many as thirty-five one season in later years. They enjoyed entertaining, and the feeling was reciprocated. Two of the stories in *Adventures in the Wilderness*, the "Ride with a Mad Horse in

37. H. Perry Smith, *The Modern Babes in the Wood or Summerings in the Wilderness* (Hartford, 1872), p. 104.
38. Edwin R. Wallace, *Descriptive Guide to the Adirondacks* (Syracuse, 1894), p. 430n.

a Freight Car" and "The Ball," convey this sense of conviviality. Of the latter story, Charles Dickens told Murray, "Write eleven more chapters as good and stop, for while the English speaking people love to laugh you will never be forgotten." [39]

Yet, in fact, just as wild horses and village dances played only a minor role in Murray's book, so he himself came to the Adirondacks for something other than sermon preaching and noisy groups. What he was really after was to leave the crowd behind and, with John Plumley as his guide and sole companion, to explore the more remote lakes and streams of the Adirondacks. It was this kind of intimate contact with the wilderness, combined with Murray's own vivid imagination, that gave birth to most of the stories in *Adventures*.

The actual committing to paper of these stories was somewhat less romantic, however, as Murray relates:

For a young man my pulpit work was tasking, for my congregation was a large and intelligent one, and from a sense of duty as truly from a wish to meet my obligations faithfully, I had to be a close student. In order to make myself more perfect in English composition, and, I may add, to keep my mind buoyant and out of conventional ruts of expression . . . I was in the habit each day of doing some small bit of work, at least, of a secular and vivacious nature. Nothing was more natural with one of my nature and habits of outdoor life than to choose Adirondack subjects both for the purpose of literary practice and mental recreation. Hence there gradually grew up a collection of original material that were [sic] unique, and being written time and again, were in the construction of the sentences and verbal discrimination as perfect as I could make them. But I certainly never anticipated that they would be published or remembered in after years by myself or others, and they never would have been but for an accident, if anything which shapes life and action may be called an accident.[40]

Among his acquaintances in Meriden was the editor and publisher of the *Weekly Recorder*, Luther Riggs. Murray goes on:

39. Quoted in connection with the promotion of Murray's collected works in the *Grand Rapids Herald*, September 18, 1898.
40. This and subsequent passages by Murray on the origins of *Adventures in the Wilderness* are from "Reminiscences," pp. 198–200.

I always liked Luther, for he was a true man at the core and praised his friends beyond discretion and cursed his enemies with most refreshing earnestness. . . .

One day Luther came running into my study in a state of mind not easily appreciated save by some country editor in like circumstances. It was one o'clock and he must go to press at five, and there was three columns of space absolutely blank. He bounded up the front steps and tore into my study without knocking, and described his predicament in language which compelled me in the interest of wise precaution to throw the matchbox into the open grate. "You must give me something, Parson," he shouted, "A section of an old sermon, a portion of a Sunday school address, a bit of temperance talk . . . , any worthless stuff to fill up the space."

With a moment's thought, Murray reached into his desk drawer and handed the editor one of his Adirondack stories in manuscript. It was promptly printed to meet the emergency, and five other stories soon followed to meet a mixed and largely local response. As far as Murray was concerned, that was the end of the matter.[41]

But it was not. A year later, when Murray moved to Boston he learned from Joseph Cook that a man was not fully established until he had a book published by the distinguished firm of Ticknor & Fields, whose authors already included such lights of American letters as Longfellow, Emerson, and Whittier. Murray immediately dismissed the possibility, for he did not have any literary ambitions. But the suggestion did not entirely die, perhaps because the office of James T. Fields was directly across Tremont Street from his own. It was not long before Murray thought of the stories from the *Meriden Recorder*. On impulse, he picked the clippings from his desk drawer, walked over, and was ushered in to see Mr. Fields himself. What happened next is again best told in Murray's own words:

41. Murray, "Among the Adirondacks," *Meriden Literary Recorder*, August 14, 1867. The following stories subsequently appeared between August 21 and November 20: "Running the Rapids," "Loon Shooting in a Thunder Storm," "Crossing the Carry," "Rod and Reel," and "Sabbath in the Woods." In 1868, further pieces by and about Murray—although not all were to figure in *Adventures*—appeared in the *Meriden Daily Republican* between April 8 and December 25 as follows: "Trout Fishing," "Farewell Sermon by the Rev. W. H. H. Murray," and "Phantom Falls or the Maid of the Mist."

. . . no sooner had I entered his presence and told him who I was than I stated briefly and frankly why I had called upon him. "I regret to say, Mr. Murray, that our list of publications was closed last week, and it would be against the custom of the house to enlarge it. And may I ask," he added, "have you the manuscript with you?" And he evidently wanted to make the fall of my expectations as easy as possible. And in return I handed him the cutting from Luther G. Riggs' paper. The change which came over Fields's face as he took the roll was simply indescribable. Pausing a moment as if to study his words, he quietly said, "This house has never printed any manuscript that has been published in small country papers." By this I was perfectly conscious of the blunder I, in my ignorance, had made, a blunder which would have been shameful to me and insulting toward him had I not proceeded innocently ignorant of the proper course to pursue in such a matter. This he perceived, and with charming adroitness and a noble wish to relieve my embarrassment, he said, "Mr. Murray, while we cannot publish this material, I do not doubt much of it will be interesting reading, and if you will kindly allow me to take the roll home with me it will give pleasure to both Mrs. Fields and myself, who have heard of your love of outdoor life, to peruse some of them at our first opportunity."

Two days after I received a note from him asking me if I would kindly come over and call on him for a moment. As soon as I could command the time I went across the street and sent up my card to his office. I shall not while I live forget a single phrase of that interview. He received me standing with several chapters of my manuscript lying loosely on the desk before him. "Mr. Murray," he said, "both Mrs. Fields and myself have read these papers attentively. They are very unique. We do not recall anything that is just like them. Here," he added, picking up several leaves, "is a descriptive bit entitled 'A Ride With a Mad Horse in a Freight Car.' May I ask, did you write that piece?" "I certainly did," I replied. "And here is a piece," he added, taking up another set of leaves, ["] called 'Fantom [sic] Falls.' May I ask, did you write that?" My reply was again in the affirmative. In like manner he questioned me on the chapter called 'Crossing the Carry,' and I gave him the same answer. Now, friends, in all my pulpit career I had never in all the ups and downs of it allowed myself the privilege of getting mad, and up to this point in the conversation I held myself perfectly in hand. But now I said, "Mr. Fields, you are aware that your interrogations are most unusual for one gentleman to address another in our position, and I feel at liberty to ask what you mean by it." "Simply this, Mr. Murray," he said, "your method of interpreting nature and your humor are unlike anything that we have ever seen. This little book, I am confident, is destined to a great career. We have decided to reopen our list this spring and illustrate it in the best manner that time will permit. . . ." And this is the way that the little volume known as "Murray's Adventures in the Wilderness" which inaugurated not only the great popular movement toward the Adirondacks and introduced the new *régime* of recreation, but which has given me a name which overshadows those by which I was christened, came to be given to the public.

On February 10, 1869, Murray signed a contract which placed the matter in Fields' hands.[42] As for Murray, he was to receive royalties of ten cents per copy after the first thousand were sold, and fifteen cents a copy if more than five thousand were sold. Within two months the book was in the stores. By June, Murray was wealthy—and famous.

Its commercial success notwithstanding, *Adventures in the Wilderness* did not enjoy a totally favorable reception by literary critics. A writer in *The Nation* had this to say about the book:

It would be hard for the honest lover of the woods and waters and forest sports to find a book concerning them which should not please him more than Mr. Murray's. And it would be harder for the person with tolerable taste in literature to find a book the tone of which would very much more displease him. "Loud" is the word that we might perhaps best apply to it. . . . The whole book is written in falsetto . . . ; is screechy from the beginning to the end, and does not inspire confidence. . . .

. . . the effect of the book might be good as leading a good many people to forsake watering-places and "loafing," and try the shanty life of hemlock-bough beds, and trout and salt pork for breakfast, and long tramps and longer sleeps in perfectly sweet air.

42. Murray's copy of the contract is in AM 69–13, and it specifies that .the publisher is to arrange for "such illustrations as may be deemed advisable" for the book. Judging from the monogram in several of the published plates, the distinguished and popular illustrator Harry Fenn got the job. Fenn also did the Adirondack subjects in William Cullen Bryant, ed., *Picturesque America* (2 vols.: New York, 1872 and 1874), II, pp. 414–35.

It would spoil the woods possibly; but it is a pity and it is a wonder that our counting-rooms and offices do not more entirely empty themselves into the Adirondacks every summer and fall. There is room yet, by the way—large room—for a good book on the Adirondack country.[43]

Despite such critical reservations, however, the book was an instant commercial success. Precisely how many copies of *Adventures* were bought by the eager public, however, we shall probably never know. Late in life Murray said that at first the book sold at the rate of five hundred copies a week.[44] Joseph Cook, in a letter to his father written on July 7 that summer of 1869, mentioned that Murray's "little book on the Adirondacks has just passed into a tenth edition," although he did not indicate the number of copies in each edition. Cook did say, however, that in the three-quarters of a year Murray had been living in Boston, "He has added $900 worth of books to his library." [45] Royalties on *Adventures* may well have accounted for this affluence. All the evidence suggests that the book was certainly a best-seller.

The book's impact on the Adirondacks the summer of 1869 was enormous. Unprecedented crowds pushed for the mountains, a stampede that ever since has been called "Murray's Rush." To meet the growing demand, the publishers in early July brought out a Tourist's Edition, in a yellow waterproof cover, complete with twelve pages of timetables, and a map in the end pocket. The railroads thoughtfully offered free copies to those buying round-trip tickets to the Adirondacks. That same month, a vivid series of letters, entitled "With the Multitudes in the Wilderness," began appearing in a Boston paper over the pseudonym "Wachusett." [46] This was the situation in the Adirondacks:

43. *The Nation*, IX (1869), p. 240.
44. "Reminiscences," p. 278.
45. Cook, *Letters*, pp. 88–89.
46. "Wachusett" was very probably George B. Wood, judging from a comparison of his articles with names in the Raquette Lake House register for 1869 (see note 34 above). His eight letters appeared in the *Boston Daily Advertiser* between July 17 and 30, 1869. All quotations from "Wachusett" which follow are from the letters published July 17, 19, and 21.

The Rush for the Wilderness. "Murray's Fools" scramble from the
train at Whitehall onto the steamer *Adirondack*. From
Harper's New Monthly Magazine, August, 1870.

. . . Mr. Murray's pen has brought a host of visitors into the Wilderness, such as it has never seen before—consumptives craving pure
air, dyspeptics wandering after appetites, sportsmen hitherto content with small game and few fish, veteran tourists in search of
novelty, weary workers hungering for perfect rest, ladies who
have thought climbing the White Mountains the utmost possible
achievement of feminine strength, journalists and lecturers of both
sexes looking for fresh material for the dainty palate of the public,
come in parties of twos and dozens, and make up in the aggregate
a multitude which crowds the hotels and clamors for guides, and
threatens to turn the Wilderness into a Saratoga of fashionable
costliness.

Like many others, "Wachusett" had followed Murray's advice as to the best route for entering the wilderness. After

"Madam, I beg pardon—is this a deer-hound?" From *Harper's
New Monthly Magazine,* August, 1870.

spending the night at Plattsburgh on Lake Champlain, he
boarded a train the following morning for an hour's ride
(twenty miles) to the Ausable River.[47] At the railhead, the
twice-weekly stage proved hardly adequate to the unusual situation, and enterprising teamsters had no difficulty getting fifteen dollars for the thirty-five-mile ride to Martin's at Saranac
Lake. "Wachusett" then goes on:

The wagon makers of the neighborhood are unable to meet the demands upon them, and the new vehicles are put on the road as
soon as they are able to go over it, without waiting for the finish-
ing and ornamental touches of the painter. . . .

One needs to be but a very short time in the Wilderness before

47. Point of Rocks, later called Rogers. The line was subsequently extended
to Ausable Forks. See Jim Shaughnessy, *Delaware & Hudson* (Berkeley, Calif.,
1967), p. 137.

he discovers that one kind of game is very plentiful here, and that another species furnishes a great deal of excitement in the hunting. The abundance is that of the mosquitoes; the excitement, hard, fervid and genuine, is that of seeking guides. The multitude of visitors who have come to the Wilderness have not been numerous enough to satiate the appetite of the insects; but they have more than exhausted the supply of guides; and the cry is still they come, though inn-keepers and guides hold up their hands in despair when we tell them that the tide of city people has only just begun to flow in upon them.

When you quit your wagon at the door of Martin's, lame and soiled and hungry as you are, the chances are ten to one that you postpone the sofa, the supper-table, and the wash basin that you may catch the extended hand of the hospitable proprietor of the inn, and selfishly strive to get ahead of the occupants of the next

"Have you no voiture, no barouche?" Unsophisticated transportation into the Wilderness. From *Harper's New Monthly Magazine*, August, 1870.

Martin's Hotel. Engraving by Samuel S. Kilburn, Jr., who also
did some of the subjects in *Adventures*. This plate appeared
in Watson's *Descriptive and Historical Guide* in 1871.

team, by whispering eagerly in his ear, "How about a guide?" Perhaps you have written to Mr. Martin a month in advance to secure
you in this respect; perhaps you have come in trusting to luck. In
either case the answer is the same. You will have to wait. There
are some people in the house who have waited several days already,
and who must be supplied ahead of you. . . .

Thus there will naturally be two reports as to the character of
the sport in the Wilderness this year, those whom the lack of
guides has kept in the north telling one story, full of the bitterness
of disappointment, while the lucky ones, who get the means of getting where the sport is, will come back with a record of enjoyment
and victory only less glowing in its colors than Mr. Murray's own.

As William Chapman White later put it, "The stampede into
the woods in June was a stampede out in August. Every stagecoach was filled with bitter people. They cried, 'Liar! Murray
wrote a re-lieable book. In it he lies over and over!' " [48] Un-

48. White, *op. cit.*, p. 115.

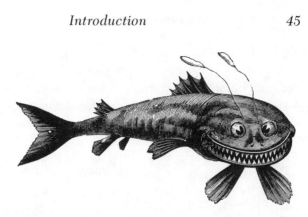

The Laker. From *Harper's New Monthly Magazine*, August, 1870.

leashing their venom on both author and book, "Murray's Fools" wrote angry letters to the newspapers, from Cincinnati and Chicago to New York, Boston, and Burlington.[49] The obvious target was Murray himself, and he became the object of personal ridicule. One anecdote going around the Adirondacks that summer was based on incredulity as to Murray's own story of "the tip of his pole crossing its butt with two trout pendulous. In order to show the sceptics how it could be done, Murray stepped into a boat, pole in one hand, placed his foot on one side of the bow, leaning upon which too heavily caused the stern to sheer suddenly in the opposite direction, and over went the Adirondack historian, *kersplash* into the water." [50]

More serious charges raised questions about the Adirondack region itself and about Murray's claims on its behalf. He was accused of murdering invalids, of attracting the wrong sort of people to the Adirondacks, and of creating a situation which severely overtaxed the region's limited facilities.

The accusation of "murder" stemmed from an account in the introduction to the book about a young man, deep in the grip

49. Press coverage of the "Murray Rush" remains to be thoroughly studied. Besides items cited elsewhere in this introduction, see the *Black River Herald* (Boonville, N.Y.), September 23, 1869, which is based on an earlier account in the Burlington, Vermont, *Free Press*. In a letter published in New York and Boston papers (see note 55), Murray himself mentions an account by a lady in a Cincinnati paper and another which was published in the *Chicago Evening Journal*.

50. Edward R. Osborne, *Letters from the Woods* [or, *Forest, Lake, and Random Rhymes*] (Poughkeepsie, 1893), p. 39.

of consumption (as tuberculosis was then called), who was actually carried into the Adirondacks. A few months of camp
life, and he was restored to robust health (pp. 12–14). The
story, his critics said, was raising false hopes and perpetrating
a "cruel hoax." They claimed that invalids coming to the Adirondacks only met the grim reaper.

This claim overlooked the fact that Murray himself had
qualified his account about the young man by calling it "extreme." In his book he cites a more typical case, that of his
own wife. "There is one sitting near me, as I write, the color of
whose cheek, and the clear brightness of whose eye, cause my
heart to go out in ceaseless gratitude to the woods, amid
which she found that health and strength of which they are
the proof and sign" (p. 14).

As it turned out, just four years after the publication of Murray's book another young man, this time a physician, was also
carried into the Adirondacks. On being lifted from the wagon
to his hotel bed, the patient heard these words from the guide
carrying him, "Why, Doctor, you don't weigh no more than a
dried lamb-skin." [51] Doctor—and patient—was Edward Livingston Trudeau, who recovered and went on to achieve inter-
national fame for his work in tuberculosis therapy.

That summer of 1869, however, there rallied to Murray's defense the authoress and lecturer Kate Field. Writing from
Raquette Lake to Horace Greeley's *New York Tribune*, she
argued:

If consumptives, with both legs in the grave visit the Adirondacks,
and after a few days or weeks leave the woods somewhat less alive
than when they entered, surely their friends display the most extraordinary absence of reason in attributing their decease to Mr.
Murray's book. . . . Newspaper writers multiply two or three dead
men by a fertile imagination, and produce "numbers of dead and
dying." Such criticism is outrageous, and such reports are willfully
malignant.[52]

51. Edward Livingston Trudeau, *An Autobiography* (Garden City, N.Y.,
1916), p. 80.
52. This and subsequent quotations from Kate Field are taken from her
"Among the Adirondacks: Murray's Fools—A Plain Talk about the Wilder-

Before and after going into the Adirondacks. From *Harper's
New Monthly Magazine*, August, 1870.

More patently self-interested howlings from the wilderness
about Murray and his book arose from disgruntled sportsmen.
Though hunters and fishermen from the cities had been visiting the Adirondacks since the 1840's, their numbers were few,
giving them a near-monopoly on the vast region. Their dismay
at seeing the invading crowd of ordinary tourists, amateur an-
glers, and even ladies, can easily be imagined. Kate Field

ness," *New-York Tribune*, August 12, 1869. Kate Field spent the last three
weeks of July in the Adirondacks, part of that time as Murray's guest. See
Lilian Whiting, *Kate Field: A Record* (Boston, 1899), p. 212.

again came to Murray's defense. "Many sportsmen," she wrote, "are rampant because their favorite hunting and fishing grounds have been made known to the public. The greatest good of the greatest number is, I believe, the true democratic platform, and if several hundred men think that the life-giving principles of the North Woods was [sic] instituted for the benefit of a few guns and rods, they are sadly mistaken."

When she reiterated these sentiments on a public lecture tour that fall, Kate Field managed to provoke a cascade of abuse upon both Murray and herself. Thomas Bangs Thorpe, a veteran sportsman, both in the Adirondacks and elsewhere, could scarcely conceal his hauteur and antifeminism:

To the genuine sportsman and true lover of Nature, nothing can be more offensive than fashionable twaddle about the "backwoods." Mr. Murray has written enough of this sort of nonsense to last a few years, at least; for it is very certain that a hunter who has shot deer, and a sportsman who understands the uses of the fly and the catching of trout, never read one word of such a book as Mr. Murray's with any other feelings than indignation . . . ; that sentiment of the highly-cultivated mind which rejoices in the wilds of Nature, is too sensitive to remain unmoved when they see "those temples of God's creation" profaned by people who have neither skill as sportsmen, nor sentiment or piety enough in their composition, to understand Nature's solitudes. . . .

And now the wilds . . . have been invaded by Miss Kate Field, and she brings some of the rude things to be seen in that wilderness, softened by her womanly imagination, into the lecture-room, and ventilates them before audiences composed of people the majority of whom have no more taste for Nature than a rosebud has for a hurricane. We do not consider the wild woods a place for fashionable ladies of the American style; they have, unfortunately, in their education, nothing that makes such places appreciated, and no capability for physical exercise that causes the attempt to be pleasantly possible. . . . Let the ladies keep out of the woods.[53]

In addition to Thorpe's complaints about the kinds of people Murray was attracting to the woods, another serious question raised by the "Murray Rush" had to do with the numbers of

53. Thomas Bangs Thorpe, "The Abuses of the Backwoods," *Appleton's Journal* (December 18, 1869), pp. 564–65.

these people and the capacity of facilities there to accommodate them. A letter written to the *New York Tribune,* signed simply "H. H." and published on August 17, 1869, considered the matter in this way:

It could not be expected that 2,000 or 3,000 persons could find accommodations or be properly cared for in a wilderness sixty or seventy miles from any market, where the roads at best are very poor, and where there are only five or six small houses within a distance of 100 miles. Heretofore small parties of from two to six persons have been in the habit of visiting that wild region, and perhaps not more than twenty or thirty parties have ever before been in the Wilderness at any one time. There are about forty guides between Boonville and St. Regus [Regis] Lake, and from sixty to eighty small boats that will carry three persons each, with the necessary baggage. Now, because 3,000 persons could not find accommodations, boats, and guides, in the center of a pathless wilderness, stretching from near the St. Lawrence on the north to the Mohawk on the south, a distance of near 200 miles, Mr. Murray is set down as a deceiver and a "murderer of helpless invalids." I hold that Mr. Murray is not responsible for these disappointments.

Inevitably the related question raises itself: just how great was the "Murray Rush" of 1869? Was "H. H." correct in his estimate of two to three thousand visitors, and, perhaps even more important, what did it amount to compared to visitation in earlier years? Definitive totals are elusive, but relative impact can be discerned from some records. For instance, a count of the names of those—including guides—who visited the Raquette Lake House shows only a few more than a hundred guests registered there the summer of 1867, close to two hundred the next year, but well over four hundred in 1869. The relative impact at hotels on the fringes of the wilderness may have been even greater.[54]

Of all the varieties of scorn which were heaped upon the head of Murray that summer, there were some situations that were clearly beyond the author's control. If professionally em-

54. For instance, see Charles Hallock, *The Fishing Tourist: Angler's Guide and Reference Book* (New York, 1873), p. 73, for 1870 figures based on names in the register of a small hotel at Franklin Falls.

ployed in the pulpit as mediator between the secular and the
divine, Murray was still in no position to exercise authority
over the aggressive black flies and mosquitoes nor over timid
trout and deer. The truth was that the discomfort and disappointment were in large measure the consequence of an unusually wet and cold summer season in the Adirondacks that
year. Kate Field confirmed this:

The stories about the woods being "white with tents" and "black
with people," are inventions of the enemy. If pleasure-seekers care
to run the gauntlet of musketoes, and are prepared for the absence
of game, they will find the Wilderness as charming as it ever was.

Murray is right in the main, but it is rash to become responsible
for either weather or Wilderness. Every one must buy his own experience. He who ventures nothing will be very sure to gain nothing.

To be sure, there was not much hope for those who preferred
hotel living, but for herself, "To come into the Wilderness and
not camp out would be to me as unnatural as to bathe in a diver's water-proof suit."

When Murray got back to Boston from his own vacation at
Raquette Lake that fall it was clear to him that a response of
his own to the furor about his book was overdue. His first impulse may well have been to save himself from the charges of
being a liar and a disgrace to his pulpit. Perhaps he had seen
an editorial in the *New York Tribune* for August 12 which said
that a plain statement of the facts would be welcomed by "the
mass of bewildered readers who have been puzzled by conflicting stories till they were almost ready to deny the existence of the Adirondacks." At any rate, he kept his temper and
concentrated his efforts on defending the Adirondacks from
slander rather than trying to defend himself. In October, 1869,
he wrote a long and important letter to the *Tribune*.[55] It is re-
published for the first time in over a century in this edition of

55. Murray, "The Adirondacks," *New-York Tribune*, October 23, 1869; reprinted in the *Boston Journal*, October 30, 1869. The sub-headlines respectively used by these papers were "Murray on Murray's Fools, His Reply to
His Calumniators" and "Mr. Murray's Reply to His Calumniators." Cited hereafter as "Reply to His Calumniators."

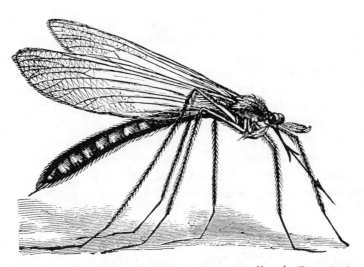

A Ha-*Bit*-U-E of Mosquito Pond. From Wallace's *Descriptive Guide to the Adirondacks*, 1887.

Adventures in the Wilderness, and it adds considerable substance and perspective to the material of the original book. In taking up the defense of the Adirondacks, Murray set himself up as speaking for all of those who were "justly incensed at the unfair and false representations which have been given to the public through the press of the country" about the region.

It seems to them greatly to be regretted that one of the loveliest and most romantic sections of our country should, even for a brief season, suffer from the aspersions of people incapable of appreciating its beauty and grandeur. . . . [I]t is due to the Wilderness itself, and also to a confused and bewildered public, that an intelligent and candid statement of the facts in the case should be published.

The newspaper article dealt with most of the specific issues which had been raised the summer of 1869 about the Adirondacks and about the book. On many of these issues, Murray merely expanded upon positions already taken by such writers as Kate Field and "Wachusett," but he also concentrated on several other points, some of which continue to have particular relevance today.

For one thing, Murray looked forward to the day in the Adirondacks, when, "Hotels will multiply, cottages will be built along the shores of its lakes, white tents will gleam amid the pines which cover its islands, and hundreds of weary and over-worked men will penetrate the Wilderness to its inner-most recesses, and find amid its solitude health and repose." He apparently had no fears that the supply of real wilderness —back from those hotels, cottages, and lake shores—would run out. "You may put 10,000 people into the Wilderness, and lo-calities can be found where, for the entire summer through, no face save your guide's shall be seen." On this proposition, how-ever, he was to have somewhat ambivalent second thoughts in later years.

Murray also rose up against the sportsmen who had com-plained that "Murray's Fools" had spoiled their private fun. In making his case, Murray drove home the point that the values inherent in the Adirondacks should be regarded as important public values.

. . . I have no sympathy at all with those two or three hundred gentlemen who would selfishly monopolize the Adirondack Wilder-ness for their own exclusive amusement and benefit. Indeed I do not look at the Wilderness as belonging to sportsmen or any class; it belongs to the country at large. . . . Its true worth does not con-sist in the game that is now there. Every deer may be killed and every trout disappear from its waters, and yet all its intrinsic ex-cellence would remain, and its value to the country be undimin-ished. We sportsmen can go elsewhere for game. . . . But this wil-derness, lying as it does within two days' ride of our great cities, is not for us to selfishly appropriate. It is, and is to be regarded in the future, a place to which not only the artist, and the lover of na-ture in her grandest aspects, but the business man and the profes-sional man, weary and jaded by months and years of over-work, can go and find in its recesses rest and recuperation for body and mind. . . .

This, as it seems to me, is the true use of the wilderness, and its value to the country at large.

Following the publication of his letter, Murray continued to contribute significantly to creating and maintaining wide-spread public interest in the Adirondacks. Particularly impor-tant, he undertook an extensive lecture tour dealing with the region and, as had been the case with *Adventures,* the impact of the tour turned out to be far greater than had been originally anticipated and its genesis no less casual.

About a year after the "rush" Murray's deacons became concerned about gossip which suggested that their pastor's success in attracting large crowds to Park Street Church was due to his use of sensational mannerisms and oratory. They came to Murray with the suggestion that the best way to protect the decorum and dignity of their historic pulpit, and to give the lie to such innuendos, would be for Murray to travel as a public lecturer, to be seen and heard in as many communities as possible. After some hesitation, Murray acceded to their urging, telling them that "If I write a lecture to kill off these charges of sensationalism I had better take a subject that is sensational, something that gives me every opportunity to be a sensationalist and an oratorical mountebank, and that subject is certainly the Adirondack life and experience in the woods." [56]

In the next three years, Murray spoke over five hundred times in the villages and cities of New England, to nearly half a million people. "Of course," he recalled, "as I got into the matter, I saw the great service that such a speech might do. . . . It literally captured the lyceum platform, and when I decided to withdraw it it became impossible to do so. At the close of its delivery I was compelled often to remain on the platform an hour, giving practical information and advice to those who intended to go to the woods the next year. It was perhaps the most influential utterance I ever made, judged by its influence on the people and the fashion of outdoor recreation which it promoted." [57]

Indeed, Murray was very probably not exaggerating this influence in the least. His book and the lecture were doing their work, although, to be sure, this work was aided considerably in the 1870's and early 1880's by continued publicity about the region, improved means of transportation to and into the Adirondacks, and by the willingness of would-be resort operators to cash in on the new clientele.

56. "Reminiscences," p. 279.
57. "Reminiscences," p. 278.

The literary and artistic record of the Adirondacks during this period is impressive. In 1870, *Harper's Monthly* published a piece by Charles Hallock which, though a heavy-handed satire of the "Murray Rush," certainly did not inhibit public interest in the Adirondacks. In this and subsequent years, a host of other magazines carried pieces on the Adirondacks, some of which were illustrated by engravings of Adirondack scenes after such artists as Homer Martin, Winslow Homer, Samuel Colman, the Smillie brothers—James D. and George— and by Fred T. Vance and T. S. Jameson. The Adirondack Wilderness, "henceforth to be a grand summer resort for Americans seeking recreation," as one of these journals put it, soon had its guidebooks as well. E. R. Wallace's guide began publication in 1872 and was issued until 1900. S. R. Stoddard's *The Adirondacks: Illustrated,* beginning in 1874, ran through annual revisions until 1916, well into the age of the automobile.[58]

An even more far-reaching record of change was written upon the face of the Adirondack region itself in these years. Thomas C. Durant's railroad from Saratoga reached North Creek in 1871. Other lines soon followed elsewhere. Regular stagecoach service was initiated on a number of hitherto

58. In addition to Charles Hallock, "The Raquette Club," *Harper's New Monthly Magazine,* XLI (1870), pp. 321–38, articles and illustrations about the Adirondacks during this period can be found in the following: *Every Saturday,* I (1870), pp. 563, 572, 838, and 849, and in II (1871), pp. 54, 57, 78, and 89; *Appleton's Journal,* IV (1870), pp. 361–66; *The Aldine,* V (1872), pp. 194–96; *Frank Leslie's Illustrated Newspaper,* XXXIII (1872), pp. 366 and 373. The various editions of the Wallace and Stoddard guidebooks are covered in entries 1208 and 1206, respectively, of Dorothy Plum, ed., *Adirondack Bibliography* (Gabriels, N.Y., 1958). Other guidebooks of the period devoted either exclusively or in part to the Adirondacks include: [Winslow C. Watson], *A Descriptive and Historical Guide to the Valley of Lake Champlain and the Adirondacks* (Burlington, Vt., 1871); S. S. Colt, *The Tourist's Guide through the Empire State* (Albany, 1871); C. A. Faxon, *Faxon's Illustrated Hand-book of Travel* . . . (Boston, 1873); and John B. Bachelder, *Popular Resorts and How to Reach Them* (3rd edition, revised: Boston, 1875). The centennial of the "Murray Rush" is recalled in "The Adirondacks: Forever Wild?" and "An Adirondack Exhibition," *American Heritage,* XX (August, 1969), pp. 44–48 and 49–63, respectively; the latter section includes colored reproductions of fourteen Adirondack paintings, and the cover of the magazine reproduces a lithograph featuring Murray.

The Dismal Wilderness. From *Harper's New
Monthly Magazine*, August, 1870.

lightly used routes in the middle 1870's, and by 1878 steamboats were plying several of the Adirondack lakes. By the 1880's, William West Durant was deeply engaged in the development of large estates and rustic camps in the vicinity of Raquette Lake, and, to top it all off, an enormous hotel, the Prospect House, opened in 1882 at Blue Mountain Lake. "One of the unnatural, almost uncanny, wonders of the wilderness," Donaldson was to say of the Prospect House, its existence deep in the central Adirondacks proclaimed visibly that the recreational use of the region had drastically altered the face of the original wilderness as Murray had originally known and loved it.[59]

59. Donaldson, *op. cit.*, II, p. 103. For hotel and resort development in the central Adirondacks during this period see particularly H. K. Hochschild, *Township 34* (New York, 1952) and the following pamphlets by the same au-

In the Adirondacks—A Carry on Racquette River. Wood engraving by John Parker Davis after Homer Dodge Martin. From *Every Saturday*, September, 1870.

The Prospect House, Blue Mountain Lake. Wood engraving by
the Liberty Printing Co., used in promoting the
hotel in its early years. About 1882.

Non-recreational exploitation in the same period was also
changing the face of the wilderness. If Murray's reaction to
recreation and vacation development in the Adirondacks may
have been somewhat ambivalent—and it was—his attitude to
logging in the region was unequivocal. In *Adventures* (pp.
16–17) Murray had written the Maine woods off as an attractive recreational resource. "Go where you will in Maine, the
lumbermen have been before you; and lumbermen are the
curse and scourge of the wilderness. Wherever the axe sounds,

thor based on his earlier work, all published at Blue Mountain Lake, N.Y.:
Doctor Durant and His Iron Horse (1961); *Adirondack Railroads, Real and
Phantom* (1962); *An Adirondack Resort in the Nineteenth Century, Blue
Mountain Lake . . .* (1962); *Life and Leisure in the Adirondack Backwoods*
(1962); *Adirondack Steamboats on Raquette and Blue Mountain Lakes* (1962).

the pride and beauty of the forest disappear. . . . In the Adirondack Wilderness you escape this." By the late 1870's, however, the impact of the logger all over the Adirondacks was severe. The development after the Civil War of chemical processes for the production of paper from softwood pulp had practically guaranteed it, and we may be sure Murray, as did so many others, looked upon the situation unhappily.[60]

As the Adirondacks moved from its Golden Age into the Gilded Age, utility and recreation had a head-on collision. By 1885, both the sale and lumbering of the 700,000 acres which then belonged to the state in the Adirondacks were prohibited. The land became part of a State Forest Preserve to be "forever kept as wild forest lands," and although initiated and justified largely on grounds of protecting the mountainous watersheds of the region, subsequent laws increasingly emphasized recreational values. The Adirondack Park law of 1892 declared that lands in the region would be maintained "as open ground for the free use of all the people." With the Park law Murray's democratic convictions about the Adirondacks received implicit legal recognition. In 1894 the lands of the Forest Preserve came under constitutional protection, and for the next seventy years the situation in the Adirondacks relative to utility and recreation would remain fairly stable.[61] But the twenty-

60. A comprehensive history of Adirondack logging remains to be written, but the following are helpful: Evelyn Mary Dinsdale, "The Lumber Industry of Northern New York: A Geographical Examination of Its History and Technology," Ph.D. dissertation, Syracuse University, 1963 (University Microfilms, 64–5650), and H. K. Hochschild, *Lumberjacks and Rivermen in the Central Adirondacks, 1850–1950* (Blue Mountain Lake, N.Y., 1962). Donaldson (*op. cit.*, I, p. 199) and White (*op. cit.*, p. 115) both, perhaps rather unfairly, take Murray to task for claiming there had been no logging in the Adirondacks prior to 1869. In the "Reply to His Calumniators," however, Murray distinguishes the interior Adirondack Wilderness—the area of his concern—from the outer Adirondacks and makes it clear that he was aware of logging taking place in the latter, particularly in the St. Regis area and along the Saranac River.

61. The best, if a somewhat biased, study of public conservation policy in the Adirondacks is Roger C. Thompson, "The Doctrine of Wilderness: A Study of the Policy and Politics of the Adirondack Preserve-Park," Ph.D. thesis, State University College of Forestry at Syracuse University, 1962; see also Thompson's "Politics in the Wilderness: New York's Adirondack Forest Pre-

Forest Destruction in the Adirondacks: A Feeder of the Hudson as it Was and
as it Is. Wood engraving by Lawson after Julian Walbridge Rix.

From *Harper's Weekly*, January 1885.

five years prior to 1894 had probably seen the greatest changes in all of Adirondack history, and "Adirondack" Murray had a great deal to do with them.

A description of the historical impact of Murray's book upon the Adirondacks in the years following upon its publication still does not explain everything important about the book. It does not tell us why the book was the success it was in its own time; it does not fully do justice to Murray's impact on the history of outdoor recreation; and, from a perspective of a hundred years, it does not tell us why the book arouses something more than mere antiquarian interest today.

In its own time, *Adventures in the Wilderness* captured readers because of its style, its substance, and its humanity. Besides these, historical circumstances at the time of its publication, including an affluent Northeast and a potentially mobile population, were optimally favorable to its success. If Murray had not written the book, someone else would have had to.

Before Murray came along, there had been quite a number of books on the Adirondacks, beginning in 1839 with one by Charles Fenno Hoffman and running right down to 1869 with others by such people as John Todd, Charles Lanman, Joel T. Headley, S. H. Hammond, and Alfred Billings Street.[62] None of these books, however, brought either fortune or fame to their authors, nor did they succeed in enticing more than a few of their readers into seeing the Adirondacks for themselves. Historical climate not even considered, Murray's book

serve," *Forest History*, VI (Winter, 1963), pp. 14–23. Also helpful are Marvin W. Kranz, "Pioneering in Conservation: A History of the Conservation Movement in New York State, 1865–1903," Ph.D. dissertation, Syracuse University, 1961 (University Microfilms, 62–1108) and Norman Van Valkenburgh, "The Adirondack Forest Preserve: A Chronology," paper prepared for the Bureau of Land Acquisition, New York State Conservation Department, 1968 (copy at the Adirondack Museum).

62. Early books on the Adirondacks included: Charles Fenno Hoffman, *Wild Scenes in the Forest* (2 vols.: London, 1839); John Todd, *Long Lake* (Pittsfield, Mass., 1845); Charles Lanman, *A Tour to the River Saguenay* (Philadelphia, 1848); Joel T. Headley, *The Adirondack; or, Life in the Woods* (New York, 1849); S. H. Hammond, *Hills, Lakes and Forest Streams* (New York, 1854)—reissued as *Hunting Adventures in the Northern Wilds* (Philadelphia, 1863)—and *Wild Northern Scenes* (New York, 1860); Alfred B. Street, *Woods and Waters* (New York, 1860) and *The Indian Pass* (1869).

succeeded partly because it omitted many of the worst aspects of these earlier books' style and substance and because Murray infused his account with a human intimacy that the others lacked.

Stylistically, Murray kept things simple and direct at all times. There is vigor and pace in his writing, and he employs a concrete and vivid diction to convey his sure grasp of the sights, sounds, and movements in the wilderness experience. If at times the sentences seem a bit short or jerky, a reading of his tales aloud around an evening campfire will dispel such an impression. Writing with enthusiasm but avoiding pomposity, Murray deliberately chose a cadence easily understood. Simple, and seemingly artless, subtleties await between the lines, but they do not obtrude.

Substantively, the long opening chapter of Murray's book presented the American public for the first time with practical information and advice about the Adirondacks that had never before been published. Earlier accounts of the region gave hardly a clue about how to get there, available accommodations, what to bring, and—just as important—what to leave at home. Murray spelled out all this, with routes and reservations, names and addresses, packing lists and menus, dollars and cents. Furthermore, he anticipated his readers' questions and anxieties, and put them to rest with solid facts and the wisdom of his own experience: plan ahead; there are no dangerous animals or snakes; avoid the insects by going in July or later, and pitching your tent on a breezy point; the guides have the skill and strength to make you comfortable; even ladies will not find the life too strenuous; and hunting and fishing are good enough "to satisfy any reasonable desire." For any reader, whether already converted to the gospel of the outdoor life or not, this compact guide and manual was well worth a dollar and a half. If Murray did not, in fact, tell all that there was to know about the Adirondacks and how to get the most out of the region, what he did tell was presented with an air of convincing authority. A reader could not help but come away from reading Murray with the belief that he too could rough it in the wilderness.

Besides the provision of plausible facts, the substance of the rest of Murray's book worked in its favor as well. His book was entertaining. The ten tales of adventure, however fanciful they may have been in many respects, were such as to both charm and delight the casual reader. If, as Donaldson put it, the public "eagerly devoured" the stories "and then as eagerly abused the writer for producing" them,[63] the fact remained that they were read. Murray himself had planned it that way, he tells us in *Adventures*, when he envisioned "a series of descriptive pieces, unencumbered with the ordinary reflections and jottings of a tourist's book, free from the slang of guides and questionable jokes and 'bear stories' with which so many works of a similar character have to a great extent been filled" (p. 7). These are precisely the flaws that make Headley, Hammond, and Street almost unreadable today. Murray also improved upon these authors and others by abandoning the conventional journalistic form. Instead of a rambling narrative, with neither unity or continuity, he constructed a series of stories, where "each stands alone by itself, having its own framework of time and character, and representing a single experience" (p. 8).

Part and parcel of the book's substance is the warm humanity which pervades it. The characterization of John Plumley is an obvious manifestation of this quality, but there is another and even more subtle expression of the human aspect throughout the book as well. James Fields touched upon this when he told Murray that his "method of interpreting nature and humor are unlike anything that we have ever seen."

In interpreting nature, Murray began from the assumption that it was a totality whose value constituted something greater than the sum of its parts. Nature as a whole—at least in the Adirondack Wilderness—had something more to yield up to man than the region's fish, game, fur, waters, forests, or even all of these put together. A newspaper reporter once asked Murray, "If you don't go into the woods to hunt and fish, what do you go for?" Murray's reply was, "Go to the woods for? Why, to have a chance to think and feel and be-

63. Donaldson, *op. cit.*, I, p. 196.

come sanctified in an unclerical and untheological manner, that last grace of God to most men." [64]

Murray's manner of expressing himself suggests that divinity lurks within wild nature, but the sentiment underlying his words is one which could be—and has been—put in strictly secular terms. This is precisely what William Chapman White did in 1954, for instance, when he wrote of those things a man might find by an Adirondack lake. They would be, he wrote, "just as they were in the summer of 1354, as they will be in 2054 and beyond. He can stand on a rock by the shore and be in a past he could not have known, in a future he will never see." [65] White's frame of reference is historical; Murray's was religious. But the sentiment is the same in both—a gentle reverence for the romantic image of wild nature.

Still, Murray did not wax lugubrious either over nature or over man in nature. If at times a touch of sentimental piety couched in an over-rich prose does creep into his writing, it is at least somewhat less obtrusive than it might have been, and as it often was in the writings of others in Murray's day. Far more important is Murray's frequent injection of humor into the man-nature confrontation. This is what saves him from triteness, and it is this particularly which lends *Adventures* its special quality of humanity.

Murray said of the laughter of the out-of-doors that it "is never bitter, never cynical. Nature brings out 'the real human' that lies latent in one." [66] In this he was distinguishing the laughter of the outdoor life from that of the indoor which, he said, was "smothered, constrained, puckered into forms of politeness. The funniest laughter is the laughter one has alone." Even in the out-of-doors, however, the insensitive sportsman is always in danger of taking himself too seriously as he teeters on the slippery possibility of failure. If he laughs at all, all too often it degenerates into a kind of uninvolved, raucous, thigh-slapping masculine jocularity. As it was, however, the Adirondack writers who had preceded Murray almost never cracked

64. Unidentified clipping in MS 69–13.
65. White, *op. cit.*, p. 264.
66. *Lake Champlain*, p. 28.

a smile of any sort. It was Murray who brought laughter to the Adirondack scene, and it was the kind of laughter which he brought that filled (and still fills) his book with vitality. Murray's laughter is that of the involved participant, and its outcome is a distillation of a sense of warm humility in the face of nature.

Style, substance, and even the intrinsic attractions of the Adirondacks notwithstanding, there is reason to believe that a good deal of the success of Murray's book in its time was due to the fact that its readership was ready for it. For one thing, the traditional American attitude toward wilderness itself as an almost totally negative entity to be "overcome" with "civilizing conquest" was beginning to change as the United States neared the limits of its geographic frontiers.[67] The transcontinental railroad was completed, dedicated, and opened just about the time Murray's book came out. At the same time, social conditions in the country—particularly in the Northeast— were changing.

The Civil War had preserved the Union, but it changed nearly every other aspect of American life. After the years of sacrifice and work, the instinct for pleasure was naturally intensified. Even before the war, Emerson had complained of "the invalid habits of this country," [68] and now everyone was concerned about health. As Murray himself put it, "An uneasiness as to the present condition of things was abroad in the land. 'Nervous prostration' began to occur. It was a new name and a new thing . . . caused by overstress and strain. . . . Clergymen, lawyers, merchants, doctors, all began to feel that the pace was too hot and too risky to keep up." [69] The old puritan prejudice against play was becoming tempered by a growing realization of its benefits. Travel and outdoor pastimes, previously the privilege of a very small aristocracy, at least in New England, were coming to be viewed as a demo-

67. A good synthesis of this subject is Roderick Nash, *Wilderness and the American Mind* (New Haven, 1967).

68. Quoted in Foster Rhea Dulles, *America Learns to Play: A History of Popular Recreation, 1607–1940* (New York, 1940), p. 183.

69. "Reminiscences," pp. 194–95.

cratic right by more and more working people seeking to escape the confining pressures of industrial urbanization. Although resistance to the idea of recreation remained in some quarters, an increasingly large part of the public was both ready and willing to be convinced that recreation was a good thing.[70] Murray was prepared to tell the public just that.

Murray's espousal of the benefits of outdoor recreation in general, we may be sure, was not without very personal as well as purely altruistic motivations. For instance, he was particularly conscious of a double standard which denied to clergymen almost entirely the recreation which was at least grudgingly being allowed to others in moralistic New England. In June of 1871, just before leaving for the Adirondacks, Murray spoke to his own congregation, and through it "to the public at large," on the delicate subject of "Ministerial Vacations: Their Necessity and Value." In behalf of the hardworking preacher, "I lift my voice in protest against the custom of the times," he said, against those "miserable 'traditions' which have put a premium on narrow-chested and shrivelled-skinned men." [71] Mental and bodily health (and presumably spiritual health) went hand in hand, he proclaimed. In later years, he took a retrospective look at "the national indifference to outdoor life and sport and the ban put upon them by the refined and wealthier class" which had dominated matters in his younger days.

No greater revolution ever occurred than that which brought about the entire change in thought and habits of the American people touching outdoor life and the sports and types of recreation representative of it.

I do not expect that you younger men around me can fully appreciate the vastness of this revolution, because you were not born under the old *régime* of ignorance as to what the body and mind of man required for health and healthy work, and accustomed to the freedom of thought and life to-day, you cannot realize the big-

70. In addition to Dulles, *op. cit.*, the changing moral attitudes of Americans towards recreation are described in Jennie Holman, *American Sports, 1785–1835* (Durham, N.C., 1931), especially Chapter 12.

71. *Sermons* (1871), pp. 267, 284, and 279, respectively.

otry and tyranny of those who controlled the religious forces of that time.[72]

What was presumably good and necessary for the minister was equally good and necessary for the harried urban layman. In the sermon on ministerial vacations, Murray urged the members of his congregation to look beyond the confines of their own ordinary life and to get out into nature. In making his case, he was not concerned so much with any one kind of outdoor recreation as against another but asserted that any kind of vacation which brought a person into the outdoors was better than none. He pleaded:

Go to the village where you were born, to the old ancestral farm where you toiled when young. . . . Go to the sea-shore, to the mountains, to the wilderness; go anywhere where you can forget your cares and cast aside your burdens. . . . Let the old, old nurse, Nature, . . . take you to her bosom again; and you will return to the city happier and healthier for the embrace.[73]

Murray's plea for the benefits of outdoor recreation in general did not mean that he failed to distinguish wilderness recreation as a specific kind of activity subsumed under the broader heading. Wilderness recreation might be a form of outdoor recreation, but not all outdoor recreation was wilderness recreation. Although liberal in his own range of activities —Murray's passion for his farm and for horses attests to this— he remained particularly identified with wilderness recreation. No doubt the publication of *Adventures* early in his career had a great deal to do with this, but Murray himself kept the identity active. The conclusion seems unavoidable that Murray himself viewed wilderness use as particularly beneficial to the individual. Presumably, because wilderness recreation was as complete an antithesis to ordinary civilized life as it was conceivable for civilized man to indulge in, the dividends of such experience proved particularly great. The man who partook of them returned to ordinary life especially refreshed.

In the case of the Adirondacks, Murray made it clear

72. "Reminiscences," pp. 194–95.
73. *Sermons* (1871), pp. 283–84.

enough in the "Reply to His Calumniators" that he himself observed the distinction between general outdoor recreation and wilderness recreation. While implying interestingly enough that the "Adirondack Wilderness" proper was something other, and geographically less, than the Adirondacks as a whole, he urged young men coming to the region "not to sit down in idleness at the hotels along the margin of the wilderness," but rather "to take a guide and penetrate into its recesses." This, he felt, constituted "the true use of the wilderness, and its value to the country at large." Once in the wilderness, any reasonably sensitive person would experience both intimately and intensely a variety of bodily and mental sensations, but among these was one Murray laid down as being particularly impressive to himself personally. In *Adventures* (p. 194) he wrote, "It is the *silence* of the wilderness which most impresses me," and twenty-one years later he confirmed this view by saying that it was the "quietude and loneliness and the absence of the coming and going of men" that made the Adirondack woods "so attractive to me when, in other years, I visited them." [74]

Murray was certainly not the first person in history to relish wilderness experience nor the first to isolate the elements of silence and solitude as being particularly striking in such an experience. Neither was he even the first person to discern such things within the limited context of Adirondack history. He did succeed, however, in doing what practically no one before him had managed to do, and that was to translate his perceptions into images so recognizable that even the man in the street could easily understand and respond to what he had to say. In short, Murray quite literally popularized both wilderness and the Adirondacks.

Late in life, he took great pride in the important role he had played in opening up the Adirondacks to the public. He was being neither modest nor mistaken when he wrote, "In most cases the Rail Roads and Hotels are first built and then they join hands in 'Booming' the region to which they wish to attract attention and travel. Vast sums of money are spent year after

74. *Lake Champlain*, p. 119.

year to draw the people there. Some time [s] they succeed—
some time [s] they do not." But in the case of the Adirondacks,
". . . long before Rail Road facilities were provided to trans-
port the people to the woods swiftly and in comfort, or hotels
builded [*sic*] and furnished to accommodate them [,] a vast
and profitable patronage was provided them and for years the
demand for accommodation far exceeded the supply." [75]

As we have seen, hotels and railroads—and private camps,
steamboats, and wagon roads—did rapidly follow Murray in
the Adirondacks. The supply began to catch up with the demand, even if it never quite exceeded it in all respects, but in
the process something else was happening in the Adirondacks.
The wilderness itself wasn't quite the same. Murray himself
sensed the beginnings of a dilemma in 1890 when he observed,
"They even say that the little wild island I loved in the Racquette, and on whose ledge of rock, under untouched trees, I
built my lodge, has been civilized by the axe and the plough,
and that the divine silence of the Sabbath air is jarred into
discord by the clang and rattle of a chapel bell!" Still, Murray
remained characteristically optimistic. It was yet possible to
preserve the cake of wilderness, he felt, even while consum-
ing it from such a civilized table as Raquette Lake might
now represent. He concluded, "But, in spite of all these sad
changes and profanations, I doubt not that the woods still
have their beauty, the mountains keep their majesties." [76]

So Murray believed in 1890. But 1890 was also the year in
which the United States Bureau of Census let it be known that
for all practical purposes the American frontier was no more.
Suddenly, the country's manifest destiny, at least in raw geographical terms, had reached fulfillment. At the same time, the
unknown wilderness which had once lain beyond was enveloped, and such pockets as might still remain in the interior
became suddenly finite, limited, and all that Americans would
ever have should they decide definitely that wilderness values

75. Letter, April 4, 1901, from Murray to Charles Bennett at Raquette Lake,
in "Adirondack Murray," *Stoddard's Northern Monthly*, II (1907), pp. 338–39.
76. *Lake Champlain*, p. 119. St. Hubert's Church, near Osprey Island, had
been built in 1882 with the help of W. W. Durant.

were important to them. On an emotional level, however, it was too much to expect that Americans—and this may well have included Murray himself—were prepared to just as suddenly throw off the expansive traditions of centuries and suppress entirely that old optimism which had sent them across the land, whether for purposes of settlement or for recreation. The beginnings of a shift in attitude were beginning to show themselves about this time, to be sure. The imposition of firm conservation controls upon parts of the Adirondacks during the 1880's and 1890's was an example, but even here, and for some time to come, the preponderance of public attention was to be focused on such bread and butter matters as future timber supply and watershed. Recreational, aesthetic, and wilderness values for the most part received either lesser or later consideration.[77]

If solutions to conflicts of a non-utilitarian nature were slow in coming, this does not mean that the problems themselves did not exist. Even as far back as 1869, some of Murray's opponents had raised such questions about the Adirondacks, if rather selfishly, when they complained about overcrowding in the woods. In those days, however, it was still possible for Murray to counter that there was plenty of room in the woods, that even with putting "10,000 people into the Wilderness" you could still find isolation. What may have been acceptable at a time when the entire population of the northeastern states amounted to little more than twelve million people, however, could be viewed in an entirely different light a hundred years later when that population had grown nearly fourfold. Rather more quickly than Murray or anyone else might have imagined, the "quietude and loneliness" of the wilderness would be in jeopardy. If there was genuine value in wilderness—and this Murray firmly believed and preached throughout his life—then the ungoverned "coming and going of men" could ultimately erode or even destroy that value.

It is at this point that Murray becomes caught up in something which has been and continues to be characteristic of

77. See W. K. Verner, "Wilderness and the Adirondacks: An Historical View," *The Living Wilderness*, XXXIII (Winter, 1969), pp. 27–46.

American cultural history. It might be called the democratic
dilemma. Murray was firmly convinced of the cultural value of
wilderness. What he had found for himself there, he asserted,
would be valuable to the public, and the public eventually responded by agreeing with him.[78] But at the same time Murray
was not about to stifle an equally powerful impulse within
himself to share that enthusiasm as widely as possible with the
public at large, even if in so doing it did create some problems. Spared, as he put it, the handicap of "incapable respectability" in youth, Murray the democrat had manifested the very
same instinct during his Boston years in his losing battle to re-
make Park Street Church, and he did the same thing in
espousing the values of outdoor and wilderness life to the public.

The fundamental problem raised by Murray, and in some
sense created by him, was (and remains) this: how is the quality of wilderness to be reconciled with quantity of use, particularly when by definition quality is contingent upon low density
of use? Put in another and more specific way, how can the wilderness of the Adirondacks be preserved while at the same
time making that wilderness and its potential values accessible
to a large public?

Murray really evolved no answer to this question. Had he
been able to undertake a visit to the Adirondacks in 1901, and
a subsequent lecture tour he had planned late in life,[79] he
might have suggested possible solutions. Ill health prevented
both the visit and the tour, however. On this count, Murray's
struggle with the dilemma was no less inconclusive than that
faced by the posterity which inherited the problem. As a student of the American wilderness wrote in the 1960's, "the final
irony in the history of the American wilderness is that this
very increase in appreciation may ultimately prove its undo-
ing. Having made such remarkable gains in the public's esti-

78. A federal Wilderness Act became law in 1964. Quotations from Murray
are included in the early hearings record, 85th Congress, 1st Session, U.S.
Senate, *National Wilderness Preservation Act: Hearing . . . June 19 and 20,
1957* (Washington, 1957), pp. 183, 187–88.

79. See letter dated April 4, 1901, from Murray to Charles Bennett, *loc.
cit.*, p. 340.

Cordially Yours
W. H. H. Murray

Murray in later years. From a souvenir program for a widows
and orphans fund benefit by Murray in 1889.

mation in the last century, wild country could well be loved out of existence in the next." [80] Murray had contributed significantly to the growth of that appreciation. Others had taken steps to see that wilderness was protected by law. And yet the problem of balancing the quality of a limited resource—particularly one that by definition required a low density of use—with equitable quantity of use in a democracy remained.

If there remains in Murray right up to the very end a certain ambivalence on this question, he left little doubt as to where he stood on the question of freedom of access to Adirondack lands. Two years before his death, billed as "The Patron Saint of the Adirondacks," Murray prepared a short article on "The Ownership of the Adirondacks." Reacting against the acquisition, posting, and fencing of large properties in the central Adirondacks by such figures as J. P. Morgan and others, Murray asserted, "There are on the earth certain creations too precious to man; too essential to his welfare to pass under private ownership." At the same time, however, he made this startling suggestion:

Broadly considered, the State of New York does not and never did own the Adirondacks. It holds them in trust. They stand for forces that affect the mind, body and spirit of men to such a degree and so salutarily that they are lifted above monetary classment. They heal the sick; they strengthen the weak; they entertain the languid; they rest the weary; they educate the spirit; they inspire and elevate the soul; they supply to knowledge and professional skill the material of noble sanitation. The Empire State does not own, has never owned, and can never own the Adirondacks. They represent values that no amount of money can match. State and personal ownership are therefore impossible. God made them and made them to stand for what money cannot buy. They save people from death, from sickness, from insanity. They restore the soul. They renew the mind. They lift up the spirit. For this the Creator made them. He owned them in the beginning and He owns them still. The State of New York is only His agent to so administer them that His bounty to the people shall not fail.[81]

80. Nash, *op. cit.*, pp. 235–36.
81. Murray, "The Ownership of the Adirondacks," *Field and Stream*, VII (1902), p. 195.

If the rhetoric is clerical, the sentiment has remained valid even in a subsequent secular age. Presumably it will remain so into the future, and so too in his own imperfections "Adirondack" Murray will be remembered as long as there is an Adirondack history.

Albany, New York
April, 1970

WARDER H. CADBURY
State University of
New York at Albany

ADVENTURES
IN THE
WILDERNESS

"O, royal sight it was to see them come one after another over the verge!"

ADVENTURES

IN

THE WILDERNESS;

OR,

CAMP-LIFE IN THE ADIRONDACKS.

BY

WILLIAM H. H. MURRAY.

"The mountains call you, and the vales;
The woods, the streams, and each ambrosial breeze
That fans the ever-undulating sky."
ARMSTRONG'S *Art of Preserving Health.*

BOSTON:
FIELDS, OSGOOD, & CO.,
SUCCESSORS TO TICKNOR AND FIELDS.
1869.

UNIVERSITY PRESS: WELCH, BIGELOW, & CO.,
CAMBRIDGE.

To my friend and companion, O. H. PLATT, of Meriden, Conn., with whom I have passed many happy hours by mountain and stream, and shared the sportsman's triumph and the sportsman's toil; in memory of many a tramp and midnight bivouac, and as a token of my very sincere regard and friendship, this book is affectionately dedicated.

W. H. H. M.

BOSTON, April, 1869.

CONTENTS.

———◆———

APPENDIX.

INTRODUCTION.

SEVERAL of the chapters composing this volume were originally published in the "Meriden Literary Recorder," during the fall and winter of 1867. Through it they received a wide circulation, and brought to the author many letters from all parts of the country, urging him to continue the series, and, when completed, publish them in a more permanent form. Lawyers, physicians, clergymen, and sporting men were united for once in the expression of a common desire. Not a few delightful acquaintances were made through this medium. It was suggested by these unseen friends, that such a series of descriptive pieces, unencumbered with the ordinary reflections and jottings of a tourist's book, free from the slang of guides, and questionable jokes, and "bear stories," with which works of a similar character have to a great extent been filled, would be gladly welcomed by a large number of people who, born in the country, and familiar in boyhood with the gun and rod, still retain, in undiminished freshness and vigor, their early love for manly exercises and field sports. Each article, it was urged, should stand alone by itself, having its own framework of time and character, and representing a single experience. The favorable reception the articles thus published received, and the cordial communications from total strangers which they elicited, together with a strong, ever-present desire on my part to encourage manly exercise in the open air, and familiarity with Nature in her wildest and grandest aspects, persuaded me into concurrence with the suggestion. The composition of these articles has furnished me, amid grave and arduous labors, with mental recreation, from time to time, almost equal to that which I enjoyed when passing through the experiences which they are intended to describe.

In the hope that what I have written may contribute to the end suggested, and prove a source of pleasure to many who, like myself, were " born of hunter's breed and blood," and who, pent up in narrow offices and narrower studies, weary of the city's din, long for a breath of mountain air and the free life by field and flood, I subscribe myself their friend and brother.

I.

THE WILDERNESS.

THE Adirondack Wilderness, or the "North
Woods," as it is sometimes called, lies between the Lakes George and Champlain on the
east, and the river St. Lawrence on the north
and west. It reaches northward as far as the
Canada line, and southward to Booneville. Its
area is about that of the State of Connecticut.
The southern part is known as the Brown Tract
Region, with which the whole wilderness by
some is confused, but with no more accuracy than
any one county might be said to comprise an
entire State. Indeed, "Brown's Tract" is the least
interesting portion of the Adirondack region. It
lacks the lofty mountain scenery, the intricate
mesh-work of lakes, and the wild grandeur of the
country to the north. It is the lowland district,
comparatively tame and uninviting. Not until
you reach the Racquette do you get a glimpse of
the magnificent scenery which makes this wilderness to rival Switzerland. There, on the very

1*

ridge-board of the vast water-shed which slopes northward to the St. Lawrence, eastward to the Hudson, and southward to the Mohawk, you can enter upon a voyage the like of which, it is safe to say, the world does not anywhere else furnish. For hundreds of miles I have boated up and down that wilderness, going ashore only to "carry" around a fall, or across some narrow ridge dividing the otherwise connected lakes. For weeks I have paddled my cedar shell in all directions, swinging northerly into the St. Regis chain, westward nearly to Potsdam, southerly to the Black River country, and from thence penetrated to that almost unvisited region, the "South Branch," without seeing a face but my guide's, and the entire circuit, it must be remembered, was through a wilderness yet to echo to the lumberman's axe. It is estimated that a thousand lakes, many yet unvisited, lie embedded in this vast forest of pine and hemlock. From the summit of a mountain, two years ago, I counted, as seen by my naked eye, forty-four lakes gleaming amid the depths of the wilderness like gems of purest ray amid the folds of emerald-colored velvet. Last summer I met a gentleman on the Racquette who had just received a letter from a brother in Switzerland, an artist by profession, in which he said, that, "having travelled over all Switzerland, and the Rhine and Rhone region, he had not met with scenery which, judged from a purely artistic point of view, combined so many beauties in connection with such grandeur as the lakes, mountains, and forest of the Adirondack region presented to the gazer's eye." And yet thousands are in Europe to-day as tourists who never gave a passing thought to this marvellous country lying as it were at their very doors.

Another reason why I visit the Adirondacks, and urge others to do so, is because I deem the excursion eminently adapted to restore impaired health. Indeed, it is marvellous what benefit physically is often derived from a trip of a few weeks to these woods. To such as are afflicted with that dire parent of ills, dyspepsia, or have lurking in their system consumptive tendencies, I most earnestly recommend a month's experience among the pines. The air which you there inhale is such as can be found only in high mountainous regions, pure, rarefied, and bracing. The amount of venison steak a consumptive will consume after a week's residence in that appetizing atmosphere is a subject of daily and increasing wonder. I have known delicate ladies and fragile school-girls, to whom all food at home was distasteful and eating a pure matter of duty, average a gain of a pound per day for the round trip. This is no exaggeration, as some who will read these lines know. The spruce, hemlock, balsam, and pine, which largely compose this wilderness, yield upon the air, and especially at night, all their curative qualities. Many a night have I laid down upon my bed of balsam-boughs and been lulled to sleep by the murmur of waters and the low sighing melody of the pines, while the air was laden with the mingled perfume of cedar, of balsam and the water-lily. Not a few, far advanced in that dread disease, consumption, have found in this wilderness renewal of life and health. I recall a young man, the son of wealthy parents in New York, who lay dying in that great city, attended as he was by the best skill that money could secure. A friend calling upon him one day chanced to speak of the Adirondacks, and that many had found help from a trip to their region. From that moment he pined for the woods. He insisted on what his family called "his insane idea," that the mountain air and the aroma of the forest would cure him. It was his daily request and entreaty that he might go. At last his parents consented, the more readily because the physicians assured them that their son's recovery was impossible, and his death a mere matter of time. They started with him for the north in search of life. When he arrived at the point where he was to meet his guide he was too reduced to walk. The guide seeing his condition refused to take him into the woods, fearing, as he plainly expressed it, that he would "die on his hands." At last another guide was prevailed upon to serve him, not so much for the money, as he afterwards told me, but because he pitied the young man, and felt that "one so near death as he was should be gratified even in his whims."

The boat was half filled with cedar, pine, and balsam boughs, and the young man, carried in the arms of his guide from the house, was laid at full length upon them. The camp utensils were put at one end, the guide seated himself at the other, and the little boat passed with the living and the dying down the lake, and was lost to the group watching them amid the islands to the south. This was in early June. The first week the guide carried the young man on his back over all the portages, lifting him in and out of the boat as he might a child. But the healing properties of the balsam and pine, which were his bed by day and night, began to exert their power. Awake or asleep, he inhaled their fragrance. Their pungent and healing odors penetrated his diseased and irritated lungs. The second day out his cough was less sharp and painful. At the end of the first week he could walk by leaning on the paddle. The second week he needed no support. The third week the cough ceased entirely. From that time he improved with wonderful rapidity.

He "went in" the first of June, carried in the arms of his guide. The second week of November he "came out" bronzed as an Indian, and as hearty. In five months he had gained sixty-five pounds of flesh, and flesh, too, "well packed on," as they say in the woods. Coming out he carried the boat over all portages ; the very same over which a few months before the guide had carried him, and pulled as strong an oar as any amateur in the wilderness. His meeting with his family I leave the reader to imagine. The wilderness received him almost a corpse. It returned him to his home and the world as happy and healthy a man as ever bivouacked under its pines.

This, I am aware, is an extreme case, and, as such, may seem exaggerated ; but it is not. I might instance many other cases which, if less startling, are equally corroborative of the general statement. There is one sitting near me, as I write, the color of whose cheek, and the clear brightness of whose eye, cause my heart to go out in ceaseless gratitude to the woods, amid which she found that health and strength of which they are the proof and sign. For five summers have we visited the wilderness. From four to seven weeks, each year, have we breathed the breath of the mountains ; bathed in the waters which sleep at their base ; and made our couch at night of moss and balsam-boughs, beneath the whispering trees. I feel, therefore, that I am able to speak from experience touching this matter; and I believe that, all things being considered, no portion of our country surpasses, if indeed any equals, in health-giving qualities, the Adirondack Wilderness.

SPORTING FACILITIES.

This wilderness is often called the " Sportsman's Paradise"; and so I hold it to be, when all its advantages are taken into account. If any one goes to the North Woods, expecting to see *droves* of deer, he will return disappointed. He can find them west and north, around Lake Superior, and on the Plains; but nowhere east of the Alleghanies. Or if one expects to find trout averaging three or four pounds, eager to break surface, no matter where or when he casts his fly, he will come back from his trip a " sadder and a wiser man." If this is his idea of what constitutes a "sportsman's paradise," I advise him not to go to the Adirondacks. Deer and trout do not abound there in any such numbers: and yet there are enough of both to satisfy any reasonable expectation. Gentlemen often ask me to compare the "North Woods" with the " Maine Wilderness." The fact is, it is difficult to make any comparison between the two sections, they are so unlike. But I am willing to give my reasons of preference for the Adirondacks. The fact is, nothing could induce me to visit Maine. If I was going east at all, I should keep on, nor stop until I reached the Provinces. I could never bring my mind to pass a month in Maine, with the North Woods within forty-eight hours of me. I will tell you why. Go where you will, in Maine, the *lumbermen* have been before you; and lumbermen are the curse and scourge of the wilderness. Wherever the axe sounds, the pride and beauty of the forest disappear. A lumbered district is the most dreary and dismal region the eye of man ever beheld. The mountains are not merely shorn of trees, but from base to summit fires, kindled by accident or malicious purpose, have swept their sides, leaving the blackened rocks exposed to the eye, and here and there a few unsightly trunks leaning in all directions, from which all the branches and green foliage have been burnt away. The streams and trout-pools are choked with saw-dust, and filled with slabs and logs. The rivers are blockaded with "booms" and lodged timber, stamped all over the ends with the owner's "mark." Every eligible site for a camp has been appropriated; and bones, offal, horse-manure, and all the *débris* of a deserted lumbermen's village is strewn around, offensive both to eye and nose. The hills and shores are

littered with rotten wood, in all stages of decom-
position, emitting a damp, mouldy odor, and sending forth countless millions of flies, gnats, and mosquitoes to prey upon you. Now, no number of
deer, no quantities of trout, can entice me to such
a locality. He who fancies it can go; not I. In
the Adirondack Wilderness you escape this. There
the lumberman has never been. No axe has
sounded along its mountain-sides, or echoed across
its peaceful waters. The forest stands as it has
stood, from the beginning of time, in all its maj-
esty of growth, in all the beauty of its unshorn
foliage. No fires have blackened the hills; no
logs obstruct the rivers; no saw-dust taints and
colors its crystal waters. The promontories which
stretch themselves half across its lakes, the islands
which hang as if suspended in their waveless and
translucent depths, have never been marred by
the presence of men careless of all but gain. You
choose the locality which best suits your eye, and
build your lodge under unscarred trees, and upon
a carpet of moss, untrampled by man or beast.
There you live in silence, unbroken by any sounds
save such as you yourself may make, away from
all the business and cares of civilized life.

Another reason of my preference for the Adirondack region is based upon the *mode* and *manner* in
which your sporting is done. Now I do not plead
guilty to the vice of laziness. If necessary, I can

work, and work sharply; but I have no special
love for labor, in itself considered; and certain
kinds of work, I am free to confess, I abhor; and
if there is one kind of work which I detest more
than another, it is *tramping;* and, above all,
tramping through a lumbered district. How the
thorns lacerate you! How the brambles tear your
clothes and pierce your flesh! How the mesh-
work of fallen tree-tops entangles you! I would
not walk two miles through such a country for all
the trout that swim; and as for ever casting a
fly from the slippery surface of an old mill-dam,
no one ever saw me do it, nor ever will. I do not
say that some may not find amusement in it.
I only know that I could not. Now, in the North
Woods, owing to their marvellous water-communi-
cation, you do all your sporting from your boat.
If you wish to go one or ten miles for a " fish," your
guide paddles you to the spot, and serves you while
you handle the rod. This takes from recreation
every trace of toil. You have all the excitement of
sporting, without any attending physical weariness.
And what luxury it is to course along the shores
of these secluded lakes, or glide down the winding
reaches of these rivers, overhung by the outlying
pines, and fringed with water-lilies, mingling their
fragrance with the odors of cedar and balsam! To
me this is better than *tramping.* I have sported
a month at a time, without walking as many miles

as there were weeks in the month. To my mind, this peculiarity elevates the Adirondack region above all its rivals, East or West, and more than all else justifies its otherwise pretentious claim as a "Sportsman's Paradise." In beauty of scenery, in health-giving qualities, in the easy and romantic manner of its sporting, it *is* a paradise, and so will it continue to be while a deer leaves his track upon the shores of its lakes, or a trout shows himself above the surface of its waters. It is this peculiarity also which makes an excursion to this section so easy and delightful to ladies. There is nothing in the trip which the most delicate and fragile need fear. And it is safe to say, that, of all who go into the woods, none enjoy the experiences more than ladies, and certain it is that none are more benefited by it.

But what about *game*, I hear the reader inquire. Are deer plenty? Is the fishing good? Well, I reply, every person has his own standard by which to measure a locality, and therefore it is difficult to answer with precision. Moreover, it is not alone the presence of game which makes good sporting. Many other considerations, such as the skill of the sportsman, and the character and ability of the guide, enter into this problem and make the solution difficult. A poor shot, and a green hand at the rod, will have poor success anywhere, no matter how good the sporting is;

and I have known parties to be "starved out," where other men, with better guides, were meeting with royal success. With a guide who understands his business, I would undertake to feed a party of twenty persons the season through, and seldom should they sit down to a meal lacking either trout or venison. I passed six weeks on the Racquette last summer, and never, save at one meal, failed to see both of the two delicious articles of diet on my table. Generally speaking, no inconvenience is experienced in this direction. Always observing the rule, not to kill more than the camp can eat, which a true sportsman never transgresses, I have paddled past more deer within easy range than I ever lifted my rifle at. The same is true in reference to trout. I have unjointed my rod when the water was alive with leaping fish, and experienced more pleasure as I sat and saw them rise for food or play, than any thoughtless violator of God's laws could feel in wasting the stores which Nature so bountifully opens for our need. I am not in favor of "game laws," passed for the most part in the interest of the few and the rich, to the deprivation of the poor and the many, but I would that fine and imprisonment both might be the punishment of him who, in defiance of every humane instinct and reverential feeling, out of mere love for "sport," as some are pleased to call it, directs a

ball or hooks a fish when no necessity demands
it. Such ruthless destruction of life is *slaughter,* —
coarse, cruel, unjustifiable butchery. Palliate it
who may, practise it who can, it is just that and
nothing short. To sum up what I have thus far
written, I say to all brother sportsmen, that, all
things considered, the sporting, both with rifle and
rod, in the North Woods is good, — good enough
to satisfy any reasonable desire. In this, please
remember that I refer to the wilderness proper,
and not to the lumbered and inhabited and therefore *over-hunted* borders of it. I have known
parties to take board at North Elba, or Malone, or
Luzerne, and yet insist that they "had been into
the Adirondacks."

WHAT IT COSTS.

This I know to some is a matter of no interest
at all, but to others, among whom, unfortunately,
the writer must number himself, it is a matter
of vital importance. The committee on "ways
and means" in our "house" is the most laborious
of all, and the six years a little woman has held
the chairmanship of it has made her exceedingly
cautious and conservative. Some very interesting debates occur before this committee, and no
demur on the part of the defeated party, as I have

often found, can change the unalterable decision.
What is true in the case of the writer is largely
true in respect to the majority of the profession
to which he belongs. Yet it is in the ministry
that you find the very men who would be the
most benefited by this trip. Whether they should
go as sportsmen or tourists, or in both capacities, a
visit to the North Woods could not fail of giving
them precisely such a change as is most desirable,
and needed by them. In the wilderness they
would find that perfect relaxation which all jaded
minds require. In its vast solitude is a total
absence of sights and sounds and duties, which
keep the clergyman's brain and heart strung up,
the long year through, to an intense, unnatural,
and often fatal tension. There, from a thousand
sources of invigoration, flow into the exhausted
mind and enfeebled body currents of strength and
life. There sleep woos you as the shadows deepen
along the lake, and retains you in its gentle embrace until frightened away by the guide's merry
call to breakfast. You would be astonished to
learn, if I felt disposed to tell you, how many con-
secutive hours a certain minister sleeps during
the first week of his annual visit to the woods!
Ah me, the nights I have passed in the woods!
How they haunt me with their sweet, suggestive
memories of silence and repose ! How harshly the
steel-shod hoofs smite against the flinty pavement

beneath my window, and clash with rude inter-
ruptions upon my ear as I sit recalling the tranquil hours I have spent beneath the trees ! What
restful slumber was mine ; and not less gently
than the close of day itself did it fall upon me,
as I stretched myself upon my bed of balsam-
boughs, with Rover at my side, not twenty feet
from the shore where the ripples were playing
coyly with the sand, and lulled by the low mono-
tone of the pines, whose branches were my only
shelter from the dew which gathered like gems
upon their spear-like stems, sank, as a falling star
fades from sight, into forgetfulness. And then the
waking ! The air fresh with the aroma of the
wilderness. The morning blowing its perfumed
breezes into your face. The drip, drip of the
odorous gum in the branches overhead, and the
colors of russet, of orange, and of gold streaking
the eastern sky. After three or four nights of
such slumber, the sleeper realizes the force and
beauty of the great poet's apostrophe, —

> " Sleep, that knits up the ravelled sleave of care,
> The death of each day's life, sore labor's bath,
> Balm of hurt minds, great nature's second course,
> Chief nourisher in life's feast."

If every church would make up a purse, and
pack its worn and weary pastor off to the
North Woods for a four weeks' jaunt, in the
hot months of July and August, it would do a

very sensible as well as pleasant act. For when the good dominie came back swarth and tough as an Indian, elasticity in his step, fire in his eye, depth and clearness in his reinvigorated voice, would n't there be some preaching! And what texts he would have from which to talk to the little folks in the Sabbath school! How their bright eyes would open and enlarge as he narrated his adventures, and told them how the good Father feeds the fish that swim, and clothes the mink and beaver with their warm and sheeny fur. The preacher sees God in the original there, and often translates him better from his unwritten works than from his written word. He will get more instructive spiritual material from such a trip than from all the "Sabbath-school festivals" and "pastoral tea-parties" with which the poor, smiling creature was ever tormented. It is astonishing how much a loving, spiritually-minded people can bore their minister. If I had a spite against any clerical brother, and felt wicked enough to indulge it, I would get his Sabbath-school superintendent, a female city missionary, and several "local visitors," with an agent of some Western college thrown in for variety, and set them all on to him!

"But how much does it cost to take such a trip?" I hear some good deacon inquire; "perhaps we may feel disposed to take your advice."

Well, I will tell you; and I shall make a
liberal estimate, for I do not think it hurts a
minister to travel in comfortable style any more
than it does Mr. Farewell and Brother Have-
enough. And if he shall chance to find a ten-
dollar greenback in his vest-pocket after he has
reached home it will not come amiss, I warrant
you.

I estimate the cost thus : —

Guide-hire, $ 2.50 per day; board for self and
guide while in the woods, $ 2.00 each per week;
miscellanies (here is where the ten-dollar green-
backs come in), $ 25.00.

If he feels disposed to take a companion, he can
do so (many go in couples), and thereby divide
the cost of guide-hire, making it only $ 1.25
per day. But I would not advise one to do this,
especially if his expenses are paid. Fifty dollars
will pay one's travelling expenses both ways,
from Boston to the Lower Saranac Lake, where
you can meet your guide. From New York the
expense is about the same. It is safe to say that
one hundred and twenty-five dollars will pay all
the expenses of a trip of a month's duration in the
wilderness. I know of no other excursion in
which such a small sum of money will return
such per cent in health, pleasure, and profit.

OUTFIT.

There is no one rule by which to be governed in this respect. Personal tastes and means control one in this matter. Generally speaking, outfits are too elaborate and cumbersome. Some men go into the woods as if they were to pass the winter within the polar circle, supplied with fur caps, half a dozen pair of gloves, heavy overcoat, three or four thick blankets, and any amount of useless *impedimenta*. Dry-goods clerks and students seem to affect this style the most. I remember running against a pair of huge alligator-leather boots, leaning against a tree, one day when crossing the "Carry" from Forked Lake around the rapids, and upon examination discovered a young undergraduate of a college not a thousand miles from Boston inside of them. It was about the middle of August, and the thermometer stood at 90° Fahrenheit. Some half a mile farther on we met the guide sweating and swearing under a pack of blankets, rubber suits, and the like, heavy enough to frighten a tramping Jew-pedler; and he declared that "that confounded Boston fool had brought in a *boat-load of clothes,*" which we found to be nigh to the truth when we reached the end of the "carry," where the canoe was. Now I wish that every reader who may visit the Adirondacks, male or female, would remember that a good-sized valise or carpet-bag will hold all the clothes any one person needs for a two months' trip in the wilderness, beyond what he wears in. Be sure to wear and take in nothing but woollen and flannel. The air at night is often quite cool, even in midsummer, and one must dress warmly. The following list comprises the "essentials" : —

Complete undersuit of woollen or flannel, with a "change."

Stout pantaloons, vest, and coat.

Felt hat.

Two pairs of stockings.

Pair of common winter boots and camp shoes.

Rubber blanket or coat.

One pair pliable buckskin gloves, with chamois-skin gauntlets tied or buttoned at the elbow.

Hunting-knife, belt, and a pint tin cup.

To these are to be added a pair of warm woollen blankets, *uncut*, and a few articles of luxury, such as towel, soap, etc. The above is a good service-able outfit, and, with the exception of the blan-kets, can readily be packed in a carpet-bag, which is easily stowed in the boat and carried over the "portages." In this connection, it should be re-membered that the Adirondack boats, while being models of lightness and speed, are small, and will not bear overloading. On the average they are some fifteen feet long, three feet wide at the mid-dle, sharp at both ends, some ten inches deep, and weigh from sixty to ninety pounds. Small and light as these boats are, they will sustain three men and all they really need in the way of baggage, but it is essential, as the reader can see, that no unnecessary freight be taken along by a party. Nothing is better calculated to make a guide cross and sour than an over-supply of personal baggage, and I advise all who attempt the trip to confine themselves very nearly to the above list. They will find that it is abundant.

For sporting outfit, this will suffice: —

One rifle and necessary ammunition.

One light, single-handed fly-rod, with "flies."

For rifles I prefer the "Ballard" or "Maynard" among breech-loaders. No shot-guns should be taken. They are a nuisance and a pest.

In respect to "flies," do not overload your book. This is a good assortment: —

Hackles, black, red, and brown, six each.

Avoid small hooks and imported "French flies."

Let the "flies" be made on hooks from Nos. 3 to 1, Limerick size.

All "fancy flies" discard. They are good for nothing generally, unless it be to show to your lady friends. In addition to the "Hackles,"

Canada fly (6), — an excellent fly.

Green drake (6).

Red ibis (6).

Small salmon flies (6), — best of all.

If in the fall of the year, take

English blue-jay (6).

Gray drake (6), — good.

Last, but not least, a large, stoutly woven landing-net.

This is enough. I know that what I say touching the salmon flies will astonish some, but I do not hesitate to assert that with two dozen small-sized salmon flies I should feel myself well provided for a six weeks' sojourn in the wilderness. Of course you can add to the above list many serviceable flies; my own book is stocked with a dozen dozens of all sizes and colors, but the above is a good practical outfit, and all one really needs.

If you are unaccustomed to "fly fishing," and prefer to "grub it" with ground bait (and good sport can be had with bait fishing too), get two or three dozens short-shanked, good-sized hooks, *hand tied* to strong *cream*-colored snells, and you are well provided. If you can find worms, they make the best bait; if not, cut out a strip from a chub, and, loading your line with shot, *yank* it along through the water some foot or more under the surface, as when fishing for pickerel. I have had trout many times rise and take such a bait, even when *skittered* along on the top of the water. To every fly-fisher my advice is, be sure and take plenty of casting-lines. Have some six, others nine feet long. There are lines made out of "sea snell."

These are the best. Never select a bright, glistening gut. Always search for the creamy looking ones. The entire outfit need not cost (rod excepted) over ten dollars, and for all practical purposes is as good as one costing a hundred.

WHERE TO BUY TACKLE.

If you buy in New York, go to J. Conroy, Fulton Street. This house is noted for its rods. No better single-handed fly-rod can be had than you can obtain at Conroy's. A rod of three pieces, twelve feet long, and weighing from nine to twelve ounces, is my favorite. A fashion has sprung up to fasten the reel on close to the butt, so that when casting you must needs grip the rod *above* the reel. This is a great error in construction. Never buy one thus made. The reel should be good eight inches from the butt, and thus leave plenty of hand-room below it. At Conroy's you can obtain such a rod, brass mounted, for some fifteen dollars ; in German-silver mountings, for seventeen. At other houses, for the very same or an inferior article I have been charged from twenty to twenty-five dollars. The first rod I ever bought at Conroy's, some six years ago, was a brass-mounted one, such as described above, which I used constantly for four years, but which I saw, on an evil day, go into four pieces, in a narrow creek, when I gave the butt to two large fish in full bolt for a snarl of tamarack-roots. Many a time have I seen that rod doubled up until the quivering tip lay over the reel. I paid fourteen dollars and fifty cents for it. I would like to pay three times that sum for another like it. If you want a rod that you can *rely* on, go to Conroy's in Fulton Street and buy one of his single-handed fly-rods.

If in Boston, William Read and Son's, No. 13 Faneuil Hall Square, is a good house to deal with. Being less acquainted in Boston than in New York, I cannot speak with such directness as I can concerning Conroy's. But having looked over Mr. Read's stock, I am quite persuaded that you can be as well served with rods by him as by any house in the country, Conroy always excepted. If I was buying in Boston, for my rod I should go to Read's. In respect to price, I am inclined to think that he sells the same class of rods cheaper than the New York house. I saw some rods at Mr. Read's the other day for *twelve dollars*, equal in all respects, so far as I could see, (and I tested them thoroughly,) to the rods for which Conroy charges fifteen dollars. At the same time I examined some split bamboo rods, price twenty-five dollars, for which many dealers in fishing-tackle, in New York, and perhaps some in Boston, would be likely to demand nearly twice that sum. Of course this firm is too well known to the sporting world for me to mention that, for a thorough hunting outfit, you can do no better than to go to this house.

For flies I advise you to go to Bradford and Anthony, 178 Washington Street. I am inclined to think that this house, in quantity, style, variety, and finish, excel even Conroy. I have looked their assortment over carefully, and know not where to find its equal. Wherever you buy, never purchase an imported fly. The French flies, especially, are most unreliable. Never put one in your book. Select only such as are tied to soft, cream-colored snells. The same holds good in respect to casting-lines or leaders. Beware of such as have a bright, glassy glitter about them. They will fail you on your best fish, and you will lose flies, fish, and temper together. For your lines I suggest, first, last, and always, braided silk. Beware of hair and silk lines. Formerly I had a great passion for fancy lines, but years of experience have caused me to settle down in favor of the braided silk line as superior to every other.

GUIDES.

This is the most important of all considerations to one about to visit the wilderness. An ignorant, lazy, low-bred guide is a nuisance in camp and useless everywhere else. A skilful, active, well-mannered guide, on the other hand, is a joy and consolation, a source of constant pleasure to the whole party. With an ignorant guide you will starve; with a lazy one you will lose your temper; with a low-bred fellow you can have no comfort. Fortunate in the selection of your guide, you will be fortunate in everything you undertake clean through the trip. A good guide, like a good wife, is indispensable to one's success, pleasure, and peace. If I were to classify such guides as are nuisances, I should place at the head of the list the "witty guide." He is forever *talking.* He inundates the camp with gab. If you chance to have company, he is continually thrusting himself impertinently forward. He is possessed from head to foot with the idea that he is *smart.* He can never open his mouth unless it is to air his opinions or perpetrate some stale joke. He is always vulgar, not seldom profane. Avoid him as you would the plague.

Next in order comes the "talkative guide." The old Indian maxim, "Much talk, no hunt," I have found literally verified. A true hunter talks little. The habit of his skill is silence. In camp or afloat he is low-voiced and reticent. I have met but one exception to this rule. I will not name him, lest it give pain. He is a good hunter and a capital guide, in spite of his evil tendency to gab. This tendency is vicious in many ways.

3 *   C

It is closely allied with that other vice, — *bragging.* Such a guide in a large party is apt to breed dispute and difference. He is very liable to give the gentleman who employs him the impression that others in the party are striving to " get ahead of him." Moreover, he is always interrupting you when you do not want to be interrupted. Silence, which is a luxury found only in the wilderness, flees at his approach. Beware of the talkative guide.

The next in order, and the last I shall mention, is the " lazy guide." Such a guide is the most vexatious creature you can have around. Nothing short of actual experience with one can give you an adequate impression. Now, a guide's duties, while not absolutely laborious, are nevertheless multiform. To discharge them well, a man should have a brisk, cheerful temperament and a certain pride in his calling. He should be quick, inventive, and energetic. With these qualities even ordinarily developed, a man makes a good guide ; without them he is intolerable. A lazy guide is usually in appearance fleshy, lymphatic, dirty, and often well advanced in years. As a rule, avoid an old guide as you would an old horse. His few years' extra experience, compared to a younger man, cannot make good the decline of his powers and the loss of his ambition. A young, active fellow of thirty, with his reputation to make, is worth two who are fifty and egotistical. The worst sight I ever saw in the woods, the exhibition which stirred me most, was the spectacle of a fat, lazy lout of a guide lying on his stomach, reading a dime novel, while the gentleman who hired him was building "smudges." If he had been my guide, I would have smudged him ! The "witty," "talkative," and "lazy guide" are the three hindrances to a party's happiness. If you find yourself or party burdened with either species, admonish kindly but firmly ; and if this mild application will not suffice, turn him mercilessly adrift, and post him *by name* on your way out, at every camp and hotel, as an imposition and a pest. Make an example of one or two, and the rest would take the hint. Every respectable and worthy guide will thank you for it, and your conscience will have peace as over a duty fulfilled.

For the most part the "independent guides" are models of skill, energy, and faithfulness. I say "independent," to distinguish the class so called from another class yclept " hotel guides." The difference between the two classes is this : the " hotel guides " are paid so much per month by the hotel-keepers, and by them furnished to their boarders and such as come unprovided. This system is faulty in many respects. The " hotel guide" is not responsible to the party for its success, and therefore is not quickened to make his

best endeavor. He has no reputation to make, as
has the independent guide, for his service is secured to him for the season, by virtue of his connection with the hotel. Furthermore, the " hotel
guide " is often unemployed for weeks if the season is dull; and, hanging around a frontier hotel
in daily proximity to the bar, is very liable to be-
get that greatest of all vices in a guide, — *drunken-
ness*. If, on the other hand, the season is a crowded
one, the proprietor finds it difficult to secure
guides enough for his guests, and so must needs
content himself with men totally unfit for the
service. Thus it often happens that a party taking
their guides at the hands of the landlord finds,
when too late, that out of half a dozen guides,
only one is capable, while the others are mere
make-shifts, the good guide being sent along as a
teacher and " boss " of the raw hands. I do not
say that there are no good guides among those
known as hotel guides, for there are ; but as a *class*
they are far inferior in character, skill, and habits
to the others.

The independent guides, so called, are, as a
whole, a capable and noble class of men. They
know their calling thoroughly, and can be relied
on. They have no other indorsement than such
as the parties to which they act as guides give them ;
and as their chances of subsequent service depend
upon their present success, they are stimulated to

the utmost to excel. Between these and the hotel guides there exists a rivalry, and I might employ a stronger term. The independent guide feels, and is not slow to assert, his superiority. He is justified in doing it. The system of hotel guiding is wrong in theory and pernicious in practice. Every guide should be immediately responsible to the party hiring him. His chances of future employment should depend upon his present success. This is the only natural, simple, and equitable method. It is beneficial to both parties. The sportsman is well served; and the guide, if he is faithful, secures constant employment from season to season. Many of the best guides are engaged a year in advance.

I cannot let this opportunity pass unimproved of testifying to the capacity, skill, and faithfulness of a great majority of the guides through the Adirondack region. With many I am personally acquainted, and rejoice to number them among my friends. I have seen them under every circumstance of exposure and trial, of feasting and hunger, of health and sickness, and a more honest, cheerful, and patient class of men cannot be found the world over. Born and bred, as many of them were, in this wilderness, skilled in all the lore of woodcraft, handy with the rod, superb at the paddle, modest in demeanor and speech, honest to a proverb, they deserve and receive the admiration of all who make their acquaintance. Bronzed and hardy, fearless of danger, eager to please, uncontaminated with the vicious habits of civilized life, they are not unworthy of the magnificent surroundings amid which they dwell. Among them an oath is never heard, unless in moments of intense excitement. Vulgarity of speech is absolutely unknown, and theft a matter of horror and surprise. Measured by our social and intellectual facilities, their lot is lowly and uninviting, and yet to them there is a charm and fascination in it. Under the base of these overhanging mountains they were born. Upon the waters of these secluded lakes they have sported from earliest boyhood. The wilderness has unfolded to them its mysteries, and made them wise with a wisdom nowhere written in books. This wilderness is their home. Here they were born, here have they lived, and here it is that they expect to die. Their graves will be made under the pines where in childhood they played, and the sounds of wind and wave which lulled them to sleep when boys will swell the selfsame cadences in requiem over their graves. When they have passed away, tradition will prolong their virtues and their fame.

I am often in reception of letters from gentlemen who wish to visit the wilderness, inquiring the names of guides to whom they can write for the purpose of engaging their services. I have been prompted to publish the following list in answer to such correspondence. I do not wish any to understand that the list is perfect, containing the names of *all* the good guides, for it does not. It contains the names of such as, through personal acquaintance or reliable information, I know to be worthy of patronage. Others, not mentioned here, there may be equally reliable. I make no invidious comparison in this selection. I seek only to give such as may be about to visit the region the names of certain guides to whom they can write with confidence, and whom, if they secure, they may deem themselves fortunate.

Long Lake Guides, or those whose Post-Office Address is Long Lake, Hamilton County, N. Y.

John E. Plumbley,
Jerry Plumbley,
Amos Hough,
Henry Stanton,
Isaac Robinson,

John Robinson,
Amos Robinson,
Michael Sabatis and Sons,
Alonzo Wood,
Reuben Cary.

Lower Saranac Guides.

Stephen Martin,
James McClellan,
Lute Evans,
Harvey Moody,
John King,

Duglass Dunning,
George Ring,
Daniel L. Moody,
Mark Clough,
Reuben Reynolds,

George Sweeny,   Alonzo Dudley,
William Ring,   Daniel Moody.

Post-office address,
Lower Saranac, Franklin County, N. Y.

St. Regis Guides.

I can recall the names of only three.

Seth Warner,   Stephen Turner,
David Sweeny.

Post-office address,
St. Regis, Franklin County, N. Y.

Concerning the guides in the "Brown Tract," and on the western side of the wilderness, around the Potsdam region, I know nothing. The Arnolds, I understand, of the Brown Tract district, owing to an unfortunate occurrence last fall, have all deserted that section of the country. The house their father kept is now unoccupied, and whether it will be opened this spring I know not.

HOW TO GET TO THE WILDERNESS.

There are several routes which you can take in an excursion to the North Woods, but only one or two which are easy and practicable for a party composed both of ladies and gentlemen. If you wish to enter at the southern end of the wilderness, and do your sporting in the Brown Tract region, go to Albany and thence to Booneville, from which place you can get transported on horseback to the first of the chain of lakes known as the " Eight Lakes." Here was formerly a hotel, known as " Arnold's." The Arnold family have now left, and I know not if the house is kept open. This entrance is not easy for ladies, nor is the region into which it brings you at all noted for the beauty of its scenery. Still many sportsmen go in this way, and to such a class it is a feasible route. You can also " go in " *via* Lake George and Minerva to Long Lake, if you choose. The distance is some eighty miles by this route, the roads bad, and the hotel accommodations poor. Long Lake is a good starting-point for a party, as it is situated midway of the forest, the centre of magnificent scenery, and the home of many guides. All it needs to make this route one of the very best is, that the roads should be improved, and a good line of coaches established. But as it now is, it is neither practicable nor entirely safe.

The best route by which to enter the wilderness is the following. It is easy and quick. The accommodations are excellent all the way through. I do not know how I can give a true impression of this route so briefly as by going, in imagination, with the reader, from Boston to the Lower Saranac, where I meet my guide. I leave Boston Monday morning, we will say, at eight o'clock, on the Boston and Albany Railroad.   At East Albany we connect with the Troy train; at Troy, with the Saratoga train, which lands you at the steamboat dock at Whitehall, Lake Champlain, at nine o'clock, P. M.   Going on board you sit down to a dinner, abundant in quantity and well served; after which you retire to your state-room, or, if so inclined, roll an arm-chair to the hurricane deck, and enjoy that rarest of treats, a steamboat excursion on an inland lake by moonlight.   At 4.30 A. M. you are opposite Burlington, Vt., and by the time you are dressed the boat glides alongside of the dock at Port Kent, on the New York side of the lake. You enter a coach which stands in waiting, and, after a ride of six miles in the cool morning air, you alight at the Ausable House, Keeseville.   Here you array yourself for the woods, and, eating a hearty breakfast, you seat yourself in the coach at 7 A. M., the whip cracks, the horses spring, and you are off on a fifty-six mile ride over a plank road, which brings you, at 5 P. M., to Martin's, on the Lower Saranac, where your guide, with his narrow shell drawn up upon the beach, stands waiting you. This is the shortest, easiest, and, beyond all odds, the best route to the Adirondacks.   You leave Boston or New York Monday at 8 A. M., and reach your guide Tuesday at 5 P. M.   So perfect are the connections on this route, that, having engaged

"John" to meet me a year from a certain day, at 5 P. M., on the Lower Saranac, I have rolled up to "Martin's" and jumped from the coach as the faithful fellow, equally "on time," was in the act of pulling his narrow boat up the beach. It is not only easy and quick, but the cheapest route also, and takes you through some of the sublimest scenery in the world. At Keeseville, if you wish, you can turn off to the left toward North Elba, and visit that historic grave in which the martyr of the nineteenth century sleeps, with a boulder of native granite for his tombstone, and the cloud-covered peaks of Whiteface and Marcy to the north and south, towering five thousand feet above his head. By all means stop here a day. It will better you to stand a few moments over John Brown's grave, to enter the house he built, to see the fields he and his heroic boys cleared, the fences they erected and others standing incomplete as they left them when they started for Harper's Ferry. What memories, if you are an American, will throng into your head as you stand beside that mound and traverse those fields! You will continue your journey a better man or purer woman from even so brief a visit to the grave of one whose name is and will ever be a synonyme of liberty and justice throughout the world. If you are mere tourists, and intend going no farther westward than North Elba, stop at Westport, above

Crown Point, and take stage to your destination. At a Mr. Helmer's (I think that is the name) you will find all necessary accommodation. If you are going into the wilderness, it is better to engage your transportation from Keeseville in advance, in order to prevent delay. To this end you can address the proprietor of the Ausable House, Keeseville, or W. F. Martin, keeper of "Martin's," as it is familiarly known to sportsmen at the Lower Saranac. This is the direct route also to reach Paul Smith's, at the St. Regis Lake. Another route, — a new one just opened, which I have never tried, — is *via* Plattsburgh, by which you can go by rail to a point within thirty miles of "Martin's." Address W. F. Martin for particulars.

HOTELS.

This subject I shall dismiss with a brief allusion. Paul Smith, or "Pol," as he is more commonly known among the guides, is proprietor of the St. Regis House. This is the St. James of the wilderness. Here Saratoga trunks and Saratoga belles are known. Here they have civilized "hops," and that modern prolongation of the ancient war-whoop modified and improved, called "operatic singing," in the parlors. In spite of all this, it is a capital house, with a good reputation, well deserved

"Bartlett's" is situated on the carry between Round Lake and the Upper Saranac. This house is well kept. The rooms are neatly furnished, the service at the tables slightly suggestive of "style." The proprietor is a brisk, business-like-looking man, pleasant and accommodating. I have never seen or heard aught to his discredit, and much in his praise. Many gentlemen leave their wives and children here while they are in the wilderness sporting. This house is conveniently located, and within easy reach of excellent hunting-ground. I heartily recommend it to public patronage.

"Mother Johnson's."—This is a "half-way house." It is at the lower end of the carry, below Long Lake. Never pass it without dropping in. Here it is that you find such pancakes as are rarely met with. Here, in a log-house, hospitality can be found such as might shame many a city mansion. Never shall I forget the meal that John and I ate one night at that pine table. We broke camp at 8 A. M., and reached Mother Johnson's at 11.45 P. M., having eaten nothing but a hasty lunch on the way. Stumbling up to the door amid a chorus of noises, such as only a kennel of hounds can send forth, we aroused the venerable couple, and at 1 A. M. sat down to a meal whose quantity and quality are worthy of tradition. Now, most house-keepers would have grumbled at being summoned to entertain travellers at such an unseasonable

hour. Not so with Mother Johnson. Bless her soul, how her fat, good-natured face glowed with delight as she saw us empty those dishes! How her countenance shone and sides shook with laughter as she passed the smoking, russet-colored cakes from her griddle to our only half-emptied plates. For some time it was a close race, and victory trembled in the balance; but at last John and I surrendered, and, dropping our knives and forks, and shoving back our chairs, we cried, in the language of another on the eve of a direr conflict, " Hold, enough !" and the good old lady, still happy and radiant, laid down her ladle and retired from her benevolent labor to her slumbers. Never go by Mother Johnson's without tasting her pancakes, and, when you leave, leave with her an extra dollar.

" *Uncle Palmer's* " is at Long Lake, and commands a view of lake and mountain scenery rarely surpassed. There are many houses open to guests in the wilderness more ostentatious; but for downright solid comfort commend me to " Uncle Palmer's." The table is well supplied; the cuisine is excellent; the beds neat and clean; the location central. Mr. Palmer is one of the most honest, genial, and accommodating men whom I have ever met. His wife is active, pleasant, and motherly. Both are full of the spirit of true kindness, and sympathetic in all their words and acts. You may be a total stranger, but no sooner are you fairly inside the house than you feel yourself perfectly at *home*. In this neighborhood live John Plumbley, and his brother Jerry, Amos Hough, Henry Stanton, Isaac Robinson and boys, Michael Sabatis and sons, and many others of the very best guides in the wilderness. Sabatis keeps a hotel on the shore of the lake, and at his house many sportsmen resort. I have heard it well spoken of, but cannot speak from experience, as I never had the pleasure of stopping over there. On the whole, I do not hesitate to say that Long Lake is, in my opinion, the best rendezvous of the wilderness, and Uncle Palmer's long table the very best spot to find yourself when hungry and tired.

"*Martin's.*" — This is the last house of which I shall speak. It is located on Lower Saranac, at the terminus of the stage route from Keeseville. It is, therefore, the most convenient point at which to meet your guides. Its appointments are thorough and complete. Martin is one of the few men in the world who seem to know how "to keep a hotel." At his house you can easily and cheaply obtain your entire outfit for a trip of any length. Here it is that the celebrated Long Lake guides, with their unrivalled boats, principally resort. Here, too, many of the Saranac guides, some of them surpassed by none, make their head-quarters. Mr. Martin, as a host, is good-natured and gentlemanly.   His table is abundantly provided, not only with the necessaries, but also with many of the luxuries, of diet.   The charges are moderate, and the accommodations for families, as well as sporting parties, in every respect ample. " Martin's " is a favorite resort to all who have ever once visited it, and stands deservedly high in public estimation.

WHEN TO VISIT THE WILDERNESS.

The purpose for which you go, and .the character of the sporting you desire, should decide this point.   If you desire river fishing for spotted trout, and trolling for the lake trout, some of which grow to weigh from twenty to thirty pounds, you should go in during the month of May or June. The objection to this time lies in the fact that the wilderness is wet and cold at this season of the year, when the snow is barely melted, the portages muddy and unpleasant, and the " black flies " in multitudinous numbers.

These objections, to my mind, are insurmounta- ble.   No ladies should go into the wilderness sooner than the middle of June.   If you want to see autumnal scenery, unsurpassed by any the world. over, and hear the " music of the hounds " in full cry after that noblest of all game for dogs, the antlered buck in swift career, go in during the month of September, and remain until snow and the cold drive you out.

My favorite season is in midsummer. I go in early in July, and remain for about two months. Late in June or early in July the "black fly" disappears. The wilderness is dry, and the climate is delightful. The thermometer stands at about seventy-five or eighty degrees. The portages are in good condition, the water not high, the lily and marsh flowers in bloom. The fishing is excellent. The trout have left the rapids and the upper portions of the streams, and gathered in great numbers at the "spring-holes," the location of which your guide is supposed to know, if not, he can easily, if he understands his business, ascertain. No better fishing can be found than spring-hole fishing, which you will find carefully described in the chapter entitled "The Nameless Creek." As for hunting, the sport is excellent during these two months. July is the best month for Jack or night shooting,—the most exciting of all shooting. The bucks by this time are in good condition, and not over-shy. These are the only months when you have shore-shooting, as it is called; that is, when you see deer feeding in broad daylight, and take them from the open boat at a good, easy range,— say from twenty to thirty rods. This is what I call good, honest sport, and not slaughter, as when

3   D

the dog drives a deer into the lake, and, rowing up beside the poor frightened and struggling thing, the guide holds him by the tail while you blow his brains out! Bah! I should be ashamed to ever look along the sights of a rifle again if I had ever disgraced myself with any such "sporting" (!) as that! At this time of the year rain-storms are unknown in this region, and the thunder-showers which occur are a source of pleasure, and not of inconvenience, to a camp. No more sublime sight can the eye behold than is presented to it when such a shower passes over these mountains.

HEALTHFULNESS OF CAMP LIFE.

I am often asked if ladies would not "catch cold" in the woods, and if the physical exertion which one must put forth is not such as to forbid that any but robust people should undertake the trip. To this I reply that I believe it to be a physical impossibility for one, however fragile or delicate, to "catch cold" in this wilderness. Remember that you are here in a mountainous region, where dampness and miasma, such as prevail in lower sections, are entirely unknown. Consider, too, how genial and equable is the climate in the summer months, and how pure and rarefied the atmosphere. Remember, also, that you breathe an air odorous with the smell of pine and cedar and balsam, and absolutely free from the least taint of impurity; and when you take all this into account, you will see how very dissimilar are the conditions and surroundings of life in the woods to life in the city or village. Acquainted as I am with many ladies, some of them accustomed to every luxury, and of delicate health, who have "camped out" in this wilderness, I have yet to meet with a single one who ever "caught cold," or experienced any other inconvenience to the bodily health in the woods.

As to the "physical exertion," there is no such exertion known here. It is the laziest of all imaginable places, if you incline to indolence. Tramping is unknown in this region. Wherever you wish to go your guide paddles you. Your hunting, fishing, sight-seeing, are all done from the boat. Going in or coming out you cross the necessary carries, which, for the most part, are short and good walking, and you can take your own time for it. In this I refer, of course, to the most frequented parts of the wilderness, and not to the portions seldom visited and more difficult of access. There are sections which I have visited by dragging my cedar shell behind me up narrow creeks and through tamarack swamps, middle deep in mud and water; but no guide would think of taking a party, unless urged by the party itself, into any such region; and, ordinarily speaking, there is no need of exertion which a child of five summers could not safely put forth, from one end to the other of a trip.

WHAT SECTIONS TO VISIT.

If you go in by way of the Saranacs, do not camp down in that section as some do, but pass over Indian Carry, through the Spectacle Lakes and Ramshorn Creek (called by some Stony Creek), into the Racquette River. Then turn up or down as you please. If you desire to see some of the finest scenery imaginable, pass up the Racquette to Long Lake, and, when some two miles up the lake, turn your face toward the north, and you will behold what is worth the entire journey to see. Then go on, and do not camp until you do so on the southern or western shore of Racquette Lake. Here you will find good sporting and scenery unsurpassed. Build here your central camp, and, as soon as you are established, take your boat and go over to the "Wood's Place," and from the knoll on which the house stands you will gaze upon one of the finest water views in the world. Then visit Terrace Lodge, on an island to the front and left of you, and, climbing up the ledge, you will either find the writer there to welcome you, or see where he and one better than he have passed many delightful hours. Only beware how you appropriate it, for we have a sort of life-lease on that camp-ground, and may appear to claim possession when you least expect us. Then paddle to Beaver Bay, and find that point in it from which you can arouse a whole family of sleeping echoes along the western ridge and the heavy woods opposite. Then go to Constable Point, and quench your thirst at the coolest, sweetest spring of pure water from which you ever drank. Go next to the southern part of the lake, so hidden behind the islands that you would never suspect such a lovely sheet of water lay beyond, with its two beautiful reaches of softly shining sand, one white as silver, the other yellow as gold; and in the waters which lave the golden, find the best bathing in the whole wilder-ness. Do not leave this region until you have made an excursion to that Lake George in minia-ture, Blue Mountain Lake, and fill your mind with an impression which will remain in memo-ry as one of the sweet and never-to-be-forgotten recollections of life. When you have retraced your progress up, and reached the mouth of Rams-horn Creek, keep on down the Racquette until you have swung round to Big Tupper Lake and lunched on the sloping ledge over which the outlet of Round Lake and Little Tupper pours its full tide in thunder and foam; and, if it be not too late in the season, and you know how to use the rod, you will

raise, amid the froth and eddies of the falls, some
of the largest, gamiest, brightest-tinted trout that
ever gladdened a sportsman's eye. Then, if you are
robust and full of pluck, force your way over the
four-mile carry, between the Falls and Round Lake,
and, hurrying on through its sluggish waters, do
not pause until you enter the narrow, secluded
stretch of Little Tupper. But the moment you
enter stop, joint your rod, and noose on your
strongest leader and largest flies, for you will
find right there, at the entrance of Bog Creek,
trout that will put your skill and tackle to the
severest test. When I passed through that region
last, I left, as John expressed it, "more than five
boat-load of fish" in that deep, sluggish pool.
Honest John Plumbley, the prince of guides, patient
as a hound, and as faithful, — a man who knows the
wilderness as a farmer knows his fields, whose instinct is never at fault, whose temper is never ruffled, whose paddle is silent as falling snow, whose
eye is true along the sights, whose pancakes are
the wonder of the woods, — honest, patient, and
modest John Plumbley, may he live long beyond
the limit so few of us attain, and depart at last full
of peace as he will full of honors, God bless him !

As you pass out, visit the St. Regis waters, by
the way of Big Wolf, and Rollin's Pond, and Long
Pine, and so circle down to " mine host " at Martin's. What a trip you will have had, what won-

ders seen, what rare experiences enjoyed! How
many evenings will pass on "golden wings" at
home, as friends draw close their circle around the
glowing grate, and listen as you rehearse the story
of your adventures, — shoot over again your "first
buck," and land for the hundredth time your "biggest" trout!

BLACK FLIES.

I will speak of these and other nuisances before
I close, in order to state the exact truth in reference to a subject concerning which newspaper and
magazine writers have given the public an erro-
neous impression. The spirit of exaggeration, and
the necessity of "getting up a good article," have
contributed to the dissemination of "anecdotes"
and "experiences" which are the merest balderdash
imaginable. I am prompted, therefore, to make,
as we were accustomed to say in college, a "plain
statement of facts," that my readers may know
precisely how much inconvenience a tourist or
sportsman is subject to, from this source, among
the Adirondacks. The black fly, concerning which
so much of the horrible has been written, is a
small, dark-colored fly, about the size of a red ant.
Its bite is not severe, nor is it ordinarily poisonous.
There may be an occasional exception to this rule;

but beside the bite of the mosquito it is comparatively mild and harmless. This fly prevails during the month of June and disappears early in July. It also invariably retires at the setting of the sun, and gives you no more trouble until late in the morning. I regard it as one of the most harmless and least vexatious of the insect family. For five years my wife and self have camped in the wilderness; we have traversed it near and far, sleeping where the night found us, but we have never been, to any extent worth mentioning, disturbed by its presence. The black fly, as pictured by "our Adirondack correspondent," like the Gorgon of old, is a myth, — a monster existing only in men's feverish imaginations.

MOSQUITOES.

In some localities these are numerous, but with care in the selection of your camp you will not be very much troubled. A headland, or a point which projects into a lake, over which the wind sweeps, or, better still, an island, is excellent ground for a camp, where mosquitoes will not embarrass you.

Gnats can also be avoided by the same care; and, in my way of thinking, they are much worse than the black fly or mosquito.

Against all these insects you can find abundant protection. The following precautions, which we have adopted with complete success, I would recommend, especially to such of my lady readers as contemplate a visit to this or any other inland region. For the hands, take a pair of common buckskin gloves and sew on at the wrists a gauntlet or armlet of chamois-skin, reaching to the elbow, and *tightly buttoned* around. Do not leave any opening, however small, at the wrist, else the gnats may creep up the arm. This gives perfect protection to the hand. For the face, take a yard and a half of Swiss mull, and gather it with an elastic band into the form of a sack or bag. Have the elastic so as to slip over the head, which when you have done, fix the elastic inside the *collar-band*, and you can laugh defiance at the mosquitoes and gnats. We, in addition to this, take in a piece of *very fine* muslin, some four yards square, which, if threatened with gnats or flies, having first thoroughly smoked the tent or lodge, we drop over the front or doorway, and behind its protection sleep undisturbed. To sportsmen, and indeed to all, I suggest this also. Take in a bottle of sweet oil and a vial of tar. These the guide will mix, and with a small bottle of the compound in your pocket you can go and come night or day as you please. All manner of insects abhor the smell of tar. When, therefore, you have need to fish or hunt or

3*

journey where they may be expected, pour out a little into the palm of your hand and anoint your face with it. To most persons the scent of tar is not offensive, and the mixture washes off on the first application of soap and water, leaving no trace or taint. To reconcile my lady readers to it, I may add, that it renders the skin soft and smooth as an infant's.

I have mentioned these various protections, not because we often resort to them, but simply from a desire to furnish my readers ample knowledge for every emergency. Last summer we were in the wilderness nearly two months, but suffered more in the first two weeks after our return, in a city in Connecticut, than during our entire stay in the woods. Care in the selection of your camp, and the employment of the above-mentioned methods of protection, will obviate every difficulty and make you as free from inconvenience as you would be in the majority of New England villages.

LADIES' OUTFIT.

A lady at my elbow, recalling how valuable a few suggestions would have been to her five years ago in respect to what is most appropriate and serviceable for a lady to wear in the wilderness, inserts the following list : —

A net of fine Swiss mull, made as we have previously described, as protection against mosquitoes, gnats, etc.

A pair of buckskin gloves, with armlets of chamois-skin or thick drilling, sewed on at the wrist of the glove and buttoned near the elbow so tightly as to prevent the entrance of flies.

For the head, a soft felt hat, such as gentlemen wear, rather broad in the brim. This is light and cool for the head, and a good protection from sun and rain.

A flannel change throughout.

Thick balmoral boots, with rubbers.

A pair of camp shoes, water-proof, warm and roomy.

Short walking-dress, with Turkish drawers fastened with a band tightly at the ankle.

Waterproof or rubber coat and cap.

A pair of Lisle-thread or kid gloves.

To this I add, as it occurs to me at this point, that no party should go into the wilderness unprovided with linen bandages, prepared lint, salve, and whatever else is needed in case of accident. You will not, probably, have occasion to use them, but if any casualty should occur they would be of the utmost service.

WILD ANIMALS.

I am often asked, especially by ladies, if it is not dangerous to take such a trip, and if wild animals do not abound in the wilderness; and I know that many are deterred from making the excursion because of their timidity. The only animals concerning which the most timid could be alarmed are the bear, wolf, and panther. The latter is a very ugly neighbor indeed, and the less you have to do with him the better. I am tolerably familiar with wood life, and the sights and sounds of such danger as one is liable to meet in the wilderness; and John and I have slept more than once, calmly enough, with our rifles inside our blankets, not knowing when we lay down what cry might awaken us; but I should not purposely put myself in the way of a panther, unless I could run my eye along the sights of my double rifle when the barrels were freshly charged. In speaking of the panther, I do not, of course, allude to the Canadian wild-cat, with which the ignorant often confound the panther, but to the *puma* itself, an animal which often measures twelve feet from tip to tip, and is the slyest, strongest, bloodiest ranger of the woods. Now, fortunately, the panther is almost wholly unknown in this region. A few still live among the loneliest defiles and darkest gorges of the Adirondack Mountains, but they never come down, unless in the depth of winter, to the shores of the lakes to the west, or the banks of the rivers. Many years have passed since one has been seen by any of the guides. The region traversed by parties is as free from them as the State of Massachusetts.

Black bears abound in some localities, but more timid, harmless creatures do not exist, all the old stories to the contrary notwithstanding. In temper and action toward men they resemble very closely the woodchuck. Their first and only anxiety is to escape man's presence. If you penetrate far enough into the wilderness, you will occasionally, at night, hear them nosing around your camp, with hedgehogs and the like, but ever careful to keep out of your sight. A stick, piece of bark, or tin plate shied in the direction of the noise, will scatter them like cats. The same is true of wolves. They are only too anxious to keep out of your sight and hearing. Touch a match to an old stump, and in two hours there will not be a wolf within ten miles of you. I wish all to take the statement as in every sense true, when I declare that there is absolutely no danger, nor indeed the least approach to danger, in camping in the wilderness. Many and many a night has my wife, when John and I were off on a hunt, slept soundly and without a thought of danger, in the depths of the forest, fifty miles

from even a hunter's cabin. It is true that her
education in woodcraft is more extensive than
that of most ladies, and, for presence of mind,
quickness and skill with the rifle, many so-called
"crack shots" might well take lessons of her; but
were this not true, I regard a camp, granted only
that it be so far in that men cannot reach it, as a
place of absolute security.

PROVISIONS.

All you need to carry in with you is

Coffee,	Pepper,
Tea,	Butter (this optional),
Sugar,	Pork, and Condensed Milk.

Always take crushed sugar; powdered sugar is
not easily picked up if the bag bursts and lets it
out among the pine-stems.

If you are a "high liver," and wish to take in
canned fruits and jellies, of course you can do so.
But these are luxuries which, if you are wise,
you will leave behind you.

BILL OF FARE.

I am often asked, "What do you have to eat up
there?" In order to answer the very natural
question, and show the reader that I do not starve,

I will give my bill of fare as you can have it served, if you will call at my camp on the Racquette next July. This is no "fancy sketch," but a *bona fide* list which I have "gone through" more than once, and hope to many times more.

Vegetables.

Potatoes, boiled, fried, or mashed.

Meats.

Venison, roast.	Venison sausages.
" steak, broiled.	" hash.
" " fried.	" spitted.

Fish.

Lake Trout (salmon).	Trout (spotted).
Boiled.	Fried (in meal).
Baked.	Broiled.
Broiled.	Spitted.
Chowder.	

Pancakes, with maple sirup (choice).
Bread, warm and stale, both.
Coffee.   Tea.

Now imagine that you have been out for eight hours, with a cool, appetizing mountain breeze blowing in your face, and then fancy yourself seated before your bark table in the shadow of the pines, with the water rippling at your feet; a lake dotted with islands, and walled in with mountains, before you, and such a bill of fare to select from, and then tell me if it looks like starvation ? If a man cannot make a pound of flesh per day on that diet, I pity him !

And now, patient reader, having given you all the information necessary to make you acquainted with the geography of the wilderness, the character of the sporting therein, the outfit needed for the excursion, the best routes of entrance, and certain suggestions as to hotels, guides, and contrivances of protection from gnats and flies, I close this chapter with the wish that you may find, in excursions which you may make thereto, the health and happiness which have, upon its waters and under its softly murmuring pines, come to me, and more abundantly — as to one who needed them more — to her who joins me in the hope of meeting you amid the lilies which fleck with snow its rivers, or in the merry circle, free from care, which, on some future evening, we hope to gather around our camp-fire.

II.

THE NAMELESS CREEK.

IT was five o'clock in the afternoon when, after
three hours of constant struggle with the current, we burst our way through a mass of alder-
bushes and marsh-grass, and behold, the lake lay
before us! Wet from head to foot, panting from
my recent exertion, having eaten nothing since
seven in the morning, and weary from ten hours'
steady toil, I felt neither weariness nor hunger as
I gazed upon the scene. Shut in on all sides by
mountains, mirrored from base to summit in its
placid bosom, bordered here with fresh green
grass and there with reaches of golden sand, and
again with patches of lilies, whose fragrance, mingled
with the scent of balsam and pine, filled the air,
the lake reposed unruffled and serene.

I know of nothing which carries the mind so far
back toward the creative period as to stand on the
shore of such a sheet of water, knowing that as you
behold it, so has it been for ages. The water
which laves your feet is the same as that which
flowed when the springs which feed it were first
uncapped. No rude axe has smitten the forests

E

which grow upon the mountains; even the grass at your side is as the parent spire which He who ordereth all commands to bring forth seed after its kind. All around you is as it was in the beginning. I know not how long I should thus have stood musing, but for a motion of John's, which broke the chain of thought and brought my mind back to the practical realization that we were wet, hungry, and tired. In the middle of the lake was a large flat rock, rising some two feet above the surface of the water. Stepping noiselessly into our boat, we paddled to the rock, and, wringing our dripping garments, stretched ourselves at full length upon it to dry. O, the pleasant sensation of warmth which that hard couch, to which the sun had given a genial heat, communicated to us! · Never was bed of eider-down so welcome to royal limbs as was that granite ledge to ours. What luxury to lie and watch the vapor roll up from your wet garments while the warm rock gave out its heat to your chilled body! In an hour we were dry, at least comparatively so, and we held a council. Our commissariat was getting rather low. Our stores, spread upon the rock, amounted to the following: two pounds of pork, six pounds of flour, four measures of coffee, one half-pound of tea. John estimated that this would last us three days, if I had ordinary success with the rod. "But what are we to do to-night?" I exclaimed; "we have

neither trout nor venison, and I am hungry enough
to eat those two pounds of pork alone, if I once
get fairly at it, and there goes the sun back of
the tree-tops now ?" "Well, unstrap your rod and
select your flies," responded he, "and we will see
what we can find. I don't mean to have you wrap
yourself around that piece of pork to-night any
way." I did as requested. For the tail fly I
noosed on a brown hackle, above it I tied a killer,
and for the dapper I hitched on a white moth.
Taking the bow seat, John paddled straight for the
west shore of the lake, and the light boat, cutting
its way through the lily-pads, shot into a narrow
aperture overhung with bushes and tangled grass,
and I saw a sight I never shall forget. We had
entered the inlet of the lake, a stream some twenty
feet in width, whose waters were dark and sluggish.
The setting sun yet poured its radiance through the
overhanging pines, flecking the tide with crimson
patches and crossing it here and there with golden
lanes. Up this stream, flecked with gold and bordered with lilies as far as the eye could reach, the
air was literally full of jumping trout. From amid
lily-pads, from under the overhanging grass, and
in the bright radiance poured along the middle of
the stream, the speckled beauties were launching
themselves. Here a little fellow would cut his
tiny furrow along the surface after a fluttering
gnat; there a larger one, with quivering fin and

open mouth, would fling himself high into the air in a brave attempt to seize a passing moth; and again, a two-pounder, like a miniature porpoise, would lazily rise to the surface, roll up his golden side, and, flinging his broad tail upward, with a splash disappear. Casting loose my flies and un-coiling my leader, I made ready to cast; but John, unmindful or regardless of the motion, kept the even sweep of his stroke. Round tufted banks, under overhanging pines, and through tangled lily-pads we passed, and at every turn and up every stretch of water the same sight presented itself. At length, sweeping sharply round a curve, John suddenly re-versed his paddle and checked the boat, so that the bow stood upon the very rim of a pool some forty feet across. Dark and gloomy it lay, with its sur-face as smooth as though no ripple had ever crossed it. No one would have guessed that beneath the tranquil surface lay life and sport.

Adjusting myself firmly on my narrow seat, un-tangling the snells and gathering up my leader, I flung the flies into mid-air and launched them out over the pool. The moment their feathery forms had specked the water, a single gleam of yellow light flashed up from the dark depth, and a trout, closing his mouth upon the brown hackle, darted downward. I struck and had him. A small trout he proved to be, of only some half-pound weight. After having passed him over to John to be disen-

gaged, I again launched the flies out, which, pausing a moment in mid-air as the straightened line
brought them up, began slowly to settle down, but
ere they touched the water four gleams of light
crossed the pool and four quivering forms, with
wide-spread tails and open mouths, leaped high
out of water. I struck, and, after a brief struggle,
landed two. From that moment the pool was literally alive with eager fish. The deep, dark water
actually effervesced, stirred into bubbles and foam.
Six trout did I see at once in mid-air, in zealous
rivalry to seize the coveted flies. Fifteen successive casts were made, and twenty-three trout
lay flapping on the bottom of the boat. But of
them all none would weigh over three quarters
of a pound; yet had I seen fish rise which must
have balanced twice that weight. I turned to John
and said, "Why don't some of those large ones
take the fly?" "Presently, presently," responded he.
"The little ones are too quick for them; cast away
quick and sharp, waste no time, snap them off, never
mind the flies, and when you have cleared the surface of the small fry you will see what lies at the
bottom." I complied. At last, after some forty
had been flung down the stream, the rises became
less frequent, the water less agitated, and, partly
to rest my wrist and partly to give John time to
adjust new and larger flies, I paused. In five
minutes the current had cleared the pool of bub-

bles, and the dark water settled gradually into sullen repose. "Now," said John, "lengthen your line and cast at that patch of lily-pads lying under the hemlock there, and if a large one rises, strike * hard." I did as desired. The flies, in response to the twist of the pliant rod, rose into the air, darted forward, and, pausing over the lily-pads, lighted deftly on the water. Scarcely had their trail made itself visible on the smooth surface, before a two-pounder gleamed out of the dark depths, and rolling his golden side up to the light, closed his jaws upon the white moth. I struck. Stung by the pain, he flung himself, with a mighty effort, high in air, hoping to fall upon the leader and snap the slender gut. Dropping the point of my rod, he came harmlessly down upon the slack. Recovering himself, he dove to the bottom, sulking. Bearing gradually upon his mouth, the only response I got was a sullen shaking, as a dog shakes a woodchuck. Fearing his sharp teeth would cut the already well-chafed snell, I bore stoutly upon him, lifting him bodily up toward the surface. When near the top, giving one desperate shake, he started. Back and forth, round and round that pool he flashed, a gleam of yellow light through the dark water, until at last, wearied and exhausted by his efforts, he rolled over upon his side and lay

---

* This word is one employed by sportsmen to denote the motion with which the fish is *hooked*.

panting upon the surface. John deftly passed the
landing-net under him, and the next minute he lay
amid his smaller brethren in the boat. I paused a
moment to admire. A bluish-black trout he was,
dotted with spots of bright vermilion. His fins,
rosy as autumnal skies at sunset, were edged with
a border of purest white. His tail was broad and
thick ; eyes prominent, mouth wide and armed with
briery teeth. A trout in color and build rarely
seen, gamy and stanch. Noosing on a fresh fly in
place of the one his teeth had mangled, I made
ready for another cast. Expecting much, I was not
prepared for what followed.

Now, all ye lovers of bright waters and green-
sward, who lift a poor half-pounder with your big
trolling-rod and call it sport, listen and learn what
befell one of your craft at sunset at the pool of the
Nameless Creek. Nameless let it be, until she who
most would have enjoyed it shall, on some future
sunset, floating amid the lilies, cast flies upon its
tide.

A backward motion of the tip, and a half-turn of
the wrist, and the three flies leaped upward and
ahead. Spreading themselves out as they reached
the limit of the cast, like flakes of feathery snow
they settled, wavering downward ; when suddenly
up out of the depth, cleaving the water in concert,
one to each fly, three trout appeared. At the
same instant, high in mid-air, their jaws closed on

the barbed hooks.   No shout from John was needed to make me strike.   I struck so quick and
strong that the leader twanged like a snapped
bow-string, and the tip of the light rod flew down
nearly to the reel.   *All three were hooked.*   Three
trout, weighing in the aggregate seven pounds, held
by a single hair on a nine-ounce rod, in a pool
fringed with lily-pads, forty by thirty feet across !

Then followed what to enjoy again I would ride
thrice two hundred miles.   The contest, requiring
nerve and skill on the fisher's part, was to keep the
plunging fish out of the lily-pads, in which, should
they once become entangled, the gut would part
like a thread of corn-silk or the spider's gossamer
line.   Up and down, to and fro, they glanced.   The
lithe rod bent like a coachman's whip to the unusual strain, and the leader sung as it cut through
the water with the whir of a pointed bullet.

At last, when at the farthest corner of the pool,
they doubled short upon the line, and as one fish
rushed straight for the boat.   Fishermen know what
that movement means.   " Give 'em the butt ! give
'em the butt !" shouted John.   " Smash your rod
or stop 'em !"   Never before had I feared to thrust
the butt of that rod out toward an advancing fish ;
but here were three, each large enough to task a
common rod, untired and frenzied with pain, rushing directly toward me.   If I hesitated, it was but
an instant, for the cry of John to " Smash her !

smash your rod or stop 'em!" decided the matter. Gripping the extreme butt with one hand, and clutching the reel with the other, I held them steadily out, toward the oncoming fish. "Good by, old rod," I mentally exclaimed, as I saw the three gleaming forms dash under the boat; "stanch as you are, you can't stand that." An instant, and the pressure came upon the reel. I gripped it tightly, not giving an inch. The pliant rod doubled itself up under the strain, until the point of the tip was stretched a foot below the hand which grasped the butt, and the quivering lance-wood lay across the distended knuckles. Nor fish nor rod could stand that pressure long. I could feel the fibres creep along the delicate shaft, and the mottled line, woven of choicest silk, attenuated under the strain, seemed like a single hair. I looked at John. His eyes were fastened upon the rod. I glanced down the stream, and even at the instant the three magnificent fish, forced gradually up by the pliancy of what they could not break, broke the smooth surface and lay with open mouths and gasping gills upon the tide. In trying to land the three, the largest one escaped. The other two averaged sixteen inches long. Within the space of forty minutes nearly a hundred trout had been taken, fifty of which, varying from one quarter of a pound to two pounds and a half in weight, lay along the bottom of the boat; the rest

4

had been cast back into the water, as unhooked by John. It was Saturday evening. The sun had gone down behind the western mountains, and amid the gathering shadows we sought a camp. We found one in the shape of a small bark lodge, which John himself had erected fourteen years previous, when, in company with an old trapper, he camped one fall upon the shores of this lake. Kindling a fire in the long-neglected fireplace, we sat down to our supper under the clear sky already thickly dotted with stars. From seven in the morning until eight in the evening we had been without food. I have an indistinct recollection that I put myself outside of eleven trout, and that John managed to surround nine more. But there may be an error of one or two either way, for I am under the impression that my mental faculties were not in the best working condition at the close of the meal. John recollects distinctly that he cooked twenty-one fish, and but three could be found in the pan when we stopped eating, which he carefully laid aside that we might take a bite before going to sleep !

Our meal was served up in three courses. The first course consisted of trout and pancakes; the second course, pancakes and trout; the third, fish and flapjacks.

"I looked at John; his eyes were fastened on the rod."

III.

RUNNING THE RAPIDS.

"NOW for the rapids," said John, as our boat left the tranquil waters of the lake, and, sweeping around a huge shelving ledge, shot into the narrow channel, where the waters, converged from either shore, were gathering themselves for the foam and thunder below.

The rapids were three miles in length, — one stretch of madly rushing water, save where, at the foot of some long flight or perpendicular fall, a pool lay, specked with bubbles, and flecked with patches of froth. The river is paved with rocks, and full of boulders, amid which the water glides smooth and deep, or dashes with headlong violence against them. And ever and anon, at the head of some steep declivity, gathering itself for flight, downward it shoots with arrowy swiftness, until, bursting over a fall, it buries itself in the pool beneath.

At the head of such a stretch of water, whose roar and murmur filled the air, we ran our boats ashore. Never until this season had these rapids been run, even by the guides; and now, untried,

inexperienced, against the advice of friends, I was
to attempt, unaided and alone, to guide my boat
past ledge, through torrents, and over waterfalls,
to the still bay below.   The preparation was
simple, and soon made.   I strapped my rifle, rod,
and all my baggage to the sides and bottom of the
boat, relaced my moccasins and tightened my belt,
so that, in case I stove the shell, or, failing to keep
her steady, should capsize her, I might take to the
water light, and have my traps drift ashore with
the wreck.   Nevertheless, I did not intend that
the boat should upset; indeed, the chances were
in my favor.   Oars and boats had been my play-
things from a boy; and wild indeed must be the
current up and across which I could not shoot
the shell in which I sat, — made of forest pine,
fourteen feet in length, sharp as an arrow, and
weighing but seventy pounds.   In addition, John
had given me valuable hints, the sum of which
might be expressed thus : " In currents, keep her
straight ; look out for underlying rocks, and smash
your oars before you smash your boat."   " Little
danger," I said to myself, " of snapping oar-blades
made of second-growth ash, and only eight feet
from butt to tip."   Yet it was not without some
misgiving that I shot my boat out into the swift
current, and with steady stroke held her on the
verge of the first flight of water, while I scanned
the foam and eddies for the best opening between

the rocks to get her through. In shooting rapids the oarsman faces down stream in order to watch the currents, direct his course, and, if need be, when within his power, and danger is ahead, to check his flight and choose another course. The great thing and the essential thing to learn and do is to take the advantage of the currents, whirls, and eddies, so as to sway your boat, and pass from this to that side of the rapids easily. The agreement was, that John should precede me in his boat; that I, watching his motions, and guided by his course somewhat, might be assisted in the descent by his experience. A good arrangement, surely ; but

> " The best laid schemes o' mice and men
> Gang aft agley,"

as we found before half a mile of the course had been run ; for my boat, being new and light, beside less heavily loaded than John's, caught at the head of some falls by the swift current, darted down the steep decline, and entering side by side, with a mighty leap, the yeasty foam, shot out ahead, and from that moment led the race to the foot of the rapids. But I anticipate.

Thus, as I said, I sat in my boat, holding her steadily, by strength of oar, in mid-stream, where the water smoothed itself for the plunge, until John, with friend Burns sitting upon his feet like a Turk, on the bottom of the boat, holding on to either side with his hands to steady himself (whether John had strapped him down or not I can't surely say), pushed from shore, and, taking the current above, brushed swiftly by, with the injunction to "follow." I obeyed. Down we glided, past rock and ledge, swerving now this side, now that, sweeping round giant boulders and jutting banks, down under the dark balsams and overhanging pines, the suction growing stronger and stronger, the flight swifter, until the boats, like eagles swooping on one prey, took the last stretch almost side by side, and, lifted high up on the verge of the first falls, made the wild leap together, and disappeared into the yeasty foam, whence, rising buoyantly, uplifted by the swelling water, shot out of the foam and mist, and, like birds fresh from sport, floated cork-like on the pool below.

We paused a moment to breathe, when, looking up, the two remaining boats, guided by Jerry and the younger Robinson, bearing Southwick and Everitt as passengers, came sweeping round the curve, and rushing, as from the roof of a house, to the brink of the fall, flung themselves into the abyss, and in a moment lay along our side. The excitement was intense. No words can describe the exhilaration of such a flight. It was thought, after mature deliberation by the company, that

Everitt's delighted yell alone, in ordinary weather, with a little wind in its favor, might have been heard easily sixteen miles. His whole being, corporal and spiritual, seemed to resolve itself into one prolonged howl of unmitigated happiness.

Having rested ourselves, we started again. By this time, brief as the experience had been, I had learned much as to the action of currents, and was able to judge pretty correctly how low a rock or ledge lay under water by the size and motion of the swirl above it. One learns fast in action; and fifteen minutes of actual experience amid rapids does more to teach the eye and hand what to do, and how to do it, than any amount of information gathered from other sources. To sit in your light shell of a boat, in mid-current, with rocks on either side, where the bed of the river declines at an angle of thirty degrees, knowing that a miscalculation of the eye, a misstroke of the oar or the least shaking of the muscles will send your boat rolling over and over, and you under it, has a very strong tendency to make a man look sharp and keep his wits about him.

Well, as I said, we started. For some fifty rods the current was comparatively smooth and slow. The river was wide and the decline not sharp. The chief difficulty we found to be in avoiding the stones and rocks with which the bottom of the river is paved, and which in many places were

barely covered. My boat, with only myself in it,
needed but some two inches of water to float in,
and would pass safely over where the other boats
would touch or refuse to go at all. It required
great care on the part of the guides to let theirs
over gently, as their bottoms are but little thicker
than pasteboard, and held by small copper tacks.
At last the shallows were past, and, bringing our
boats in line, one behind the other, we made all
ready for another rush. The sight from this point
was grand. Our boats were poised as on the
ridge-board of a house, while below, for some
twenty rods, the water went tearing down ; now
gliding over a smooth shelving ledge, with the
quick, tremulous motion of a serpent, and now
torn to shreds by jagged rocks at the bottom, and
again beat back by huge boulders which lifted
themselves in mid-current, presenting to the
eye one continuous stretch of mad turmoil and
riot. At the foot of the reach the eye could just
discern the smooth, glassy rim of a fall, we knew
not how high, while far down the river, shut from
view by a sharp curve, the rush and roar of other
falls rose sullenly up through the heavy pines and
overhanging hemlocks, which almost arched the
current from side to side. At a word from John,
who, leading the van, sat as a warrior might sit
his steed, bareheaded and erect, the oars were
lifted, and the freed boats, as though eager for

flight, started downward. Away, away they flew. If before they went like birds, they went like eagles now. No keeping in line here; each man for himself in this wild race; and woe to boatman and to boat if an oar should break or oar-bolt snap. Close after John, gaining at every rush, my light boat sped. No thought for others, all eye and nerve for self, with a royal upleaping of blood, as my face, wet with the spray, clove through the air, I flashed until the fall was reached, and, side by side, with trailing oars, we took the leap together. Down, down we sank into the feathery foam; the froth flung high over us as we splashed into it. Down, down, as if the pool had no bottom, we went, our boats half full of spume and foam, till the reacting water underneath caught the light shells up and flung them out of the yeast and mist, dripping inside and out, from stem to stern, as sea-birds rising from a plunge. No stop nor stay for breathing here. Around the curve, by no effort of mine leading the race, I went, swept down another reach and over another fall, and, without power to pause a moment, entered into the third before I had time to think. Steeper than all behind, it lay before me, but straight, and for a distance smooth, for aught I could see as I shook the spray from my eyes, until it narrowed, and the converging torrent met between two overhanging rocks in one

4 *   F

huge ridge of tossing, swelling water. What lay below I knew not ; how steep the fall, or on what bottom I should land. In rapids, John had told me, the wildest water was the safest, and so I steered straight for the highest swell of water and the whitest foam. Fancy a current, rods in width, converging as it glides, until the mass of rushing water is brought as into an eaves-trough five feet across, with sharp, jutting rocks for sides, where the compressed water flings itself wildly up, indignant at the restraint put upon it; and then fancy yourself in a boat weighing but seventy pounds, gliding down with a swiftness almost painful into the narrow funnel through which, bursting, you must shoot a fall you cannot see, but whose roar rises heavily over the dash of the torrent, and you can realize what it is to shoot the rapids of the Racquette River, and my position at the time.

Balancing myself nicely on the seat, dipping the oar-blades until their lower edges · brushed along the tide, I kept my eyes steadily upon the narrow aperture, and let her glide. Nothing but the pressure of the air upon the cheek, as the face clove it, and the sharp whistling of the seething current, bespeaks the swiftness with which you move. When near the narrow gorge, — which you must take square in the centre, and in direct line, or smash your boat to flinders, — while the width would yet allow, wishing some steerage-way before I entered the chasm, I threw my whole strength upon the oars. The lithe ash bent to the strain, and the boat quivered from stem to stern under the quick stroke. Then, bending forward upon the seat, with oars at a trail, I shot into the opening between the rocks. For an instant the oar-blades grated along their sides, and then, riding upon the crest of a wave, I passed out of the damp passage, and lo! the fall whose roar I had heard yawned just beneath me. Quick as thought, I swung the oars ahead, and as the billow lifted me high up upon the very brink, gave way with all my might. Whatever spare strength I had lying anywhere about me, at that particular point of time, I am under the impression was thrown into those oar-blades. The boat was fairly lifted off the wave, and shot into the air. For an instant, it touched neither water nor foam, then dropped into the boiling caldron. Another stroke and it darted out of the seething mass with less than a gallon of water along the bottom.

The rapids were run! Wiping the sweat from my face, and emptying the water from the barrels of my rifle, I rested on my oars, to see the boys come down. O, royal sight it was, to see them come, one after another, — John leading the van, — over the verge! As boats in air they seemed, with airy boatmen, as they came dashing along.

O, royal sport, to see them glide like arrows down the steep, at an angle so sharp that I could see the bottom board in each boat, from stem to stern! O, noble sight to see them enter in between the mighty rocks, — the chasm shutting them from view a moment, — from which, emerging in quick succession, with mighty leaps, quivering like sporting fish, they shot the falls triumphantly!

What sports have we in house and city like those which the children of wood and stream enjoy? — heroic sports which make heroic men. Sure I am, that never until we four have done with boats and boating, and, under other pilotage, have entered into and passed through the waters of a colder stream, shall we forget the running of the Racquette Rapids, on that bright summer day. And often, as we pause a moment from work, above the harsh rumble of car and cart, the sound of file and hammer, rises the roar of the rapids. And often, through the hot, smoky air of town and city, to cool and refresh us, will drift, from the far north, the breeze that blows forever on the Racquette, rich with the odors of balsam and of pine.

That night I slept upon the floor at Palmer's, proud to feel that I was the first "gentleman" — in the language of the guides — "that ever ran the rapids"; prouder of that than of deeds, attempted or done, of which most men would longer dream. I nearly forgot to state that several unearthly yells in the chamber overhead, during the night, revealed the fact that *somebody*, in dreams, was still running the rapids.

IV.

THE BALL.

WE were seven in all, — as jolly a set of fellows as ever rollicked under the pines, or startled the owls with laughter, that summer of '67, when camping on the Racquette. Our company represented a variety of business and professions; but, happily, we were of one temper and taste.

There was Hubbard, a gentleman faultless in bearing and speech; the fit of whose coat and the gloss of whose boots, whether you met him in Wall Street or at his manufactory in Connecticut, might well stir the envy of an exquisite. There was Everitt, to whose name you could write photographer, artist, violinist; the most genial, sunny, kind-hearted, and rollicksome fellow that ever enlivened a camp, or blest the world with his presence. Southwick, when at home, supplied half the city with soles; who sells boots and shoes in such a manner as to make you feel, as you go stamping away from his presence, that he has done you a special favor in condescending to take your money at all; a man who crossed the Isthmus, and tunnelled the gulches of California for gold in 1848 ; a shrewd, wide-awake Yankee, such as are grown principally in that smartest of all our States, — the Nutmeg State. And there, too, was Fitch, who had handled the saw and lancet in the army during the war. And Fay, the lawyer, who had fought the battle all young lawyers must fight, and won. And Burns, and the Parson. A goodly set of fellows, one and all, equally ready for business or fun.

We were on our way " out," bronzed and tough from exposure to the sun, water, and wind; and with hearts as free from care and as light as children's, we clomb the hill, at the base of which we had run our boats ashore, and entered, with merry greetings, Uncle Palmer's house. What a hungry set we were, when, at four o'clock that afternoon, we drew up to that never-to-be forgotten table ! What jokes and stories and peals of laughter enlivened the repast, and made the table and dishes shake and clatter as the meal progressed. No coarseness nor rudeness there ; each man a gentleman still, amid the liveliest sally of wit and loudest roar of merriment. At last the meal was over, and we adjourned to the open air to smoke or lounge, or to engage in rivalry of skill, until the day, rich in its summer loveliness, should fade away. Several matches with the rifle — the result of boastful banter— at last engage the attention of

the entire party.   Our targets were pennies stuck
into the end of a slender stick, two or three feet
long, which Jerry held out some thirty paces off;
the rule being that no bullet must graze the
stick.   Pretty close work it was, requiring steady
nerves and an exact eye; but penny after penny
had been dashed out of the slot, and hurled into
the oat-field beyond.   The blue smoke from the
muzzle of my rifle was curling gracefully into the
air as I closed the contest, when Everitt exclaimed,
"What shall we do to-night, boys?"   "Let us
have a dance," shouted Hubbard; "Uncle's dining-
room is just the place to trip the light fantastic
toe."   And he jumped up from the log on which
he had been sitting, and struck into a double-
shuffle, which sent the chips flying in all directions.

"Hurrah! a ball, a ball!" screamed Southwick,
"unless the Parson objects.   A speech from the
Parson! hear, hear!" he continued, as he turned a
double summersault over Fay's back, and landed
some distance down the slope in an onion-bed.
Unfortunately for the Parson, Southwick's yell
was taken up, and the words "Speech!" "Ball!"
"Parson!" "Dance!" resounded on all sides.
Being thus called upon, I could not refuse to
give my opinion.   Indeed, I may be pardoned
when I admit that I felt quite flattered by the
heartiness of the call.   It was more direct and

unanimous than I ever expect to receive from any
church whatever. Moreover, for I wish the true
state of the case to be thoroughly understood, I
had not made a speech for nearly three weeks.
Now, as all my readers know, "making speeches"
is about the only *bona fide* perquisite of the profession. This is the great advantage we have over
laymen. The moment you take this away from
a clergyman, you rob him of his great prerogative,
and he becomes no better than an ordinary man.
My clerical readers will, I am sure, sympathize
with me in my position. For three weeks I had
been of no importance whatever to the world, but
here was a chance to do some good; here, unex-
pectedly, an opportunity to make a speech had
presented itself. I mounted a pile of cedar slabs,
and, trying to feel modest, began : —

"Dancing, my friends, I remark in the first
place, is a very pernicious habit." That was a
good beginning. Even three weeks of constrained
and cruel deprivation had not deprived me of my
"gift." Pausing a moment to note the effect of
my opening sentence upon the audience, I was
slightly embarrassed at the sight of Southwick
dropping small chips down the neck of Burns's
shirt. Rallying in an instant, I resumed : "It has
been the means, my hearers, of getting many a
young man into a scrape." Here I paused again.
Whatever weakness the first sentence had in it,

this had the true sermon ring.   No, I had not lost
my power.   My birthright had not been filched
from me.   I began to feel the oratorical impulse
once more.   I drew myself up, closed the thumb
and two middle fingers of my left hand, and pointing the other two directly at the audience, as I had
seen some of our celebrated orators, clenched the
right fist, and shook it at an invisible foe over
my head, — a gesture borrowed from some of our
Congressmen, — and shouted : " Dancing will be a
perilous amusement to you to-night ; because —
because — "   I lost the connection here, but re-
membering what a slight matter such a lapse is
in a sermon, before most congregations, and feeling that it would not do to stop just there, continued, — "*because* it leads to a promiscuous mingling of the two sexes.   On this ground I am
to-night, and ever shall be, opposed to it.   I warn
you against Mr. Southwick's suggestion."

At this point I was interrupted by the most
uproarious tumult.   Intense and indecorous merriment seized the entire group.   Hubbard was
pressing his hands against his sides in the
most suggestive manner.   Everitt was hammer-
ing Southwick with both fists upon his back, in
the hope of saving him from death by stran-
gulation.   It was impossible to proceed.   I was
conscious that I ought to go on. · I had several
splendid sentences all ready for utterance.   I felt

that every moment I was losing my hold upon the audience. Still the uproar grew. In wrath, mingled with love, I descended from the slabs, and taking Burns gently but decidedly by the collar, demanded the cause of his unseemly mirth.

Sobered slightly by my attitude, which was sternly affectionate, Burns managed to articulate, " How can there be a ' promiscuous mingling of the sexes' in this crowd ? "

I stood perfectly dumb. I saw the justness of the criticism and the dilemma suggested. I realized, at that moment, the value of logical connection.

Had my audience been in a church, and devoutly drowsy or piously asleep, such a slight slip would never have been noticed, and the report of the sermon, written out by a godless expert, who had not left his hotel during the day, would have appeared excellently in Monday's papers.

I retired in haste and mortification from the yelling and writhing group ; nor did I regain my composure until the sounds of Everitt's violin charmed the darkness from my soul as the harp of David exorcised by its melody the wicked spirit from the bosom of Saul.

Now Everitt is a natural fiddler. He fiddles as easily as a rabbit runs. While camping on Constable Point, on the Racquette, we had several concerts. They were, in every sense, impromptu affairs.   The audience was small, but very appreciative.   (That sentence is not original.   I borrowed it from the musical column of the New York Herald.)   These concerts were especially well sustained; that is, for about four hours and a half each time.   We had some very fine singing at those *soirées*.   (*Soirées* is a good word.   It sounds well.   That's why I use it.)   I hesitate to instance individual members of this troupe, lest it should seem invidious.   Hubbard is an excellent singer.   He missed his chance of eminence when he went into business.   He should have taken to the stage.   The Parson would have distinguished himself, had he lived before notes were invented. Nothing in the world but notes prevents him from ranking first class.   Even this fact did not preclude him from standing high in this company. Nevertheless, I am still impressed with the thought that he was born too late.   I never listened to a circle of amateurs who seemed to rise so superior to the arbitrary *dictum* of the masters as did this. Not one of them, so far as I could observe, allowed any such artificial impediments as notes, pitch, time, and the like, to obstruct the splendid outbursts of nature.   In point of *emphasis*, which is, as all my readers know, the great desideratum in music, I judge them to be unrivalled.   In that classic stanza,

" There sat three crows upon a tree,"

their emphasis was magnificent. But I was telling about Everitt's fiddling. Nature dealt bountifully with my friend in this respect. His capacity and perseverance in drawing a bow border on the marvellous. Indeed, he is a kind of animated musical machine. Set him going, and he will play through the entire list of known tunes before he comes to a halt. His intense activity in this direction afforded the only possible solution for the greatest mystery of the camp, — Everitt's appetite while in the woods. I find in my "notes" a mathematical calculation, made the fifth night in camp. It was the result of the gravest deliberation on the part of the whole company, and is beyond doubt nearly correct. This is the formula : —

"Exhaustion of muscular fibre through fiddling, two pounds per night. Consumption of venison steak, three and a half pounds.

"Net gain to Everitt, one pound and a half per night."

This conclusion contributed materially to relieve the minds of the company from an anxiety concerning the possible results of the trip to Everitt.

When I entered the room, drawn thither, as I have said, by the tones of the violin, the company were in full career. The intricacies of the Virginia reel were being threaded out with a rapidity which, with ladies for partners, would have been rather embarrassing. After the quadrille, Spanish

dance, and several others had been gone through,
the floor was cleared for individual exhibitions
of skill. Then was the double-shuffle executed
with an energy never excelled. Gentlemen and
guides contended in friendly rivalry. Everitt
was in prime condition, and drew the bow with
a vehemence which, if long continued, would
have sent him out of the woods lighter in flesh
by several pounds than when he came in. At last
the floor was again cleared, partners chosen, and
with every rule of etiquette observed, good old
money-musk was honored, — partners gallantly
saluted as if they were ladies, jewelled and fair,
and the company seated.

At this point the proceedings assumed a new
character. The conversation might be reported
thus : —

Guide. " I suppose you folks down in the settlements don't dance as we do ? "

Everitt. " Well, no, not exactly. Our dances
are largely French."

Guide. " Do tell ! Well, now, how is that ? "

Everitt. " I do not think I could give you a correct idea of them ; they are very peculiar."

Guide. " Come, now, could n't some of you give
us a notion about it ? We would like to see how
you dance down in the cities."

Everitt. | " The fact is, we have more *action* in
our dancing than you have in yours. It would

make your eyes stick out to see a French dance."

Guides. "Come, now," they all shouted, "show us how it is done; we all want to see. Give us one of your tip-top French dances. Come, now."

"Well, fellows," said Everitt, giving us the wink as he tuned his violin, "what say you, shall we show our friends how to dance a real, swinging French dance? If so, shall we put Hubbard or Southwick on the floor?"

"O, Southwick by all means!" shouted Burns. "No disparagement to Hubbard, but Southwick is the man; especially if he will give us the dance he danced last summer on our fishing-trip 'Down East.'" So it was arranged, and Southwick took the hint and the floor.

Now Southwick was the best dancer there; that is, he covered the most ground. His performance was the theme of universal remark. His style was superb. There was a certain *abandon* in it, which few Americans could rival. I know of but one word which can at all describe Southwick when dancing; it is — omnipresent. This epithet is moderately accurate.

The room was some thirty-five feet long, but he was often at both ends of it at the same time. If to rivet the attention of the audience is success, my friend certainly achieved it. There was but one thought on the part of the whole company whenever Southwick danced; it was to get out of the way. Greater unanimity in this respect was never seen. Never, before that evening, did I desire that a room might have more than four corners, but I more than once devoutly wished that that room had had sixteen. Sixteen would not have been one too many, with my friend on the floor. I called Uncle Palmer's attention to the terrible lack of corners in his house. At the time I made the suggestion, the old gentleman was trying to force himself in between the door-post and the sheathing. He appeared to appreciate it. After a few preliminary flourishes, Everitt shouted the word "Go!" and Southwick struck out. I saw him coming, and dodged; I escaped. The next time he swung round, I was prepared for him. There were several wooden pins driven into the logs near the ceiling, such as our forefathers were wont to season their beef-hams on. Spying one of these just over my head, as I stood flattened against the wall, I vaulted from the floor and clutched it. The scene from this point of view was very picturesque. The fellows had observed my movement, and followed my example: it affected them like an inspiration. In an instant the whole company were suspended from pins around the room. A sense of the ludicrous overcame my terror, and I began to laugh. That laugh grew on me. I found myself unable to stop laughing. My eyes began to moisten and run over. Now, a man cannot laugh in that fashion, and hang on to a pin at the same time. I have tried it, and know. First one finger began to slip, then another loosened and gave way a little; the muscles of my hand would not obey my will to contract. I found it impossible to retighten my grip; I knew it would probably be fatal to drop. I endeavored to stop laughing. Now, it is a well-known fact, that when one tries to stop laughing he can't. If you ever doubted this, reader, never doubt it again. If any man strove to stop, I did. My effort was vain. I fairly shook myself off the pin, and dropped. That sobered me. The instant I struck the floor, all laughter departed. I saw Southwick coming. I seized hold of the window-sill, the wood of which was cedar; I sunk my nails deep into it; *it held*. The next time he swung round the circle I was saved by a miracle, that is, in a way I cannot account for. I was just poising myself for a plunge at the door, when the music ceased, and my friend sat down. We all cheered him immensely. I cheered louder than all the rest. I never had greater cause to cheer. Everybody complimented him. One exclaimed, " What a free action!" another, " How liberal in style!" I said, " Astonishing!" We all saw that it had made a great impression on the guides. They said that " they had no idea folks danced *so*, down in the settlements." "It is n't anything to what I could do if the room was only larger, is it?" said he, appealing to me. "No; this room is terribly cramped," I responded, thinking of my narrow escape, and fearful that he might repeat the performance; "no educated dancer can do himself justice in it; I would not try again, if I were in your place."

At this point of the entertainment a delightful addition was made to the party. Certain messengers, who started early in the evening on horses and in boats, had scoured the country and lake shore, and returned accompanied by a bevy of young ladies. Their entrance caused great commotion. Hubbard glanced uneasily at his unpolished boots. Burns had fished a pair of old kids from the depth of his hunting-shirt pocket, and was inspecting their condition behind Southwick's back. Everitt suddenly discovered that he could keep his seat without the use of three chairs. The Parson brightened up at the prospect that his philippic against dancing, and the "promiscuous mingling of the sexes," might yet be delivered with effect. There was a dead pause. All were introduced to the ladies, each guide presenting "his man." Uncle Palmer's benignant face appeared at the door, looking perfectly jubilant.

Here the writer would gladly pause. He feels that the narration has proceeded far enough.

Would that he might record that the company played "blind-man's-buff," or "roll the trencher," or those refined "ring plays" where healthy and moral exhilaration is experienced by each man hugging and kissing his partner. But his duty as a historian forbids. Truth must not be mutilated through partiality for friends; and, as a chronicler of facts, he is bound to say, affirm, and transmit to posterity, that the company actually *danced*! Yes, that is the word, — *danced*. *O tempora*! *O mores*! which, freely translated, signifies, "What is the world coming to!" Reader, pardon this exhibition of virtuous feeling, this generous outburst against the vices of the day. Even Herodotus could not have restrained himself, in my position. But I must return to the historic style, — the plain narration of facts.

First, Uncle Palmer led off with his wife, — age countenancing the foibles of youth! Then Uncle Ike Robinson tripped down the floor with his daughter. Next, O ye gods! Hubbard whirled away with a nimble-footed damsel. Burns shot by with little Miss Palmer, and Southwick, the indomitable, careered along the floor with Jerry, his guide. (Which was the lady I cannot say.) And last of all, "John," the trusty, honest John, whizzed past with a lovely attachment to his arm. The costumes of the dancers were unique. In cut and color no one could complain of sameness.

Uncle Ike was in his stockings. John had on tightly-laced moccasins. Southwick sported a pair of bright scarlet slippers. Hubbard shook the floor with boots that had seen service on the "carry." All were mingled together; while above the din made by heavy boots smiting the resounding floor, the merry laugh of girls, and peals of irrepressible mirth, the voice of Everitt, who sat perched upon the back of a chair, sawing away with all his might, rang out the necessary orders. It has been reported that at this juncture the Parson himself was swept by the centripetal attraction into the revolving mass, and that the way he "cut it down" revealed a wonderful aptness for the "double-shuffle," and that a large amount of the old Adam remained yet to be purged out of his natural constitution. The probabilities are that this report is entirely unfounded, or at least grossly exaggerated.

At last, well along in the fashionable hours, the revelry ceased, the company separated, and silence settled down over the household. With the sounds the scene itself would have passed away and been forgotten save by the actors, had not the pen of the Parson rescued it from threatened oblivion, and in these pages preserved it for transmission to posterity. He thus avenges himself on those who interrupted him in the exercise of his right, by recounting the folly his speech would undoubtedly have prevented, had he been permitted to proceed.

V.

LOON-SHOOTING IN A THUNDER-STORM.

THE shrill cry of a loon piercing the air broke my heavy slumber, and brought me to my feet in an instant, rifle in hand. The night before, late in the evening, we had run our boat ashore, and, stretching ourselves on either side of the quickly lighted camp-fire, with no shelter but the overhanging trees, dropped instantly to sleep. From that slumber, almost as deep as that which is endless, the cry of a loon had aroused me. Directly in front of the camp, with his long black head and spotted back glistening in the sun, some fifteen rods from the shore, the magnificent bird sat, eying the camp. If there is any sound which will start a fellow to his feet quicker than the cry of a loon under his camp, about six in the morning, I have yet to hear it. Wide awake the instant I struck the perpendicular, I dropped my rifle — never in those woods, by day or night, beyond reach — into the extended palm, and simultaneously the sharp concussion broke the surrounding silence. The sight was good, and the lead well sent; but the agile bird,—well named the Great Northern

Diver, — ever on the alert, had gone under with the
flash ; and the bullet, striking the swirl made by
his dive, glanced up, and went bounding, in ever-
lessening skips, across the lake.   The crack of the
rifle awoke John from a slumber such as men sleep
after fourteen hours of constant rowing ; and, starting up, the fire was soon rekindled, and the coffee
boiling.   Soon all was ready, and we were pro-
visioning ourselves for the coming day.   Trout,
coffee, and the inevitable flapjacks made up the
bill of fare.

The morning, in its atmospheric appearances, was
peculiar.   Not a breath of air was stirring.   The
little lake was as liquid glass, without ripple or
seam.   Even the forest, that, like the sensitive
strings of a harp, is rarely, if ever, silent, sent
forth no sound, and its dim recesses were still as
death.   Above, the clouds were dull and slaty.
They, too, hung motionless.   No scud drifted
athwart their surface ; no rift broke their smooth
expanse.   The sun, with its broad face barred with
streaks of cloud, looked red and fiery.   It had
a hot, angry look, as if enraged at seeing the ob-
structions in its upward path.   In the west, out
of the slaty cloud, the white and feathery heads of
some cumuli upreared themselves, suggesting rain
and the hot blaze of lightning.

"John," said I, as we each sat with a warm
trout in one hand and a pint-cup of coffee in

the other, — "John, we shall have a tough day of it."

"Yes," said he, pausing a moment in his eating to listen, and holding on with one hand to the tail of a fish, of which the front half was already beyond human sight; "there goes some thunder now"; and even as he spoke a jar shook the earth under us, and a heavy roar rolled up sullenly out of the west.

We finished our meal, and then, lighting our pipes, seated ourselves on the shore of the lake, in counsel. The air was heavy, thick, and oppressive; not a sound broke the stillness. Had the heavens above us been the roof of a cavern a thousand fathoms under earth, the breathless quiet could not have been deeper. The colloquy ran something in this wise : —

"How long is the next carry, John ?"

"Three miles, if we go to Bottle Pond; a mile and a half, if we go to Salmon Lake," was the answer.

"How is the carry to Bottle Pond ?" I asked.

"A mere trapper's line," said John; "it is n't cut out; two miles and a half by blazed trees, and half a mile of slough."

"That 's delightful !" I exclaimed; "how is it by way of Salmon Lake ?"

"It 's a mile and a half to Salmon," was the response; "not cut out; crossed only in winter by hunters; half a mile of swamp."

"Well, we 'll go to Salmon Lake; that 's the nigher," I said. "Shall we get rain?"

As John was about to reply, a dull, heavy sound came up from the depths of the forest, — a solemn, ominous sound, breaking the dead silence. Another and another followed; a muffled roar, filling the air, so that one might not tell from what quarter it came.

"Yes," said John, as the noise died away,— "yes, it *will* rain. The old trees never lie. Those sounds you have just heard are made by falling trees. You always hear them before a storm."

"But, John," I exclaimed, "what makes them fall this morning? There is not a breath of air stirring."

"I don't know," responded John, "what makes them fall. I have often thought how queer it is. Many a time have I sat in my canoe on a morning like this, when there was not wind enough to float a feather, and seen the old fellows come crashing down. I tell you what," continued he, "it makes a man feel solemn, to see tree after tree, great, giant chaps, a hundred and. fifty feet high, begin all of a sudden to quiver and reel, and then fall headlong to the ground; when, for aught you can see, there is no earthly cause for it. Let us sit still a moment and hear them."

I did as requested. Now, far away in the forest, the same dull, heavy roar would arise, linger a moment in the air, then die away. Then, nigh at hand, a rushing sound, as the broom-like top of some mighty pine swept through the air, would fall upon the ear, followed by the crash of broken boughs and the heavy thump of the huge trunk as it smote the earth. Then, far away, half smothered between the mountains, would rise again the dull roar, and we knew another monarch of the woods had yielded its life at an unknown summons.

I am free to confess, that John's remark as to the effect of such a phenomenon upon one, was then and there fully verified by myself. I know nothing more mysteriously solemn than this sound of falling trees coming up from the forest, — falling, so far as you can see, without cause. What unseen hand smites them ? What pressure, unfelt by man, pushes their vast trunks over ? Is it to the Spirit of the coming Storm they bow, prostrating themselves in anticipation of his chariot's approach ? Is there some subtle and hostile chemistry in the air which penetrates their fibres, weakening them to their fall ? Or do these aged patriarchs of the wood, with fearful prophecy, foresee their hour of doom, and, in the breathless lull ere the tempest breaks, yield like an ancient Roman to their fate ?

"Perchance," I said to John, "He who noteth the falling of a sparrow and marketh the boundary

5 *

of human life, hath given the trees a limit also, which they may not pass; and these are being summoned, and so go down."

We sat a moment in silence; then, with a common impulse, without a word, arose, and, gathering up our traps, made ready for a start. As we pushed out into the lake, we saw that the clouds in the west were blacker; a flash of lightning ran along their upper verge, and the mountain above us caught up the heavy boom, and, as if enraged at the intrusion on its silence, hurled it back angrily toward the cloud. At the same instant the shrill, mocking cry of a loon rose into the air, mingling with the reverberations of the thunder, as light treble notes break sharply through a heavy volume of bass.

" There 's the confounded loon," exclaimed John, " that frightened the deer from the shore last night. If it was n't for that thunder-shower in the west, we 'd teach her to keep her mouth shut before we left the pond. I think you might start the feathers off her back any way, tube or no tube."

The last sentence needs explanation. Loons are the shyest and most expert swimmers of all waterfowl. Twenty rods is as near as you can get to them. When under fire, they sink themselves into the water so that nothing but the feathers along their backs and heads are in sight, and so quick are they that they dive at the flash, getting under in time to escape the bullet. Yet I have killed them repeatedly on Long Island Sound, driving my bullet through the butt of the wing, thirty rods away.   There are two styles of gun-tubes; the first kind is so open as to allow the powder to pass up to the cap.   When the cap explodes, this powder must burn grain by grain, and so comparatively slow.   The other kind is so made as to prevent the powder from passing up into it; and the lightning-like percussion has free course to the centre of the charge in the chamber.   Slight as the difference would seem to be, it is a vital one in loon-shooting.   With tubes of either make in the barrels of my rifle, loading with the same charge, I have killed with the one and invariably failed to kill with the other.   Unfortunately, the tubes in my barrels this season were both *open* ones; and to this John alluded in his closing remark.

"John," said I, counting out fifty bullets and laying them on the bottom of the boat within easy reach, "there are fifty bullets; and if you say the word, shower or no shower, we 'll give that old loon a lively time before we strike the carry."

"Well," said John as he ran his eye over the western heavens, now black as night, save when a bright flash clove the darkness or leaped crinkling along the inky mass, "let 's give her a try.   We shall have an hour, anyway, before the rain reaches us, and I would like to see that loon in the bottom of the boat."

Dipping his paddle into the water with a strong
sweep, he turned the bow of the light boat about,
and started toward the bird. Light as a cork the
loon sat upon the water, some sixty rods away, its
neck, marked with alternate rings of white and
black, proudly arched, and almost at every breath
sending forth its clarion cry, as if in boastful challenge.

"Sound away, you old pirate you!" exclaimed
John, as he swept along; "we 'll make you shorten
your neck, and sit lower in the water before we
are through with you."

And even as he spoke the bird settled slowly
down, until nothing but a line of feathers lay along
the water, and the quick, restless head, with its
sharp-pointed bill, was barely above the surface.

"See her," said John; "I warrant she has smelt
powder and heard the whistle of lead before this.
I wish she did n't know quite so much, or else that
that cloud would pass back of the mountains."

The plan proposed was to keep her under water, giving her no time to rest after her long dives,
and so tire her out that she would be forced to rise
often to the surface to breathe. Before we had
come within forty rods the loon went under.

"Now," shouted John, as he shot the boat toward the wake, "the Lord only knows where she 'll
come up; but we will take that swirl of water for
our centre, and, when she breaks, you show her
what she may expect."

"There she rises," I exclaimed, as we swept over the wake. "Steady with your paddle, there"; and as I spoke, catching the line of feathers along the sights, I launched the bullet toward her.

"Well done!" said John, as the spray made by the smitten water broke over her webbed feet, jerked out of the lake by her frantic effort to get under; "load quick, and save the other barrel for emergencies."

After some twenty shots she began to come more quickly to the surface; and as we took the wake she made in diving for our centre, the circumference described through her position when she arose grew nearer and nearer to the boat.

"Now," said John, as the loon went under for the twenty-fifth time, "when she rises again take her before she shakes the water out of her eyes. I saw the direction of the dive, and she will come up in the line of that dead hemlock there."

I fastened my eyes upon the spot, and, catching the first ripple through the sights, the ball struck above her back before a feather was in sight. Whether the bullet had ruffled her plumage somewhat, or from some other cause, for the first time she rose in the water and shook her narrow wings, uttering a defiant cry.

"Steady there," I whispered hoarsely to John. For an instant the tottlish boat, which the weight of my ramrod would jar, stood, held by the paddle,

as motionless as though embedded in ice; and as
the sharp crack of the other barrel sounded, the
loon was knocked flat over upon her back.

"There, you old — "

I don't know exactly what John was about to
say, for he did not say it; for as he spoke the loon,
with a mighty splash, went down, leaving a hundred feathers around her wake. The bullet had
rasped along her side, shearing off the speckled
plumage, but had not penetrated sufficiently deep
into her body to disable her. By this time the
heavens, toward the west, even to the zenith, were
black as ink. The red lightning darted its zig-
zag course this way and that, amid the gloom;
white, fleecy clouds raced athwart the dark expanse,
and ever and anon a fierce whirlwind, in minia-
ture, would settle down upon the water, and spin
across the glassy bosom of the lake; while the
thunder, peal on peal, crashed above the mountains, until the very air and water shook and quivered at the shock. To a looker-on the scene would
have been grand in the extreme. Amid the gathering gloom, now dense as twilight, the light boat
went moving hither and thither, now gliding straight
ahead, now swerving in lessening circles around the
spot of the anticipated rising, while above the crackling thunder rose the clear report of the rifle, whose
barrels, choked with smut, and dangerously hot
from rapid firing, rang fiercely sharp, as if in angry

"Steady there!"

protest at the abuse. The gloom grew darker.
The wind, in quick, nervous puffs, broke over the
mountain, and where it touched the lake lifted
the spray high into the air. A few plunging drops
of rain smote the water and boat like bullets.
The hot lightning fairly hissed through the murky
atmosphere above us; so sharp, so bright, so close,
that the lake at times seemed as on fire, burning
with a blue, ghastly light. The thunder was inces-
sant. The dwellers in lowland countries know
nothing what thunder is amid the hills. No single
clap or peal was there, but rush and roar continuous, and crackling bolts and rumble and jar. Across
the lake, over our heads, the volleys· went. The
mountain eastward, receiving a bolt against its
sides, would roll it back, while the mountain opposite, catching the mighty boom as players do a
ball, would hurl it sharply home. And so the wild
play went on. Mountain besieging mountain, hill
pelting hill; while we, amid the deepening gloom
and tumult, swept hither and thither, keeping sight
of the loon, whose rises were frequent and breath
nearly gone.

"John," said I, shouting so he could hear me amid
the confusion, — "John, pull for the shore; it's
time to go."

"Give her one more," said John; "here she rises,
over your left"; and as the smoke from the discharge floated up, split by a gust, John shouted:

" Ready with your other barrel there. The loon
is tiring. I hear her blow when she comes up.
She can't stay under long. I 'll run you down
upon her soon. HERE *she is !* " he screamed,
" *under your very muzzles !* "

I turned, and sure enough there sat the loon
within six feet of the boat, in the very act of shaking the water from her eyes. The rifle lay across
my knee, the barrels in direct line with the bird.
Without lifting it, or moving an inch, I pulled,
and water, smoke, and feathers flew into the air
together. A loud " quack " from the loon, and a
convulsive yell from John, his mouth opening and
shutting spasmodically as roar after roar of almost
hysterical laughter came pouring out, followed the
discharge. I was just fitting a cap to a freshly
charged barrel, when the loon broke the water
again at short range, her back nearly bare of
feathers ; and as she dived another tuft flew up,
cut by the passing ball, and John pronounced her
" nearly picked." But now the storm broke over
the mountain. The rush and roar and crash of
wind and thunder drowned the report, and only
by the flash might a spectator know I was firing.
The gloom grew thicker. A cloud settled over the
lake, and we were wrapped within its fleecy folds.
Only once more, as a flash clove through the fog, I
saw the loon, and fired. Then dense and dark the
storm swept down around us. Wild, fitful gusts

tore through the air. The lightning crinkled through the fog; white patches of froth and splashing drops of rain drifted over and fell into the boat; while, as a bass to the wild minstrelsy of bursting bolts, the dull, monotonous, roar of the storm, whose heavy-footed squadrons were charging over the mountain's brow, rose with dread, augmenting grandeur. The quivering of the frail boat told me that John was vigorously plying his paddle; and in a moment we shot into the lily-pads, and, pulling our boat ashore, turned it bottom side up and crawled under it, just as the grayish sheet of plunging water swept over us, and the floods came down.

There we lay, safely sheltered, regretting the storm, and recounting the ludicrous passages of the contest, until the water, gathering in a pool beneath the boat, saturated our garments and warned us to be moving. Suggesting to John that "we had better not stay under that boat until it floated off," we crawled out from under our temporary shelter; which, John remarked, "had a good roof, but a mighty poor cellar." Standing, as a preliminary caution, long enough in the rain to get thoroughly wet, we prepared for the start. An uncut carry for nearly two miles lay before us, the first half of which ran directly through a swamp, now filled to overflowing with water. We had a tough experience in getting through, which the reader will find described in the next chapter.

H

VI.

CROSSING THE CARRY.

"JOHN," said I, as we stood looking at each other across the boat, "this rain is wet."

"It generally is, up in this region, I believe," he responded, as he wiped the water out of his eyes with the back of his hand, and shook the accumulating drops from nose and chin; "but the waterproof I have on has lasted me some thirty-eight years, and I don't think it will wet through to-day."

"Well!" I exclaimed, "there is no use of standing here in this marsh-grass any longer; help me to load up. I'll take the baggage, and you the boat."

"You'll never get through with it, if you try to take it all at once. Better load light, and I'll come back after what's left," was the answer. "I tell you," he continued, "the swamp is full of water, and soft as muck."

"John," said I, "that baggage is going over at one load, sink or swim, live or die, survive or perish. I'll make the attempt, swamp or no swamp. My life is assured against accidents by fire, water, and mud ; so here goes. What 's life to glory ? " I exclaimed, as I seized the pork-bag, and dragged it from under the boat ; " stand by and see me put my armor on."

Over my back I slung the provision-basket, made like a fisherman's creel, thirty inches by forty, filled with plates, coffee, salt, and all the *impedimenta* of camp and cooking utensils. This was held in its place by straps passing over the shoulders and under the arms, like a Jew-pedler's pack. There might have been eighty pounds weight in it. Upon the top of the basket John lashed my knapsack, full of bullets, powder, and clothing. My rubber suit and heavy blanket, slung around my neck by a leather thong, hung down in front across my chest. On one shoulder, the oars and paddles were balanced, with a frying-pan and gridiron swinging from the blades; on the other was my rifle, from which were suspended a pair of boots, my creel, a coffee-pot, and a bag of flour. Taking up the bag of pork in one hand, and seizing the stock of the rifle with the other, from two fingers of which hung a tin kettle of prepared trout, which we were loath to throw away, I started. Picture a man so loaded, forcing his way through a hemlock swamp, through whose floor of thin moss he sank to his knees ; or picking his way across oozy sloughs on old roots, often covered with mud and water, and slippery beyond description, and you have me daguerreotyped in your mind. Well, as I said, I started. For some dozen rods I got on famously, and was congratulating myself with the thought of an easy transit, when a root upon which I had put my right foot gave way, and, plunging headlong into the mud, I struck an attitude of petition; while the frying-pan and gridiron, flung off the oars and forward by the movement, alighted upon my prostrated head. An ejaculation, not exactly religious, escaped me, and with a few desperate flounces I assumed once more the perpendicular. Fishing the frying-pan from the mud, and lashing the gridiron to my belt, I made another start. It was hard work. The most unnatural adjustment of weight upon my back made it difficult to ascertain just how far behind me lay the centre of equilibrium. I found where it did not lie, several times. Before I had gone fifty rods, the camp-basket weighed one hundred and twenty pounds. The pork-bag felt as if it had several shoats in it, and the oar-blades stuck out in the exact form of an X. If I went one side of a tree, the oars would go the other side. If I backed up, they would manage to get entangled amid the brush. If I stumbled and fell, the confounded things would come like a goose-poke athwart my neck, pinning me down. As I proceeded, the mud grew deeper, the roots farther apart, and the blazed trees less frequent.

Never before did I so truly realize the aspiration of the old hymn, —

" O, had I the wings of a dove ! "

At last I reached, what seemed impossible to pass, — an oozy slough, crossed here and there by cedar roots, smooth and slippery, lay before me. From a high stump which I had climbed upon I gave a desperate leap. I struck where I expected, and a little farther. The weight of the basket, which was now something over two hundred pounds, was too much for me to check at once. It pressed me forward. I recovered myself, and the abominable oars carried me as far the other way. The moccasins of wet leather began to slip along the roots. They began to slip very often ; and, at bad times. I found it necessary to change my position suddenly. I changed it. It was n't a perfect success. I tried again. It seemed necessary to keep on trying. I suspect I did not effect the changes very steadily, for the trout began to jump about in the pail and fly out into the mud. The gridiron got uneasy, and played against my side like a steam-flapper. In fact, the whole baggage seemed endowed with supernatural powers of motion. The excitement was contagious. In a moment, every article was jumping about like mad. I, in the mean time, continued to dance a hornpipe on the slippery roots. Now I am con-

scientiously opposed to dancing. I never danced.
I did n't want to learn. I felt it was wicked for
me to be hopping around on that root so. What
an example, I thought, if John should see me!
What would my wife say? What would my deacons say? I tried to stop. I could n't. I had
an astonishing dislike to sit down. I thought I
would dance there forever, rather than sit down, —
deacons or no deacons. The basket now weighed
any imaginable number of pounds. The trout
were leaping about my head, as if in their native
element. The gridiron was in such rapid motion,
that it was impossible to distinguish the bars.
There was, apparently, a whole litter of pigs in the
pork-bag. I could not stand it longer. I concluded to rest awhile. I wanted to do the thing
gracefully. I looked around for a soft spot, and
seeing one just behind me, I checked myself. My
feet flew out from under me. They appeared to be
unusually light. I don't remember that I ever sat
down quicker. The motion was very decided.
The only difficulty I observed was, that the seat I
had gracefully settled into had no bottom. The
position of things was extremely picturesque.
The oars were astride my neck, as usual. The
trout-pail was bottom up, and the contents lying
about almost anywhere. The boots were hanging
on a dry limb overhead. A capital idea. I thought
of it as I was in the act of sitting down. One

piece of pork lay at my feet, and another was sticking up, some ten feet off, in the mud. It looked very queer, — slightly out of place. With the same motion with which I hung my boots on a limb, as I seated myself, I stuck my rifle carefully into the mud, muzzle downward. I never saw a gun in that position before. It struck me as being a good thing. There was no danger of its falling over and breaking the stock. The first thing I did was to pass the gridiron under me. When that feat was accomplished, I felt more composed. It's pleasant for a man in the position I was in to feel that he has something under him. Even a chip or a small stump would have felt comfortable. As I sat thinking how many uses a gridiron could be put to, and estimating where I should then have been if I had n't got it under me, I heard John forcing his way, with the boat on his back, through the thick undergrowth.

"It won't do to let John see me in this position," I said; and so, with a mighty effort, I disengaged myself from the pack, flung off the blanket from around my neck, and seizing hold of a spruce limb which I could fortunately reach, drew myself slowly up. I had just time to jerk the rifle out of the mud and fish up about half of the trout, when John came struggling along.

"John," said I, leaning unconcernedly against a tree, as if nothing had happened, — "John, put down the boat, here's a splendid spot to rest."

"Well, Mr. Murray," queried John, as he emerged from under the boat, "how are you getting along?"

"Capitally!" said I; "the Carry is very level when you once get down to it. I felt a little out of breath, and thought I would wait for you a few moments."

"What's your boots doing up there, in that tree?" exclaimed John, as he pointed up to where they hung dangling from the limb, about fifteen feet above our heads.

"Boots doing!" said I, "why they are hanging there, don't you see. You did n't suppose I'd drop them into this mud, did you?"

"Why, no," replied John, " I don't suppose you would; but how about this?" he continued, as he stooped down and pulled a big trout, tail foremost, out of the soft muck; "how did that trout come there?"

"It must have got out of the pail, somehow," I responded; "I thought I heard something drop, just as I sat down."

"What in thunder is that, out there?" exclaimed John, pointing to a piece of pork, one end of which was sticking about four inches out of the water; "is that pork?"

"Well, the fact is, John," returned I, speaking

"It is pleasant for a man, in the position that I was in, to feel that he has something under him."

with the utmost gravity, and in a tone intended to suggest a mystery, — "the fact is, John, I don't quite understand it. This Carry seems to be all covered over with pork. I would n't be surprised to find a piece anywhere. There is another junk, now," I exclaimed, as I plunged my moccasin into the mud and kicked a two-pound bit toward him; "it 's lying all round here, loose."

I thought John would split with laughter, but my time came, for as in one of his paroxysms he turned partly around, I saw that his back was covered with mud clear up to his hat.

"Do you always sit down on your coat, John," I inquired, "when you cross a Carry like this?"

"Come, come," rejoined he, ceasing to laugh from very exhaustion, "take a knife or tin plate, and scrape the muck from my back. I always tell my wife to make my clothes a ground color, but the color is laid on a little too thick this time, anyway."

"John," said I, after having scraped him down, "take the paddle and spear my boots off from that limb up there, while I tread out this pork."

Plunging into the slough, balancing here on a bog and there on an underlying root, I succeeded in concentrating the scattered pieces at one point. As I was shying the last junk into the bag, a disappointed grunt from John caused me to look around. I took in the situation at a glance. The

6

boots were still suspended from the limb. The paddle and two oars had followed suit, and lay cosily amid the branches, while John, poising himself dexterously on the trunk of a fallen spruce, red in the face and vexed at his want of success, was whirling the frying-pan over his head, in the very act of letting it drive at the boots.

"Go in, John!" I shouted, seizing hold of the gridiron with one hand and a bag of bullets with the other, while tears stood in my eyes from very laughter; "when we've got all the rest of the baggage up in that hemlock, I'll pass up the boat, and we'll make a camp."

The last words were barely off my lips, when John, having succeeded in getting a firm footing, as he thought, on the slippery bark, threw all his strength into the cast, and away the big iron pan went whizzing up through the branches. But, alas for human calculation! The rotten bark under his feet, rent by the sudden pressure as he pitched the cumbrous missile upward, parted from the smooth wood, and John, with a mighty thump which seemed almost to snap his head off, came down upon the trunk; while the frying-pan, gyrating like a broken-winged bird, landed rods away in the marsh. By this time John's blood was up, and the bombardment began in earnest. The first thing he laid his hand on was the coffee-pot. I followed suit with the gridiron. Then my fishing-basket and a bag of bullets mounted upward. Never before was such a battle waged, or such weapons used. The air was full of missiles. Tin plates, oar-locks, the axe, gridiron, and pieces of pork were all in the air at once. How long the contest would have continued I cannot tell, had it not been brought to a glorious termination; but at last the heavy iron camp-kettle, hurled by John's nervous wrist, striking the limb fair, crashed through like a forty-pound shot, and down came boots, oars, paddle, and all. Gathering the scattered articles together, we took our respective burdens, and pushed ahead. Weary and hot, we reached at length the margin of the swamp, and our feet stood once more upon solid ground.

At this juncture another cloud from out of the west swept up the heavens, and its distended borders, heavy with rain, parted, and down the plunging torrents came. The wind, sweeping through the lofty pine-tops over our heads, sounded like the rush of airy squadrons charging to battle. The lightning blazed amid the descending sheets of water, lurid and red, or shot its electric currents amid the trees; while, overhead, peal and boom and rattling volleys rolled and broke. Forcing our way along through spruce and balsam thickets, and heavy undergrowth of deer-bush, which flapped their broad flat leaves, loaded with water, into our eyes, we came upon a giant pine, which some descending bolt had struck, far up amid the topmost branches, and riven to the very roots. Huge slabs, twenty feet in length, and weighing hundreds of pounds, torn out from the very heart, thrown a dozen rods on either side, and the ground strewn with yellow splinters, bore palpable witness of the lightning's power. Pausing a moment amid the wreck and ruin, looking into the yellow heart of that riven pine, weeping great drops of odorous gum, how weak the effort of man appeared beside the power of nature. What is our boasted strength of brawn and muscle compared with the terrific forces which lie hidden amid the elements? And what is ours or theirs beside the power of Him who holds their violence in check, and uses at will the wild chemistry of the skies?

At length (for all journeys have an end) we tore our way through the last opposing thicket, and stood upon the coveted beach. The dreaded Carry was crossed; and, as if to reward our toil and cheer our drooping spirits, even as we lay panting upon the wet sands, the cloud above us parted, and the bright sun came out, gemming the dripping trees with jewels, and swathing the lake in golden sheen. Patches of fleecy fog rose from the shores, and, changing to yellow mist as the sun warmed them, floated lazily along the mountain's side. Kindling a fire, we cooked some coffee, watching, as we drank it, the bright vermilion bow which grew upon the eastern cloud, until it spanned the horizon from north to south; from under whose arch of gold and azure the heavy-tongued thunder rolled its dying cadences far away eastward over the Racquette.

VII.

ROD AND REEL.

"MR. MURRAY, wake up! the pancakes are ready!" shouted John.

Aroused by the familiar cry, I arose, and, walking down to the shore of the lake, waded out into its tide, and, plunging my head under water, held it there for a moment, while the delicious sense of coolness ran through my system; then I raised it, turning my dripping face straight toward the bright, warm sun. O the sweet experience of that moment! How cool the water; how fresh the air; how clear the sky; how fragrant the breath of balsam and of pine! O luxury of luxuries, to have a lake of crystal water for your wash-bowl, the morning zephyr for a towel, the whitest sand for soap, and the odors of aromatic trees for perfumes! What belle or millionnaire can boast of such surroundings?

Fresh as an athlete in training, I returned to camp and to breakfast. Breakfast in the wilderness means something. No muttering about "those miserable rolls"; no yawning over a small strip of steak, cut in the form of a parallelogram, an inch and a half by three; no lying about tawny-colored water by calling it "coffee." No; but up in the woods you take a pancake, twelve inches across (just the diameter of the pan), and one inch thick, and go conscientiously to work to surround it. You seize a trout ten or fourteen inches long, and send it speedily to that bourne from whence no trout returns. You lay hold of a quart pan full of liquid which has the smack of real Java to it, made pungent with a sprinkling of Mocha; and the first you know you see your face in the bottom of the dish. And the joke is, you keep doing so, right along, for some thirty minutes or more, rising from each meal a bigger, if not a better man.

The meal was finished. It did not take long to wash the dishes; and over the remnants of what had once been a feast we sat in council.

" John, what shall we do to-day ? "

" Well, I think," said John, " we 'll take some trout. I told you, when we started, you should see a three-pounder before we got back; and here we are within twenty miles of the Racquette, and my promise unfulfilled. I know a little lake, hidden away back of that hard-wood ridge yonder, which is one huge spring-hole; and when scouting through here on my own account, some six years ago, I took some fish from it such as you seldom see. I doubt if there has been a fly on it since; and if the breeze will freshen a little, you 'll have rare sport."

Soon after, John shouldered the boat, and we started. Some forty minutes' tramp, and we reached the shore and made our camp. From it the scene was delightful. The lake was nearly circular, some half a mile across, its waters deep and clear. Into it, so far as we could see, no water came; out of it no water went. It was, as John had called it, one huge spring-hole; the mountains on all sides sloped gradually up, an unbroken sweep of pine and balsam, save where, at intervals, a silver-beech or round-leaved maple relieved the sombre color with lighter hues. Thus secluded, seldom visited by man, the little lake reposed, mirroring the surrounding hills in its cool depths, and guarded safely by them. We stepped into our boat and glided out toward the centre of the pool. Not a motion in the air; not a ripple on the water. At last the beeches along the western slope began to rustle. The mournful pines felt the pressure of airy fingers amid their strings, and woke to solemn sound. The zephyr at length reached the lake, and the cool water thrilled into ripples at its touch; while the pool, which an instant before shone under the sun like seamless glass, shook with a thousand tiny undulations.

"Now," said John, "if the fish have n't all drowned since I was here, you 'll see 'em soon. When one rises I 'll put you within casting distance of the wake, and if he likes it he 'll take the fly. If one takes, strike hard; for their jaws are stout and bony, and you must hook them well or you'll lose them in the struggle."

We sat and watched. "There!" suddenly shouted John; "one is n't dead yet." And whirling the boat about, he sent it flying toward a swirl in the water, some twenty rods away, made by a rising fish whose splash I had heard but did not see. We had traversed half the distance, perhaps, and all alert I sat, holding the coil and flies between my fingers, ready for a cast, when, as we shot along, a bright vermilion flash gleamed for an instant far below us, and a broad, yellow-sided beauty broke the surface barely the length of my rod from the boat. The swoop of a swallow is scarcely swifter than was the motion of the boat as John shied it one side, and, with a stroke which would have snapped a less elastic paddle, sent it circling around the ripples where the fish went down. Twice did I trail the flies across the circle and meet with no response; but hardly had the feathers touched the water at the third cast, when the trout came up with a rush. He took the fly as a hunter might take a fence, boldly. I struck, even as he hung in mid-air, and down he went. After a sharp fight of some ten minutes' length the trout yielded, the fatal net enclosed him, and he lay flapping within the boat. Thus five were captured in little more than an hour's time, good two-and-a-

half-pound fish each of them, — a string which a
man might contemplate with pride.   We paused
a moment to give John time to inspect the tackle
to see if it was all right.   The trout had made
sad work with the flies.   The largest and strongest
came out of their mouths bare to the shank.   Five
ruined flies lay with the five captured trout on
the bottom of the boat.

"Mr. Murray," said John at length, as he sat
looking at the mangled flies ; " have n't you something larger ?   These trout are regular sharks."

"Nothing," replied I, running over the leaves
of my fly-book, "except these huge salmon-flies " ;
and I held half a dozen gaudy fellows out toward him, the. hooks of which were nearly two
inches in length, covered with immense hackle of
variegated floss, out of whose depths protruded
a pair of enormous wings, and brilliant with hues
of the ibis and the English jay.

"Let 's try one, anyway," said John, laughing.   "Nothing is too big for a fish like that !"
and he nodded his head toward a deep swirl made
in the water as a monstrous fellow rose to the surface, closed his jaws on a huge dragon-fly that had
stopped to rest a moment on the water, and, throwing his tail, broad as your hand, into the air, darted
downward into the silent depths.   "There," continued he, as he tossed the tuft of gay feathers
into the air, "that 's the first pullet's-tail I ever

noosed on to a leader. A trout that takes that will be worth baking. Lengthen your line to the last foot you can cast, and when a big one rises I'll put you within reach of his wake."

We sat for several minutes in silence, watching. At last, some fifteen rods away, a magnificent fish shot up out of the water after a butterfly which chanced to be winging its way across the lake, and missing it by only a few inches, fell back with a splash into the very ripple he made in rising.

" Now !" shouted John, as he sent the light boat skimming over the water, " give him the feathers, and if he takes, sink the hook to the very shank into his jaws."

I pitched the coil into the air, and by the time it had fairly straightened itself out the boat was in reach of the wake ; and, obedient to the quick turn of the wrist, the huge fly leaped ahead. It had not reached the surface by a yard, when the water parted and out came the trout, his mouth wide open, quivering from head to tail with the energy of the leap ; missed, as he had before, and fell back flat upon his side.

" Quick, quick ! cast away !" shouted John, as with a stroke of the paddle he sent the boat sheering off to give me room for the cast.

Feeling that there was not an instant to lose, by a sudden jerk I caused the fly to mount straight up into the air, trusting to the motion of the boat to straighten the slack as it fell. John understood the motion; the boat flew round as on a pivot, and glided backward under the reversed stroke. It was well done, as only John could do it; nor was it a second too soon; for as the tuft of gay plumes alighted amid the ripples, the huge head of the trout came out of water, his mouth opened, and, as the feathers disappeared between his teeth, I struck with all my might. Not one rod in twenty would have stood that blow. The fish was too heavy even to be turned an inch. The line sung, and water flew out of the compressed braids, as though I had sunk the hook into an oak beam.

Reader, did you ever land a trout? I do not ask if you ever jerked some poor little fellow out of a brook three feet across, with a pole six inches around at the butt, and so heavy as to require both hands and feet well braced to hold it out. No, that's not landing a trout. But did you ever sit in a boat, with nine ounces of lance-wood for a rod, and two hundred feet of braided silk in your double-acting reel, and hook a trout whose strain brought tip and butt together as you checked him in some wild flight, and tested your quivering line from gut to reel-knot? No one knows what game there is in a trout, unless he has fought it out, matching such a rod against a three-pound fish, with forty feet of water underneath, and a clear,

unimpeded sweep around him! Ah, then it is
that one discovers what will and energy lie within the mottled skin of a trout, and what a miracle of velocity he is when roused. I love the
rifle, and I have looked along the sights and held
the leaping blood back by an effort of will, steady-
ing myself for the shot, when my veins fairly
tingled with the exhilarating excitement of the
moment; but if one should ask me what is my
conception of pure physical happiness, I should
assure him that the highest bodily beatitude I
ever expect to reach is, on some future day, when
the clear sun is occasionally veiled by clouds, to
sit in a boat once more upon that little lake, with
John at the paddle, and match again a Conroy
rod against a three-pound trout. That 's what I
call *happiness!*

Well, as I said, I struck; and, as we afterwards
discovered, the huge salmon-hook was buried to
the shank amid the nerves which lie at the root of
a trout's tongue. Then came a fight for the mas-
tery such as never before had I waged with anything that swims. Words should have *life* in them
to depict the scene. Quick as a flash, before I
had fairly recovered my balance, partially lost by
the energy with which I struck, the trout started,
and before I could get a pressure upon the line,
not twenty yards were left on the reel. A quick
stroke from John, and the boat shot one side; and

bearing stoutly on him, tasking the rod to the last ounce of resistance, I slowly swayed him about and recovered a little slack. After a few short sweeps he doubled on the line and shot straight for the boat as an arrow from a bow.

"Double, and be hanged to you!" shouted John, as he shied the light shell to one side and swung it round so as to keep me facing the fish. "If you get under this boat it will be because this paddle breaks."

Failing in his attempt to run under us, he dove to the bottom. "Let him rest a moment," said John; "recover your line; you'll need it all when he rises. He's big and ugly, and his next rush will be like lightning."

After I had stowed away some forty yards of line upon the reel, winding it on hard and evenly, so that it would render well, I began to feel of the fish. The first pressure elicited only a shake. At the next he described a circle, still keeping to the bottom, then came again to a stand-still. He acted ugly. I felt that, when the rush came, it would try nerve and tackle alike. Enjoining John to watch the fish and favor me all he could, and by no means to let him pass under the boat, I gave a quick, sharp jerk. My arm was still in the air and the rod unstraightened, when I caught a gleam far down below me, and before I had time to wink the huge fellow parted the water almost within reach of my arm, and when high up in mid-air he shook himself, the crystal drops were flung into my very face. Perhaps I shall live long enough to forget the picture, as that trout for an instant hung in the air, his blue back and azure sides spotted with gold and agate, his fins edged with snowy white, his eyes protruding, gills distended, the leader hanging from his jaws, while a shower of pearly drops were shaken from his quivering sides. He fell; but while still in air the boat glided backward, and when he touched the water I was thirty feet away and ready for his rush. It came. And as he passed us, some forty feet off, he clove the water as a bolt from a cross-bow might cleave the air. Possibly for five minutes the frenzy lasted. Not a word was uttered. The whiz of the line through the water, the whir of the flying reel, and an occasional grunt from John as the fish doubled on the boat, were the only sounds to be heard. When, suddenly, in one of his wildest flights, the terribly taxed rod straightened itself out with a spring, the pressure ceased, the line slackened, and the fish again lay on the bottom. Wiping the sweat from my brow, I turned to John and said, "What do you think of that?"

"Mr. Murray," replied John, laying the paddle down and drawing the sleeve of his woollen shirt across his forehead, beaded with perspiration, —

"Mr. Murray, that fish is ugly; if he should get the line over his back, he'd smash the rod like a pipe-stem!"

"He won't get it over his back," replied I. "Ready with your paddle; he's getting too much breath."

"But I say," said John, looking affectionately at the rod as he took up the paddle; "if I was in your place, and he *did* get the line over his shoulder, I would part my tackle before I smashed that rod."

"I won't do either, John"; and as I answered I gave a jerk, and the trout started again. But why repeat? Why tell of flights and rushes which followed? Twice did he break the surface a hundred feet away, flinging himself out like a black bass. Once did he partially get the leader over his back and dashed away like lightning; while John, anxious to save so true a rod from ruin, shouted to me, "Part the gut!" But who ever knew a fisherman, when his blood is up, refuse a risk to save the game? I screamed to John to shoot the boat one side; and when the last foot of silk was given I advanced the butt. The heavy fish and pliant rod were pitted one against the other. Three days later, in another struggle, the old rod parted; but this time it triumphed. For a moment the quivering tip rattled upon the bars of the reel. The fish struggled and shook himself,

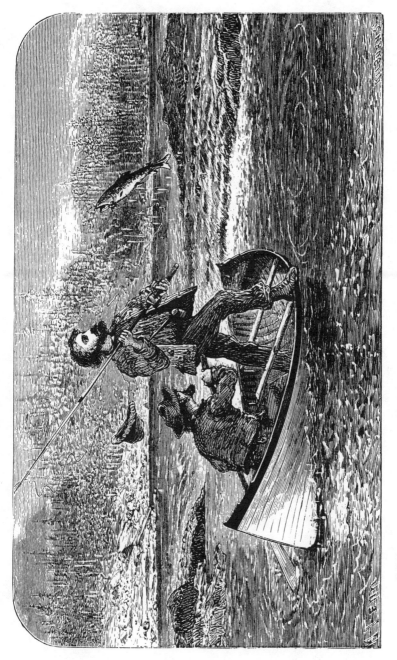

"When, high in mid-air, he shook himself, the crystal drops were flung into my very face."

but the tenacious fibres would not part. He ceased to battle, came panting to the surface, and rolled over upon his side. The boat shot toward him, and as it glided by John passed the landing-net beneath him, and the brave fighter lay upon the bottom board. His tail, across its base, measured five inches; and his length from tip to tip was *seventeen inches and three quarters!*

"John," I said, twisting round in my seat and facing him, — "John, I should have lost that fish or smashed the rod, if it had not been for your paddle."

"Of course, of course," replied John; "that's my business. Those fly-rods are delicate things. Like women, they should n't be put to heavy work if you can help it, but they are able to bear a heavy strain if necessary. But with all I could do I thought it was gone once. I don't think I ever came so near breaking this paddle as on that last sweep. It made my flesh creep to hear the old rod creak. I really believe my own back would have snapped if it had parted."

We had captured six trout in two hours, whose average length was sixteen inches and a half. I asked John if we should take another.

"I don't think it will be sin to take one more," he responded. "I saw a tail show itself out there," — and he nodded over his left shoulder, — "which looked like a lady's fan. If there is a larger trout

than that last one lying anywhere about this pond,
I would like to see him"; and as he spoke he
swept his paddle through the water, and the boat
started. I looked at my fly. The teeth of the
trout had torn the hackle half away, and shorn
off from the body one gaudy wing. An exclama-
tion from John started me. The fish had risen
again. I too saw his tail as he disappeared, and it
was as broad as a fan.

"Mr. Murray," exclaimed John, "that fish is the
biggest trout I ever saw." 'T is full two feet long.
I saw him fair, broad side on. His mouth was
like a bear-trap. Ready for a cast. Send the fly
straight for the centre of the wake, and if he
takes, strike like thunder!"

John was evidently getting excited, and the
glimpse I had of the trout had thrilled me as
the blast of a bugle might thrill a warrior har-
nessed for battle. The boat was forty feet away
when the tuft of gay plumes, mangled but still
brilliant, floated downward, and lighted amid the
glistening bubbles. I had not trailed it a yard
when a gleam of blue and yellow passed me, and
with a splash and plunge which threw the water
in silvery spray high into the air, the trout broke.
I saw the feathers disappear within his monstrous jaws, and, lifting myself involuntarily half
off my seat, I struck. I think John was convinced that I struck hard enough that time, for

the strong nine-foot leader parted under the quick stroke, and down into the depths went the trout, with leader and flies streaming from his mouth.

"Well," said John, as I swung myself around so as to face him, "for twenty-seven years I 've boated up and down the waters of this wilderness, and rarely will you strike a lake or stream, from the Horican to the St. Lawrence, above whose surface I have not seen fish leap; but never before this day have I seen, on lake or stream, a spotted trout as large as that which has just carried fly and leader to the bottom. Well, let him go," he continued; "he 'll manage, some way, to get that hook out of his jaw, and live to take another fly. And you and I will build our camp-fire some evening next summer upon the shore of this pond again; and when the sun comes over those pines there, I 'll warrant we 'll find the old fellow active as ever."

So speaking, he turned the boat about, and headed toward the camp. That afternoon we lay on the beach and watched the leaping trout sporting before us; or gazed, dreaming of absent friends, into the deep blue sky, across whose cerulean dome the snow-white clouds drifted, urged silently onward by the pressure of invisible currents. The sun at last withdrew his beams. One moment, and the pines that crested the western slope were all ablaze. The next, gloomy and dark they stood, their dense and sombre foliage unlighted by a ray. The shadows deepened. The ripple left the lake, and its unruffled surface stretched from shore to shore like a sea of glass. One by one the stars came out in quick succession. The waters contended in rivalry with the skies, and every star which shone in the heaven above shone in the depths below. Thus we sat and saw dark-featured but brilliant Night succeed to the throne of blond and gentle Day. Suddenly, breaking the profound silence, the solemn hoot of an owl echoed through the forest. It was answered in a moment by the prolonged howl of a wolf, hunting amid the hills far to the north. Throwing some huge logs on the fire, and wrapping our blankets around us, we stretched ourselves beside the blaze, and, with malice in our hearts toward none, sank peacefully to our night's repose.

VIII.

PHANTOM FALLS.

" JOHN," I exclaimed, as I stood emptying the
water out of my boots, — " John, I will surely
write an account of this night's adventure."

" No one will believe you if you do," replied he.
" If it was not for this water," he continued, as he
gave his soaked jacket a wring with both hands, " I
should doubt it myself, and declare that we have
only been dreaming, and had not shot two miles of
those rapids to-night, nor dragged our boat from
under the suction of Phantom Falls."

" I do not care whether people believe it or not,"
I replied. " There lies your broken paddle,"— and I
pointed to the piece of shivered ash, — " and there
you stand, wringing the water of the rapids from
your jacket, and we *know* that something more
than human has now for two nights appeared off
our camp, and that we did, two hours ago, take
boat and follow it until it vanished into mist ; and
I shall tell the story of what we have seen and
done, not expecting any one will believe it."

Gentle reader, I keep the promise made to John,
as we stood by our camp-fire under the pines, and

advise you to believe no more of it than you see fit. Perhaps the reading will serve to entertain a circle of friends some winter evening, when the wind moans dismally without, as the writing will rest him who, in front of a glowing grate, on a December night, for his own amusement even more than for your own, tells you the story of

PHANTOM FALLS.

"John," said I, "since eight o'clock we have made good forty miles, and my fingers are so stiff that I can scarcely unclasp them from this paddle-staff. Let us make camp before the sun goes down."

"Well," replied he, "fifteen years ago I camped one night by that big rock there at the mouth of the rapids, and I would like to see how the old camp looks, for I saw something there that night that I could not account for; I will tell you about it after supper to-night."

Of course I assented, and bent myself to the paddle with renewed energy.

We were in the heart of the wilderness, where even trappers seldom penetrated. For fifty miles on either side not even the smoke of a hunter's cabin colored the air. For weeks I had not seen a human face or heard a human voice other than our own. Day after day we had been pushing our light, narrow shell up unexplored creeks, building our fire each night on the shore of some lake or pond where it is doubtful if fire was ever kindled before. As we proceeded down the lake, the roar of the rapids came more and more distinctly to our ears, and as the shores converged the boat began to feel the action of the water beneath it, where were the beginnings of the current. As John felt the movement, he lifted his oars, and, laying them carefully along the bottom of the boat, pointed toward a huge pine that stood to the west of a projection of land along the other side of which rushed the rapids. Understanding the motion, I turned the bow of the boat toward the tree, and then, with easy stroke, urged it along.

"How well I remember the night I camped here," said John, speaking half to himself. "How naturally that old pine looks, and the three hemlocks on the point, and the rock against which I built my fire. I wonder if the old story is true, and if I did see her, or whether it was only a dream!"

By this time the boat had run into a little notch or bay, and a few sharp strokes sent it to the shore with a force that urged it half its length up over the yielding sand. We stepped to the beach.

Supper having been prepared and eaten, we

threw some heavy logs upon the fire, and, reclining upon our blankets, gazed off over the lake. The moon was nearly at the full. Her rounded orb was just appearing above the eastern mountains, and across the tranquil water she poured her pure white radiance. The lake lay motionless; not a wave, not even a ripple, broke the smooth surface. Above, the sky was cloudless. Suspended in the still ether, a few of the larger stars struggled for existence. Weak and vain such rivalry! for the queen of night held open audience, and their lesser lights paled in her more brilliant presence. The woods were dumb. Silence brooded in the heavy pines and amid the darker firs. The balsams, through their spear-like stems, yielded their fragrance upon an air too motionless to waft it. Even the dull roar of the rapids was so even in tone, that, instead of disturbing, it seemed rather to deepen the all-pervading silence.

"Mr. Murray," said John, at length, "do you know that we are camped on haunted ground?"

"Haunted ground!" I returned, raising myself upon my elbow, and turning toward him. "What do you mean? You don't believe in ghosts, do you?"

"Well, I don't know," replied John, "what to believe; but some of the old trappers tell queer stories about this place, and I know that, just fifteen years ago this month, I made my camp

under this very pine, and that during the night
I saw something off the camp which was n't
human!"

"So that was what you were muttering about,
was it, John, when we were running in?" I responded. "Give us the story, as you promised; this
is the very night and place to hear a ghost-story.
I can almost catch the soft, cat-like tread of old
Indian warriors gliding through the shadows, and
the dip of unseen paddles along the motionless
water. So go ahead, John; give us the whole
story, and take your own time for it."

"Well, it won't take long," replied John; "and I
would like to know what you think of it, anyway.
The story which the old trappers tell is this:—

"'The tribe of Indians that once hunted around
the shores of this lake, and over these mountains,
was called the Neamski. It was a branch of
the great Huron family, and their chief was
Neosko, which means thunder-cloud, or some such
thing. Well, this chief had a daughter, Wisti by
name. The French called her the Balsam, because
of the richness of her dark beauty. This girl fell
in love with a young Frenchman, a Jesuit priest,
whom the missions in Canada had sent down to
this tribe to convert them. Her love, it seems,
was returned with ardor, and here in this little
cove they were wont to hold their nightly tryst.
At last the young priest, impelled by his passion

7   J

for the girl, determined to visit Montreal, get discharged by his superiors from the service, return for his mistress, and, striking through the lakes eastward, reach Albany, where he could embark for France. He left in the early spring, with the understanding that he would meet her at this spot on a certain night in June. For some reason, perhaps because he could not get a release, perhaps piety prevailed at last over love, or, more probable still, because he was ambushed on his journey by hostile Indians and killed, he never returned. Night after night, as the story runs, Wisti would take her canoe, paddle to this point, where, not finding her lover, she would return dejected to her father's camp. She had many lovers, of course. Chiefs from near and far, even from the big lakes, came seeking her hand. She refused each and all. In vain her father threatened, her relations urged, her tribe insisted. To every suitor she returned the same answer: "My heart is far away in the North, and will not come back to me." A year came and went. The snow for a second time melted from the mountains, and the ice deserted the streams. Her lover had been sick, she said to herself, and could not keep his promise; but now he would surely come. Thus she kept her hope up as she watched and waited. Night after night she would visit this spot, only to be disappointed. The burden was too heavy for her to bear. The light deserted her eyes and agility her limbs. With the leaves of autumn she faded, and one September night she launched her canoe and left her father's camp. When last seen, she was directing her course toward this point. It is possible that, caught in the sweep of the rapids, she was swept down, or else, broken in spirit by the continued absence of her lover, and weary of a life, every day of which brought only a new and bitterer disappointment, she purposely paddled out into the current, and sought, through the white foam and mist of the rapids, a meeting with him who was, as she believed, no longer on earth.' And they say," continued John, "that thrice each year, about this time in June, there comes up out of the rapids a canoe, which leaves, as it glides, no wake, urged by a noiseless paddle, and in it a figure sits, clothed in raiment whiter than the mist."

"Well, John," I said, after a slight pause, "is that all? Do you believe the story? Did you ever see her?"

"Mr. Murray," said John, solemnly, "I do believe the story; and I have seen her."

"What!" I exclaimed, now thoroughly interested; "do you say that you have seen her, John? When, and how? Tell me all about it."

"It was just fifteen years ago this moon," continued he, "and I was returning from a trip down the Black River country, when, late in the evening,

I ran my boat into this little bay. The moon, the lake, the mountains, all looked as they do at this moment. Against this very rock I built my fire, and, being tired, quickly dropped to sleep. I lay that night in the same position in which you are now lying. How long I had been sleeping I do not know, when a low, uneasy whine from my hound, and his nose rubbing against my face, aroused me. Thinking that some wild animal had approached the camp, I seized my rifle and peered steadily into the forest. Not a twig snapped. Twice did the dog walk around the fire, lift his nose into the air, and whine. I did not know what to make of it. I was about to order him to be quiet, when he started to his feet, took a step toward the lake, and then crouched, shivering, to the ground. Quick as thought I turned, and there, Mr. Murray," said John, speaking in a low but steady voice, and pointing with his brawny hand toward the east, "there, just rounding that point, I saw a sight which made my blood curdle. A boat, or what seemed to be a boat, was there, — a birch canoe, curved up at either end, — and in it sat a girl, or what seemed a girl, all clothed in white, and airy as a cloud. In her hand she grasped a paddle, and her head was turned as in the attitude of listening. Up to the very margin of the water the canoe came, and twice did that face, or what seemed a face, look steadily into mine. Then, with a motion as when one shakes his head with disappointment, it turned away, and the canoe, as if impelled by a paddle, described a circle, and glided, with the white form in it, around the point."

John paused. That his narrative was honest I had no doubt. Every tone and syllable proved it. I did not know precisely what to say, so we sat for a while in profound silence. At last John started up, seized hold of the end of a large log which the fire had burned through in the middle, ended it over upon the pile of glowing coals, and as he seated himself said, —

"Well, Mr. Murray, what do you think of it?"

Rising to my feet, I turned about so as to face him, and responded : —

"John, I do not doubt that you think you saw what you say you did see ; but I do not believe that you really saw any such sight after all. The fact is, John, it was what the doctors would call a mental delusion. You were very tired ; you had heard the old story about the place — Be still, Rover, will you!" I exclaimed, interrupting myself to touch the old dog with my foot, as he rose to his feet, lifted his nose into the air, and began to whimper, — "it is nothing but a wolf or a wildcat, you old fool you ; lie down. — The fact is, John," I resumed, "you were very tired that night ; you had often heard the story about the place ; you

were here all alone, and dropped asleep thinking
of it, and, being in a feverish state, you dreamed
that you saw — "

"Mr. Murray," whispered John, hoarsely, interrupting me, "for God's sake, look there."

There was something in his voice, and in the
quick motion of his hand as he thrust it out
toward the lake, which startled me.   Scarcely
knowing why or what I was doing, I turned and
saw what was enough to quicken the blood in
cooler veins than mine.   Within a hundred feet
of the beach on which I was then standing was
what seemed at least to be a canoe, and in it a
form sat, bent slightly forward as in the act of
listening.   A moment it sat thus, and then the
attitude became erect, and a face, as it were the
face of a girl imprinted on the air, looked directly
into mine.   I neither spoke nor moved, but stood
steadfastly gazing at the apparition.   I was not
frightened to bewilderment.   All my faculties
seemed supernaturally active.   I noted the form
of the canoe.   It was as John had described it, —
curved up at either end, and delicately shaped.   I
noticed the paddle, slender and polished ; the white
drapery, the shadowy face.   I remembered afterward that the moonlight fell athwart the prow, as
it projected from the dark shadows of the pines
into the unimpeded radiance.   It may have been a
minute that the apparition faced us ; then, with a

movement of the head as when one seeks in vain for something not to be found, the paddle sank into the water and the phantom boat, urged as by a steady stroke which stirred no ripple, glided, with the white figure in it, along the shore and around the point, and then, heading toward the rapids, vanished from sight.

It must have been several minutes before either of us spoke. Then John broke the silence with the words, " Well, Mr. Murray, what do you think about it now ? "

" I think," said I, " that imagination has played a trick on me, or else the old story is true and this is haunted ground."

" Did you notice the canoe," continued John, " how it was curved and ornamented at either end; and the paddle, what a delicate shaft it had; and the face, was it not as the face of a girl ? "

" Yes," I returned, solemnly, " it was as you describe it, John, save that it did not seem like a real boat or paddle, and the face looked like the outline of a face printed on the air, rather than a solid head."

" So it did, so it did," responded he ; " but does not the good Book say somewhere that we shall all be changed at death, and that our bodies will not look as they do now ? "

" Well, John, we won't talk any more about it to-night," I replied ; " I want to sleep on it. Toss me my blanket there, and roll those two logs on to the fire, and we will go to sleep. In the morning we will hold a council, and decide what to do. If there is any truth in the old story, you and I might as well find it out."

John did as he was requested, and, coming round to where I stood, we wrapped ourselves in our blankets, and side by side, with Rover at our feet, prepared ourselves for slumber. "What's that?" I exclaimed, as a sharp, quick cry, followed by a prolonged howl, came up from the depth of the forest.

"A wolf has killed a deer," murmured John, "and he is calling in the pack"; and then we slept.

The sun was high in the heavens before we awoke. Our sleep had been a heavy, oblivious slumber, which took as it were so many hours clean out of our lives, — a gap across which was stretched not even the filament of a dream by which the memory could afterward connect the lying down and the rising up.

"John," said I, when breakfast was ended, "I tell you what we will do to-day. We will explore the rapids and mark us out a course down as far as Phantom Falls, and we will lay in wait off our camp to-night, when, if the apparition makes us another visit, we will run alongside of that canoe or shadow, whichever it may be, and solve the mystery. What say you?"

"I say anything you say, Mr. Murray," promptly responded John. "I never yet saw a canoe I
was afraid to run my boat alongside of; but what
shall we do if it goes from us? Shall we give
chase?"

"Certainly," I responded; "and I don't believe
that anything short of a ghost can out-paddle us,
if we fairly settle ourselves down to it."

"Nor I either," returned John, laughing; "but
what if it leads down the rapids? I heard an old
trapper say that he followed it once to the very entrance of them, down which it glided and escaped
him."

"Well, as I said, John, we will explore the
rapids to-day, and map us out a course. The river
is high, and with the full moon we can easily run
them. It is a good mile, you say, before we reach
the falls, and it must be ghost or devil if, with a
good paddle at either end of this shell, you and I
cannot catch it in a mile race."

So it was arranged, and, taking up our paddles,
we stepped into our boat and started for the
rapids. In a moment we had turned the point and
shot out into the current, in which, with reversed
strokes of the paddles, we held the light shell
stationary while we scanned the reach of tremulous water below. No prettier sight can a man
gaze at, nor is there one more calculated to quicken
the blood, than to see two men sit bareheaded and

7*

erect at either end of their cedar boat, paddle in
hand, in the smooth water which gathers like a
pool at the mouth of rapids. And many a wild,
ringing cheer have I heard rise, mingling with the
roar of waters, from those who glided in their
skeleton boats over the verge, and passed from the
gazer's sight amid the foam and rocks below.

"John," said I, as we sat looking downward,
"it's all clear ahead; let her glide."

"All right," replied John; "the waters are
high, and we shall have a clean run of it. The
small rocks are covered, and the boulders we can
dodge. We will aim for the centre, and let the
current take us. I guess we shall ride fast enough.
Only one thing before we start. We shall find
several small falls, which we must jump; but
when you hear the roar and see the smoke of
Phantom Falls, look well to your paddle and mind
what you are about. It won't do to go over them.
Twenty-five feet are more than I care to jump."

"Exactly my sentiment," returned I, "but
which side are we to land? If you and I shoot
this boat out of such a current as that," and I mo-
tioned downward, "it must be with a stroke quick
as lightning and well together."

"I know that," said John. "I explored the
banks above the falls, one day, not knowing but
that I might be swept down some time, and about
thirty rods up stream, right abreast of a dead hem-

lock, there is a large whirlpool. We will strike it to the right, and when exactly abreast of the tree we must jump our boat with one stroke under cover of the bank. Do you understand?"

"Perfectly," replied I.

"Ready, then," said John. "Steady as you are. *Now!*"

At the word "Now!" we lifted our paddles and glanced like an arrow down the slope.

Three times that day we ran the rapids, and each time without a mishap. Indeed, it was not a difficult matter, as the water was very high; and as soon as we got accustomed to the extreme swiftness of the motion, we found no difficulty at all in handling our boat. The most trying spot was where we had to run out of the current, to do which it was necessary that the stroke of our paddles should be as one, and made with our united strength.

"There," said John, as for the third time we ran under the bank, "I am not afraid to run these rapids night or day, even if chased by a ghost. Come, let us go and see the falls."

Forcing our way through the underbrush, we clambered down the bank, and, walking out upon the shelving rock, stood where the mist and spray fell on us. The falls were some twenty-five feet high, perpendicular as the face of a wall. The edge of the rock over which the water rushed must have been notched or chipped; for, starting from the very rim of the cataract, spouts of water leaped into the air, and, falling in feathery spray, formed a veil through which the dark green torrent might be seen as it fell behind it. In one spot only did the current flow unimpeded. Near the middle of the stream, for some eight feet in width, the down-rushing waters rolled to the brink and curved over without jet or seam, smooth as a sheet of glass. Underneath, the water was churned into foam, boiling and tossing about in the wildest confusion.

For several minutes we stood admiring the wild scene in silence. "Mr. Murray," at length shouted John, putting his mouth close to my ear, so as to make himself heard amid the uproar, "if any poor fellow should ever get caught in the rapids alone, and have to shoot the falls, he should steer for that smooth water, and, when on the very brink, put his whole strength into one stroke of his paddle; and if he could project his boat so that, when it struck, it would fall on the outside of that upheaving ridge, he would be safe, but if he fell inside of that white line of foam, he would be sucked under the falls and torn to pieces on the jagged bottom."

"John," said I, "it could be done, I verily believe, as you say, but not one man in fifty could hold his paddle or sit his boat steadily, gliding downward to such a fearful leap; but will and nerve could do it, only Heaven keep us from trying it."

"Amen," said John, "and yet there is no telling what may happen to those who boat by day and night up and down this wilderness as much as we do; and if you ever have to do it, Mr. Murray, steer for that smooth water, and, as you love your life, when on the brink, do as I have told you."

"Well," said I, changing the subject, "if that poor Indian girl did really come down the rapids, she must have met her death under these falls."

"Yes, that is why they call them Phantom Falls," answered John. "An old trapper told me once that he camped in the bend of the river there one night, and as he was rebuilding his fire about midnight, he saw a canoe and a white form rise slowly out of the mist and go sailing up the rapids. He was so frightened that he took boat and paddled all night down stream till he reached the settlement."

"Well," said I, as we turned from the falls and clambered up the bank, "to-night we will see if the old story is true or not. Let us go to camp." So saying we shouldered our boat and started for the camp above.

It might have been eleven o'clock when, taking up our paddles, we stepped into our boat and pushed off into the lake. We took our position in the shadow of a hemlock which grew on the very margin of the bank, some fifty yards to the west of the camp, and waited. I cannot say that I expected anything unusual would show itself. I am no believer in Spiritualism. I am not nervous by nature. I never dream. It was these facts which made it so hard for me to account for the appearance of the night before. The more I had reflected the more had I been puzzled.

"John," said I, at length, speaking in a guarded whisper, "this is the queerest ambush you and I ever made."

"I was just thinking of that very same thing," responded he; "but I am very glad we are here. For fifteen years I have wanted to do this very thing, but never found any one to attempt it with me. How do you feel?"

"Never better in my life," I replied; "although I must say that I hope we may not run the rapids. Moonlight is not sunlight, after all; and if you should make a mistake, or — "

"Mr. Murray," broke in John, "did you ever know me make a mistake? Have not you and I run rapids worse than these, time and again? and when have we taken anything but foam and spray into our boats? I tell you I am not afraid to run the rapids; only if we do go down, remember the dead hemlock. It would n't do to go over the falls."

"Never fear on that point, John; when I am ready to die, I shall choose another grave than that boiling hell of water to sleep in. When I feel the tap of your paddle-staff on the boat, I will do my part; never fear."

Here the conversation ceased, and we sat in silence, — a silence so profound as to be almost painful. Ten, twenty, thirty minutes passed, and nothing appeared. I grew impatient, incredulous. I even began to feel that I would not like my friends to know what a fool I was making of myself. "John," said I at length, taking out my watch, and holding its face up to a bright beam of light which had found its way through the dark foliage overhead, — "John, it is five minutes to twelve, and we have made fools of ourselves long enough. I don't think the Indian girl will make her toilet under the falls to-night, even if we should sit cramped up here till morning. Come, shove into the —"

A low moan, almost human in its piteousness, arose on the midnight air. Again the hound, by a supernatural instinct, had divined the approach of the spirit. I looked toward the camp. The dog sat on his haunches, facing the lake, his nose lifted into the air. Outlined as he was against the fire, I could see the uneasy tremulousness of his body. He opened his mouth, and up through the stillness swelled the saddest of all sounds, — the prolonged cry of a hound, when, in unknown grief, he wails out his feeling. At the same instant I felt the boat shake. Never did I obey that signal to be on the watch more quickly. Never was I signalled before to look at such an object. A canoe, and in it a figure like a girl's, was in the very act of turning the point. A living girl could not have kept a steadier stroke, or urged a boat along more naturally. And yet I felt that it was not flesh and blood, nor a real boat, nor ashen paddle before me. Onward the apparition came. Up to the very border of our camp that spectral boat glided, then paused. A human face could not have gazed more searchingly into the fitful firelight; a human form could not have taken a truer attitude of search. I saw a shadowy arm move through the air, and the formation of a hand rested for a moment on the brow, — as when one shields his eyes, peering into darkness, — then sank upon the paddle-staff, and the boat moved forward.

That motion roused me. It started John also. An instant more and we had solved the mystery. But even as our boat glided out of the deep shadow, the apparition turned her head full on us. I wonder we did not stop. But, with that ghostly face not fifty feet away, looking through the bright moonlight steadily into mine, I gave a stroke which bent my paddle like a sword-blade when you throw your weight suddenly upon it. The deed was done.

"*Never was I signalled before to look at such an object.*"

Devil or saint, spirit or flesh, we had her ! I thrust
my hand out to grasp the garments of the girl. I
clutched the empty air ; the girl was gone full
twenty yards away, and speeding toward the point.
Not thus were we to be eluded. John had not
missed his stroke, and, seizing my paddle again, we
sent our boat flying over the surface of the lake in
hot pursuit. Never, as I believe, was boat of bark
or cedar sent faster over the water. Our paddles
were of choicest ash, smooth as ivory, three feet in
the staff and thirty inches in the blade, while the
shell that floated us turned barely sixty pounds, with
a bottom like polished steel, and so cork-like that,
balanced carefully at stem and stern, as it was now,
it seemed to rest upon, rather than part, the water
on which it sat ; and as we cast our utmost strength
into our paddles as only boatmen can, the lithe thing
fairly flew, while its delicate framework of cedar
roots and paper-like sides quivered under the nervous strokes from stem to stern. Around the point
we rushed, pursuer and pursued. Into the swift
suction we shot almost side by side ; down over the
verge and through the white rift into the gloom of
overhanging pines, leaped a cascade, and with hands
and faces wet with spray, and garments flecked
with patches of froth and foam cast high over us as
we splashed through the rapid torrent, plunged
down the second reach and over a second fall
without losing a stroke. Still, just ahead, the boat

and spectre glided.   At one moment entering into
the shadow of some dark pine or hemlock which
overhung the stream, her white form with the whiter
face looking back at us would show an outline as
clearly marked as though of flesh and blood ; the
next, as it passed out of the gloom, it would melt
away into the moonlight, until it seemed only as an
airy formation, making no obstruction to the eye, —
a thing of mist and air.   Once, as we leaped a fall, I
thought our race was over ; for even as we hung in
air, I reached to seize the phantom.   I closed my
hand, but grasped *the atmosphere.*   I felt it was in
vain.   No mortal hand might ever touch it, or if it
might, the human senses were too gross to feel the
contact.   At that moment the white figure arose,
and, standing erect, pointed with one hand downward, and with the open palm of the other waved
us as in warning back.   The moon shone full upon
her face.   The look was sad, almost plaintive.   An
indescribable expression of patience possessed it.
" Living or dead, form or spirit, the years have
brought no hope to you, poor girl ! " said I to
myself.   In a moment her posture changed.   Her
hands dropped to her side.   Her head was bent, as
though in the attitude of listening, down the stream.
Then, suddenly starting, she stood erect, and, flinging her arms over her head with a gesture which
had in it both warning and supplication, she waved
us back.   *That instant I heard the roar of Phantom*

Falls. I tapped the side of the boat with my paddle-staff. In a moment I felt an answering jar from John, and knew that he had caught the heavy boom which warned us to end the race. Down, down we went, past rock and bulging ledge, swept round a curve, and lo ! the hemlock was in sight. Right glad was I to see it. It looked like a friend standing there, leaning out, as it was, over the swiftly gliding water, which hissed and quivered under it. I saw the eddying pool which spun abreast of it, and marked the white line of foam fringing the black circle, and noted with joy how surely John was sending the boat to the identical spot from which, with one brave stroke, we were to jump her out of the fierce suction under the projecting banks. I had no thought of accident. The faintest suspicion of failure had not crossed my mind. With the thunder of the falls filling the air with a deafening roar, barely thirty rods away, with the siz-z of the current around me as we dashed down the decline, I felt as calm and confident as though the race was over and we were standing on the bank. Nearer and nearer to the line of froth we flew ; straight as an arrow from the bow the light boat shot. I grasped my paddle, reaching my left hand well down to the blade, holding it suspended and stretched far out ahead, ready for the stroke. The moment came. I dashed the paddle into the current and bent upon

the staff.   Even as I bent to the stroke, the sound
of rending wood, a crash, a quick cry, piercing
sharply through the roar of the falls, smote upon my
ear.   No words were needed to tell me what had
happened.   *John had broken his paddle!*   The
treacherous ash had failed him even in mid-stroke.
I did my best.   I felt that life, sweet to all at all
times, doubly sweet as it seemed to me then, lay in
the strength of my arms.   I threw the last ounce
of power I had into that stroke.   The elastic staff
bent under the sudden pressure like a Damascus
blade.   It held ; but all in vain.   The suction was
too strong.   It seized John's end of the boat,
whirled it round, and sent it flying out into the
middle of the stream.   It is said that men grow
cool in danger ; that the mind acts with supernatural quickness in moments of peril.   Be that as it
may with others, so it was with me in that fearful
moment. .   *I knew that we must go over the falls.*   I
felt that John must make the awful shoot.   I had
more confidence in him than in myself.   As the
boat spun round upon the eddy, I seized advantage of the current, and righting it, directed the bow
down stream.   Then, calmly turning in my seat,
reversed my paddle, and, holding it by the blade,
reached the staff to John.   He took it.   Never
shall I forget the look of John's face as his fingers
closed on it.   No word was uttered by either of us.
No voice might make itself heard in that uproar.

The moon made everything almost as discernible as in the day. He took the paddle, understanding my thought, looking straight at me. Upon his face was an expression, plain as speech might make it, which said, " All that man can do, Mr Murray, all that man can do." Then he passed the blade into the water. I saw him take two strokes, steady and quick, then turned. Down, down we went. O, how we shot along that tremulous plain of quivering water ! I felt the shell tremble and spring as John drove it ahead. A joy I cannot express thrilled me as I felt the boat jump. Hope rose with every nervous stroke of that paddle, as it sent us flying toward the verge. No matter how we struck, provided our projection carried us beyond the deadly line of bubbles and the suction inward. I held my breath, seizing the rim of the boat on each side with either hand, and crouched low down for the leap. The motion was frightful. My face seemed to contract and sharpen under the pressure of the air as I clove through it. How John could keep his stroke, rushing down such a decline, was and will ever be to me a matter of increasing wonder. Yet, quick and smiting as his stroke was, it was as regular as the movement of a watch. Down, down we glanced, straight for the middle of the falls and the smooth opening along the jagged rim. Lower and lower I crouched. Quicker and quicker jumped the boat, until the verge was reached, and, quivering like a frightened fish, the shell, driven by what seemed to be more than mortal strength, with a mighty leap, sprang out into the air.   So nicely had long custom taught us to balance it, that, keeping the inclination given it by the current, it clove through the cloud of rising mist, passing clean out of it before we touched the water ; for even as we hung above the abyss, I saw the deadly line was passed and we were saved.   The boat, keeping the angle of declination, struck the water, and went under like a pointed stake hurled from the hand, and John and I were left struggling in the current.

We swam to the edge of the deep pool, and, climbing upon the sloping ledge, lay for a brief time motionless, and, side by side in the deep shadow of the pines, our faces prone on our crossed arms, filled with the sweet sense of life delivered, and with emotions known only to Him with whom, with the roar of the falls, out of whose hell of waters we had been snatched, rising around us, we held communion.

At the lower end of the pool we found our boat drifted ashore and John's broken paddle beside it. Shouldering the shell, and striking eastward, we soon came to the carry, traversing which we quickly reached the lake, and launching out upon it, in five minutes stood where the opening sentences of our story found us wringing our clothes beside our rekindled camp-fire.   And there, reader, we will leave you standing in fancy by the flickering fire-light, with Rover at your feet and the lake shimmering, like a sea of silver under the white radiance of the full-orbed and perfect moon, lying tranquilly before you.

"Just one word, Mr. Murray, before you stop. Did you *really* see a ghost, and is there any such place as Phantom Falls?" To which query of yours, gentle reader, pausing only one moment to answer, before I quarter this Christmas orange, I respond, "*Ask John.*"

IX.

JACK–SHOOTING IN A FOGGY NIGHT.

WE were camping on Constable Point, John and I, in the summer of 1868, when the following experience befell me. I tell it because it represents one phase of Adirondack life, and because it will enable me to enjoy over again one of the most ludicrous and laughable adventures which ever assisted digestion.

It was the 8th of July, and a party of Saranac guides, consisting of Jim McClellan, Stephen Martin, and a nephew of his, also a Canadian, name unknown, at least unpronounceable by me, had come up from the Lower Saranac, and were going through to Brown's Tract for a party of German gentlemen (and gentlemen in the best sense of the word we afterward found them to be), who had arranged the year before to camp on the Racquette for a while. The guides were instructed to select and build a camp as they came through, and then, leaving one of their number to keep it, to come after the party, who were to await them at Arnold's. The spot the guides selected was only some twenty rods to the north of us, and there they pitched their tent, close by the little projection of yellow sand which thrusts itself out into the deep blue waters of the lake. The following morning all the guides save the elder Martin started for Arnold's, leaving him to keep camp. Soon after dark Martin, having put everything in order to receive the party, dropped over to our lodge, in the door of which John and I were sitting, smoking our pipes, and chatting of this or that, as men will in the woods.

"Well," said I to Martin, as he came up, "I suppose you have all your arrangements made for the party to-morrow."

"Yes," returned he. "I don't know as I can do much more; only I do wish I could have a big buck hanging by his gambrels when they come pulling in. It would please Mr. Schack mighty well, I tell you. The fact is," he continued, "I came over here to see if you did n't want to go out to-night with your jack. We might take a short stretch up Marion River there, and I think find a venison without much trouble." Of course I was ready to go. Indeed, I was exceedingly glad of the chance. The fact is, one deer a week was all John and I could manage to dispose of; and as I never permit myself to shoot more than the camp can eat or give away, and as no parties had as yet come in, I had very little sport, and eagerly hailed the opportunity which Martin's

8

proposition gave me of "drawing it fine" on a deer's head once more.

So it was settled that we should go jack-shooting up Marion River; and, after a few minutes of further conversation as to our outfit, Martin left to prepare his boat. I proceeded to discharge my rifle, which was loaded with conical balls, in order to recharge with round ones, which are far better for short range and night work.

Perhaps, as a matter of interest to sportsmen, and for the information of the uninitiated reader, I should pause a moment in my narration to describe, not only "jack-shooting," but also "my jack."

Be it known to all, then, that a deer is a very inquisitive as well as a timid animal. His curiosity is generally greater than his timidity, and at the sight of anything new or strange he is impelled by this feeling to inspect it. Hence it is that, instead of flying from a blazing torch or lighted candle at night, he is more apt to stand stock still and gaze at it. Hunters avail themselves of this peculiarity, and hunt them by torchlight in the night-time. Ordinarily speaking, they take a piece of bark some two feet long by ten inches wide, and, bending it into the shape of a half-moon, tack it to a top and bottom board of the same shape. Into this box of bark, shaped like an old-fashioned half-moon lantern, they in-

sert one or more candles, and fasten it to a stick
some three feet in length.   The stick is then stuck
into the bow of the boat, and the "jack" is ready.
The hunter, rifle in hand, seats himself close behind and under the jack, and the paddler at the
other end of the boat or canoe.   Thus equipped
they start out.   The guide paddles quietly along,
until a deer is heard feeding, as is their custom
at night, upon the edge of the bank, or walking
in the water nipping off the lily-pads, which they
love exceedingly.   The jack is then lighted and
the boat run swiftly down toward the deer.   If
he is young, or has never seen a jack before, he
will let the boat (which he does not see, so intently
is he gazing at the light) come very near him,
and he is easily shot.   If he is old and shy, it is a
far more difficult task to get near him.   The de-
fects of this jack are evident.   It is worthless on any
but a perfectly still night, for the least current of
air will blow the light out.   It necessitates also
the scratching of a match previous to "lighting
up," and the noise incident to such an opera-
tion in the open air at night, when every object
about you is damp and wet, and in the presence
of game, does not tend to steady the nerves of
an amateur.   It is also stationary, and if you
run past the deer, as you are liable to do, it is
difficult to turn the light on him.   If, furthermore, the deer is in motion in any but a straight

line from you, the jack is of no service at all. Now, when deer are scarce and shy, or the nights windy, such a jack is almost useless, and the sportsman is often driven to change his camp or starve, although deer are all around him. Having in seasons previous experienced the disadvantages of the old jack, I determined to invent and construct one which should absolutely overcome all these imperfections. This is what I hit upon. I took a common fireman's hat, and, having the rim removed, had the crown padded with wadding, and lined with chamois-skin. I caused a half-moon lantern of copper to be made with a concave bottom which fitted closely to the hat, and was fastened thereto with screws. Through the top of the hat a hole was made large enough for the burner to pass; the lamp itself, containing the oil, was fitted and held by brass studs to the crown, between it and the head. In the back side of the lantern was placed a German-silver reflector, heavily plated. The screw which lifts and lowers the wick was connected with a shank that projected through the side of the lantern, so that by a touch of the finger the light might be let on or cut off. A large, softly padded throat-latch buckled the jack firmly to my head. Observe the advantages of this jack over the old style. Being enclosed by an air-tight glass front, it might be used in a tornado. When floating for

deer you could turn the wick so low down that
no light was visible, and when one was heard you
could run down toward him, and, with your finger
on the adjusting screw, turn on the light just when
you wanted it, and not an instant before, and this
too without a moment's pause. If the deer was
on the jump, it made no difference. The reflector
was so powerful, that, if you turned the wick well
up, it made a lane some three rods wide and fifteen
rods long as light as day, and the jack being on your
head, the blaze was never off the leaping deer,
whose motion your eye would *naturally* follow,
and as your head turned, so, without thought or
effort on your part, turned the jack. Moreover, as
all hunters know, one trouble with the old style
of jacks is, that as you hold your rifle *under* it,
when taking aim, only the *front* sight is lighted
up ; and the rear sight being in the dark, you cannot " draw it fine," but are ever liable to "shoot
over." Shooting with the old style is but little better than *guess* shooting, any way. To be sure, you
might discard the rifle, and with an old blunder-
buss, charged with slugs or buck-shot, which scatter twenty feet in going forty, get your deer. But
this is simply slaughter, — a proceeding too shameful for a sportsman ever to engage in. A man
who drops his deer with anything but a single
bullet should be hooted out of the woods. Now
the jack I am describing, when placed firmly on

the head, casts its light from lock to muzzle, and so enables the hunter to draw his bead as "fine" as he may choose. Nothing need be said in favor of this jack, — which is here for the first time described, and thus made common property, — beyond the fact that, during the whole season in which I hunted, mostly nights, I never marked a deer with a bullet back of the ears, unless he was on the jump when I shot. And time and again, as John Plumbley and many friends can testify, on nights good, bad, and indifferent, sitting, kneeling, or standing in the bow of a tottlish boat, I have sunk my bullet as squarely between the eyes as one may place his finger. One word more touching the advantages of this jack. All my readers who have hunted deer at night know that full one half of them started will go out of the river on a jump, and, when ten or twelve rods from the bank, come to a stand-still. Now this distance is too great for an old-style jack to illuminate; and often the hunter must signal his guide to paddle on, when he knows the buck he wants stands not a dozen rods away, looking straight at him. Now, with the aid of a reflector, my jack will throw a lane of light from fifteen to twenty rods; and if the deer stops within that distance, as three out of five will, and you hold steady, he is sure to come into your boat. Never shall I forget an old buck I laid out one night up South

Inlet, on the Racquette, as he stood with his nose stuck into the air and blowing away like an animated trumpet. It was just seventeen rods from the bow of the little shell I stood in, and the lead went in at one ear and came out of the other.

So much for jack-shooting and my jack. I have been thus minute in my description, because I thought it might assist my brother sportsmen to enjoy what I regard the most exciting of all sport,— deer-shooting at night. I take this way also of answering the many letters of inquiry concerning my jack recently addressed me by gentlemen who have heard of my invention from the guides, and who would like to avail themselves of it. It is rather expensive, but a *sure* thing, if well made.

Well, to return to my narration. I was driving the ball into the right barrel of my rifle when I heard the soft dip of a paddle abreast of the camp, and in a moment Martin stepped up the bank and entered, paddle in hand, the circle of the firelight. Many who read this may remember Martin, brother to him of the Lower Saranac House; but for the sake of others, who have never seen him, I will give a sketch of him. I recall him perfectly as he stood leaning on his paddle in my camp that night. A tall, sinewy man he was, in height some six feet two, in weight turning perhaps one hundred and seventy pounds,— every ounce of superfluous flesh

" sweated " off his body by his constant work at the paddle and oars, which gave him a certain gaunt, bony look, to be seen only in men who live the hunter's life and eat the hunter's fare along our frontiers. Yet there was a certain litheness about the form, a springy elasticity in the moccasined foot, a suppleness of motion, which, if it was not grace, was something next akin to it. His hair was sandy, short, crisp, and curly. His shoulders were brought the least trifle forward, as boatmen's generally are, and especially such as leave their boats to follow, with cat-like tread and crouching posture, the trail. Pants and hunting-shirt of Scotch gray ; a soft felt hat of similar color, and the inevitable short, thin knife stuck in a leathern sheath, made up his outfit. A wiry, nervous man, I said to myself, as I looked him over ; none the less nervous because a certain backwoodsman's indifference and *nonchalance* veiled the dash and fire within. A good guide I warrant, easy and pleasant of temper when fairly treated, but hot and violent as an overcharged and smutty rifle when abused.

"Martin," said I, as I dragged my jack from under a bag where it had lain concealed (for I did n't wish every one to copy my invention the first season), "what do you think of that ?" and, touching a match to the wick, I lifted the jack to my head and buckled the throat-latch.

" Well," said he, after looking at it a moment,
" that 's a new idea, anyway.   Should n't wonder
if it worked ; but I have seen so many new-fangled
notions brought into the woods that were not
worth a toadstool, that I have about given up
ever seeing anything better than a piece of bark,
and a tallow dip, mean and tricky as that is."

" Well," said I, moistening my finger and lifting it into the air, " if that current of wind comes
out of the north, we shall want something better
than a tallow dip to see through the fog with before ten o'clock."

" That 's the fact," broke in John ; " I saw, an
hour ago, by the way that hard maple brand
snapped and glowed, that it was getting colder. By
the time you reach the river the fog will be thick
enough to cut, and the best thing you can do, both
of you, is to bunk in here with me, and help me
lessen this bag of ' Lone Jack.' "

" No," said I, " fog or no fog, we 'll go out.   I
know how much it would please the party to-morrow to see a good buck hanging in front of the
camp as they come down the lake ; and, Martin,
if you will do your part at the paddle, I 'll show
you how Never Fail acts when a deer stands looking into the muzzles " ; and I patted the stock of
my double rifle, of which it is enough to say that it
has " N. Lewis, Troy, N. Y.," etched on either barrel.

" Well," replied Martin, as he turned toward

8 *   L

the beach, "it's thirty-five years since I raised the first blister on these hands with a paddle-staff, and though it is a mighty silent paddle that is usually back of you, yet we Saranac boys don't admit that any man in this wilderness can beat us in a still hunt."

With this allusion to John's reputation at the paddle, he headed his long, narrow boat out into the lake, and steadied it between his knees until I was seated in the bow; then, with a slight push, sent the light shell from the beach, vaulting at the same instant, with a motion airy as a cat's, into his own seat astern.

Who that has ever visited the Adirondacks does not grow enthusiastic as he recalls the beauty and solemn splendor of the night, as he has beheld it while being paddled across some one of its many hundred lakes ? The current of air which I had noted at the camp, cool and refreshing after the hot summer's day, was too steady and slight to stir a ripple on the glassy water. The sky was in its bluest tint, sobered by darkness. In the southern heavens, and even up to the zenith, the stars were mellow and hazy, shorn of half their beams by the moist atmosphere through which they shone. A few, away to the south, over the inlet of that name, lying back of a strata of air saturated almost to the density of vapor, beamed like so many patches of illuminated mist. But far to the north and west, whence at intervals a thin gleam of lightning shone reflected from some far-off nether region, the low growl of thunder was occasionally heard. Above, in the clear, cool blue, the star which never moves, the Dipper, and countless other orbs, differing in glory, revealed in sharp, clear outlines their stellary formations. The waveless water was to these heavens a perfect mirror; and over that seamless surface, over planets and worlds shining beneath us, over systems and constellations the minutest star of which was visible we softly glided. With bowed head I gazed into that illuminated sea. I thought of that other sea which is "of glass like unto crystal" before the throne, and the glory which must forever be reflected up from its depths. "Is this the same world of cities and cursing in which I lived a week ago?" I said to myself, "or have I been translated to some other and happier sphere?" Around me on all sides, as I gazed, Night dusky and dim sat on the mountains, and brooded over the starry sea, and the all-enveloping silence of the wilderness rested solemnly over all. As I sat and mused, — yea, and worshipped, — memory stirred within me; the words of the Psalmist came to my lips, and I murmured, "This is night which showeth wisdom, and the melody of which has gone out through all the world."

My meditations were somewhat rudely interrupted by the grating of lily-pads against the sides of the boat. We had crossed the lake, and were entering the river. My mood changed with the change of locality. The lover of nature was instantly lost in the sportsman, and as we shot into the fog, which, rising above the river, from the lake looked like a great fleecy serpent twined amid the hills, eye and ear were all alert to detect the presence of game. But we were doomed to delay. For nearly two miles we crept through the damp and chilly fog, hearing nothing to interrupt the profound silence save the occasional plunge of a muskrat or the sputter of a frog skating along the surface of the water. But all of a sudden, when heart and hope were about to fail, some distance ahead of us we heard the well-known sounds, k-splash, k-splash, and knew that a deer, and a large one too, was making for the shore. Here our adventures began. I signalled Martin, by a desperate " hitch " on the thwart, to run the boat at full speed toward the sound. He did. The light shell shot through the fog, and when in swift career struck the bank, bow on. Martin was tremendous at the paddle, and a little more force would have divided that marsh from side to side; as it was, the thin, lath-like boat was buried a third of its length amid the bogs and marsh-grass. With much struggle, and several suppressed but suggestive exclamations from Martin, we extricated the boat from the meadow and shoved out into clear water.   We had heard nothing from the deer since he left the river.   Thinking that possibly he might have stopped, after gaining the bank, to look back, as deer often do, I rose slowly in the boat, turned up the jack, and peered anxiously into the fog. The strong reflector bored a lane through the fleecy mass for some fifty feet, perhaps ; even at that distance objects mingled grotesquely with the fog.   At the extreme end of the opening I detected a bright, diamond-like spark.   What was it ?   I turned the jack up, and I turned it down.   I lowered myself until my eyes looked along the line of the grass. I raised myself on tiptoe.   Nothing more could be seen.   " It may be the eye of a deer, and it may be only a drop of water, or a wet leaf," said I to myself.   Still it looked gamy.   I concluded to launch a bullet at it anyway.   Whispering to Martin to steady the boat, I sunk my eye well down into the sights, and, holding for the gleam amid the marsh-grass, fired.   The smoke, mingling heavily with the fog, made all murky before me, while the explosion, striking against the mountains on either side, started a dozen reverberations, so that we could neither see nor hear what was the result of the shot.   After waiting in silence a few moments, hoping to hear the deer " kick," without any such happy result, I told Martin I would go ashore to load, and see what it was I had shot at.   He paddled

forward, and, seizing the tall grass, while he forced
the boat in against the bank with his paddle, I
clambered up. Being curious to ascertain what
had deceived me, I strode off into the marsh
some forty feet, and, turning up the jack, lo and
behold a dead deer lay at my feet! " Martin,"
shouted I, " here the deer is, dead as a tick!"

" The d — l!" exclaimed the guide from the fog.

" What did you say?" again I shouted.

" I said I did n't believe it," returned Martin,
soberly.

" Paddle your canoe up here, then, you old scep-
tic, and see for yourself," I rejoined, taking the
deer by the ear and dragging him to the bank.
" Here he is, and a monster too." Martin did as
directed. " Well," exclaimed he, as he unbent his
gaunt form from the curve into which two hours
of paddling had cramped it, and straightened himself to his full height, until his eyes rested upon the
buck, — " well, Mr. Murray, you are the first man
I ever saw draw a fine bead in a night like this,
standing in the bow of a Saranac boat, at the twin-
kle of a deer's eye, and *kill*. That jack of yours is
a big thing, and no mistake." By the time he had
finished, the boat had drifted off into the river, —
for the current was quite strong at that point, —
and I was alone. I was just fitting a cap to the
tube of the recharged barrel, when I felt a movement at my feet, and, casting my eyes downward,

I saw that the deer was in the act of *getting up*! The ball, as we afterward discovered, had glanced along the front of the skull, barely creasing the skin.   It had touched the bone slightly, and stunned him so that he dropped; but beyond this, it had not hurt him in the least.   Quick as thought, I put my foot against his shoulder and pushed him over.   "Martin," I cried, "this deer is n't dead; he 's trying to get up.   What shall I do ?"

"Not dead!" exclaimed he, shouting from the middle of the river through the dense fog.

"No, he is n't dead; far from it.   He is mighty lively, and getting more and more so," I returned, now having my hands full to keep the deer down. "Come out and help me.   What shall I do ?"

"Get hold of his hind leg; I 'll be with you in a minute," was the answer.

I did as directed.   I laid hold of his left hind leg, just above the fetlocks, and sprang to my feet.

Reader, did you ever seize a pig by the hind leg ?   If so, multiply that pig by ten; for every twitch he gives, count six; lash a big lantern to your head; fancy yourself standing alone on a swampy marsh in a dark, foggy night, with a rifle in your left hand, and being twitched about among the bogs and in and out of muskrat-holes, until your whole system seems on the point of a separation which shall send you in a thousand infinitesimal parts in all directions, like fragments of an exploding buzz-wheel, and you have my appearance and feelings as I was jerked about that night amid the mire and marsh-grass, as I clung to the leg of that deer. Now, when I fasten to anything, I always expect to hold on. This was my determination when I put my fingers round that buck's leg. I have a tremendous *grip*. My father had before me. With his hands at a two-inch auger-hole in the head of a barrel, I have seen him clutch, now with his right, now with his left hand, twenty-two house-rats as they came darting out to escape the stick with which I was stirring them up, and dash them dead upon the floor, without getting a single bite; and everybody knows that a rat, in full bolt, comes out of a barrel like a flash of lightning. I fully expected to maintain the family *prestige* for grip. I did. I stuck to that deer with all my power of arm and will. I felt it to be a sort of personal contest between him and myself. Nevertheless, I was perfectly willing at any time to let go. I had undertaken the job at the request of another, and was ready to surrender it instantly upon demand. I shouted to Martin to get out of that boat mighty quick if he wanted to take his deer home, for I should n't hold on to him much longer. It took me about two minutes to deliver that sentence. It was literally jerked out of me, word by word. Never did I labor under greater

embarrassment in expressing myself. In the mean
while Martin was meeting with difficulty. The
bank of the river was steep, and the light cedar
shell, with only himself in it, was out of all balance, and hard to manage. It may be that his
very strong desire to get on to that meadow
where I was holding his deer for him operated
to confuse and embarrass his movements! He
would propel the boat at full speed toward the
bank, then jump for the bow; but his motion
forward would release the boat from the mud,
and when he reached the bow the boat would be
half-way across the river again. Now Martin is a
man of great patience. He is not by any means a
profane person. He had always shown great respect for the cloth. But everybody will see that
his position was a very trying one. Three several
times, as he afterward informed me, did he drive
that boat into the bank, and three several times,
when he got to the bow, that boat was in the middle of the river. At last Martin's patience gave
way, and out of the fog came to my ears ejacula-
tions of disgust, and such strong expletives as
are found only in choice old English, and howls
of rage and disappointment that none but a guide
could utter in like circumstances. But human
endurance has a limit. I was fast reaching a
condition of mind when family pride and trans-
mitted powers of resolution fail. What did I care

for my father's exploit with the rats at the two-inch auger-hole? What did the family grip amount to after all? I was fast losing sight of the connection such vanities sustained to me. I was undergoing a rapid change in many respects, — of body as well as mind! When I got hold of that deer's leg, I was mentally full of pluck and hope; my hunting-coat, of Irish corduroy, was whole and tightly buttoned. Now, mentally, I was demoralized; every button was gone from the coat, and the right sleeve hung disconnected with the body of the garment. The jack had been jerked from my head, and lay a rod off in the marsh-grass. I could hold on no longer. I would make one more effort, one more appeal. I did. "Martin," said I, "are n't you EVER going to get out of that boat?"

The heavy thug of the boat against the bank, an explosive and sputtering noise which sounded very much like the word "damn" spoken from between shut teeth, a splash, a scramble, and then I caught sight of the gaunt form of Martin, paddle in hand and hunting-knife between his teeth, loping along toward me, through the tall, rank grass. But, alas! it was too late. The auspicious moment had passed. My fingers one by one loosened their hold, and the deer, gathering all his strength, with a terrific elevation of his hind feet sent me reeling backward, just as Martin, doubled up into

a heap, was about to alight upon his back. He
missed the back, but, as good luck would have it,
even while the buck was in the air, — the deer
going up as Martin came down, — the fingers of
the guide closed with a full and desperate grip
upon his *tail*.   Quick as a flash I recovered myself
from the bogs, replaced the jack, which fortunately had not been extinguished, upon my head,
and stood an interested spectator of the proceedings. Now everybody knows how a wild deer
can jump when frightened; and the buck, with
Martin fastened to his tail, was thoroughly
roused. The first leap straightened the poor fellow
out like a lathe, but it did not shake him from his
hold. If the reader has ever seen a small boy
hanging to the tail-board of a wagon, when the
horse was at full speed, he can form a faint idea
of Martin's appearance as the deer tore like a
whirlwind through the tall grass. Blinded and
bewildered by the light, frenzied with fear, the
buck, as deer often will, instead of leading off,
kept racing up and down just within the border
of light made by the jack, and occasionally making a bolt directly for it. My position was
unique. I was the sole spectator of a series of
gymnastic evolutions truly original. Small as the
audience was, the performers were thoroughly in
earnest. Had there been ten thousand spectators,
the actors could not have laid themselves out with

greater energy.   No applause could have got another inch of jump out of the buck, or another inch
of horizontal position out of Martin.   Whenever,
at long intervals, his feet did touch the ground, it
was only to leave it for another and a higher aerial
plunge.   Now and then the buck would take a short
stretch into the fog and darkness, only to reappear
with the same inevitable attachment of arms and
legs streaming behind.   The scene was too ludicrous to be endured in silence.   The desperate expression of Martin's face, as he was swung round and
jerked about, was enough to make a monk explode
with laughter while doing penance.   I rested my
hands on either knee, and laughed until tears rolled
down my cheeks.   The merriment was all on my
side.   Martin was silent as death, save when the
buck, in some extraordinary and desperate leap,
twitched a grunt out of him.   Between my paroxysms I exhorted him : it was my time to exhort.
" Martin," I shouted, " hang on ; that 's *your* deer.
I quit all claim to him.   Hang on, I say.   Save
his tail anyhow."

Whether Martin appreciated the advice, whether he exactly saw where the " laugh came in," I
cannot say, and he could not explain.   Still I am
led to think that it was to him no trifling affair,
but a matter which moved him profoundly.   At
last the knife was jerked from his teeth, either
because of the violence of his exertion, or because

"Martin," shouted I, "hang on; that's your deer. I quit all claim to him."

he had inadvertently loosened his grasp on it. Be this as it may, Martin's mouth was at last opened, and out of it were projected some of the most extraordinary expressions I ever heard. His sentences were singularly detached. Even his words were widely separated, but brought out with great emphasis. He averaged about one word to a jump. If another got partially out, it was suddenly and ruthlessly snapped off in mid utterance. The result of his efforts to express himself reached my ears very much in this shape : " Jump — *will* — you — be-e—*damned*— I 've-e—GOT — you! I 'll — hold-d — ON — till — your — ta-i-l — comes — off-f. — *Jump-p-p* — be D-D-DAMNED — I 'VE — got — you-u-u."

When the contest would have ended, what would have been the result had it continued, whether the buck or the guide would have come off the winner, it is not easy to say. Nor is it necessary to speculate, for the close was speedily reached, and in an unlooked-for manner. The deer had led off some dozen jumps out of the circle of light, and I was beginning to think that he had shaken himself loose from his enemy, when all at once he emerged from the fog with Martin still streaming behind him, and made straight for the river. Never did I see a buck vault higher or project himself farther in successive leaps. The Saranacer was too much put to it to articulate a word ; only a series of grunts, as he was twitched

along, revealed the state of his pent-up feelings.
Past me the deer flashed like a feathered shaft,
heading directly for the bank. "Hang on, Martin!"
I screamed, sobered by the thought that he would
save him yet if he could only retain his grip, —
"hang to him like death!" He did. Never did my
admiration go out more strongly toward a man than
it did toward Martin, as, red in the face and unable to relieve himself by a single expression, he
went tearing along at a frightful rate in full bolt
for the river. Not one man in fifty could have
kept his single-handed grip, jerked, at the close
of such a struggle as the Saranacer had passed
through, and twitched mercilessly as he now was
being through the tall bog-grass and over the un-
even ground. But the guide's blood was up, and
nothing could loosen his clutch. The buck reached
the bank, and, gathering himself up for a desperate leap, he flung his body into the air. I saw a
pair of widely separated legs swing wildly upward, and the red face of Martin, head downward,
and reversed, so as to be turned directly toward me
by the summersault he was turning, disappeared
like a waning rocket in the fog overhanging the
river. Once in the water, the buck was no match
for his foe. I hurried to the edge of the bank.
Beneath me, and half across the river, a desperate
struggle was going on. Martin had found his voice,
and was using it as if to make up for lost time. In
a moment a gurgling sound reached my ears, and

I knew that the deer's head was under water; and shortly, in answer to my hail, the guide appeared, dragging the buck behind him. The deer was drowned and quite dead. Drawing my knife across the still warm throat, we bled him well, and, waiting for Martin to rest himself a moment, slid him down into the boat and stretched him at full length along the bottom. Taking our places at either end, and, lifting our paddles, we turned our faces campward. Down through the dense, damp fog, cleaving with dripping faces its heavy folds, we passed; glided out of the mist and darkness of the lowland upon the clear waters of the lake, now lively with ripples, and under the brightly shining stars, nor checked our measured stroke until we ran our shell ashore in the glimmer of the fire, by the side of which, rolled in his blanket, with his jacket for his pillow, John was quietly sleeping. At the touch of the boat on the beach he started up, and the coffee he had made ready to boil at our coming was shortly ready, and, as we drank the warming beverage with laughter which startled the ravens from the pines, and woke the loons, sleeping on the still water of Beaver Bay, we told John the story of our adventure with a buck up Marion River on a foggy night. And often, as I sit in my study, hot and feverish with toil which wearies the brain and wrinkles the face, I pause, and, throwing down pen and book, fancy myself once more upon that bank, enveloped in fog, with the buck and Martin at his tail, careering before me. Then, with brain relaxed, and eyes which had been hot with the glimmer of the gas on the white sheet cooled and washed in mirthful tears, I turn to pen and book, and graver thoughts, refreshed and strengthened. Blessed be recollection, which, while it allows the ills and cares of life to fade away, enables us to carry all our pleasures and joys forever with us as we journey along !

MY JACK.

X.

SABBATH IN THE WOODS.

I AROSE early, that I might behold the glory of morning among the mountains. As my eyes opened, the eastern sky was already overspread as with a thin silvery veil, with the least trace of amber and gold amid the threads; while one solitary star, like a great opal, hung suspended in the translucent atmosphere, with its rich heart glowing with red and yellow flame.

My camp was made on the very ridge-board of the continent. Below me, to the south, stretched the silurian beach, upon which, as Agassiz believes, the first ripples broke when God commanded the dry land to appear. As I lay reflecting upon the assertion of science, — that these mountains were among the first to rise out of the Profound, that here the continent had its infancy, that amid these heights the earth began to take shape and form, — I seemed to be able to overlook the world. Nor was it at the cost of any great effort of the imagination that I seemed to hear, as the dawn brightened in the east and the rose tints deepened along the sky, as the darkness melted, the vapors floated up, and the atmosphere grew tremulous as the lance-like beams began to pierce it, the Voice which, in the beginning, said, " Let there be light ! " As I gazed, novel emotions arose within me. The experience was fresh and solemn. The air was cool, delicious. The earth was clothed as a queen in bridal robes ; and Morn, with garments steeped in sweet-smelling odors, her golden curls unbound and lifted by unseen winds, streaming abroad as a yellow mist, — like a maiden at the lattice of her lover, — stood knocking at the windows of the East, and saying : " Open to me, my love, my undefiled : for my head is filled with dew, and my locks with the drops of the night."

If a person would know how sensitive his na-ture is, how readily it responds to every exhibition of beauty and power, how thoroughly adapted it is, in all its faculties, to religious impressions, he must leave the haunts of men, — where every sight and sound distracts his attention, and checks the free exercises of his soul, — and, amid the silence of the woods, hold communion with his Maker. It is the *silence* of the wilderness which most impresses me. The hours of the Sabbath pass noiselessly. No voice of conversation, no sound of hurrying feet, no clangor of bells, no roll of wheels, disturb your meditations. You do not feel like reading or talking or singing. The heart needs neither hymn nor prayer to express its emotions. Even the Bible lies at your side unlifted. The letters seem dead, cold, insufficient. You feel as if the very air was God, and you had passed into that land where written revelation is not needed; for you see the Infinite as eye to eye, and feel him in you and above you and on all sides. It is true, at intervals, you turn to the Bible. You have your reading moods, when some apt passage, some appropriate selection or chapter, is read, with a profit and rapture never before experienced. But this mood I believe to be the exception. Ordinarily, the spirit is above the letter. The action of eye and voice interfere with the sentiment. You do not want to read, but think. When you feel the presence of a friend, have his hand in yours, see him at your very side, you do not need to take up a letter and read that he is with you. So with God: in the silence of the woods the soul apprehends him instinctively. He is everywhere. In the fir and pine, which, like the tree of life, shed their leaves every month, and are forever green; in the water at your feet, which no paddle has ever vexed and no taint polluted, rivalling that which is as " pure as crystal "; in the mountains, which, in every literature, have been associated with the Deity, you see Him who of old time was conceived of as a " Dweller among the hills." With such symbols and manifestations of God around, you need not go to the lettered page to learn of him. The Bible, with its print and paper, is a hindrance rather than a help. Like a glass with too narrow a field, it concentrates the vision too much. It clips the wings of the imagination, and narrows the circle of its flight. The spirit which, for the first time, perhaps, has escaped the bonds of formal worship, for the first time tasted of freedom and tested its capacities to soar, returns regretfully to the restraint and bondage of book and speech. It takes these up as an angel, whose hands have once swept a heavenly harp, touches again the strings of an earthly instrument.

This I have always observed, that the memory is unusually active, and takes great delight in recalling texts of Scripture and devotional hymns, when brought under the influence of nature. Passages from the Psalms, which I do not remember that I ever committed ; fragments of old and solemn hymns, hewn I know not from what block, long forgotten if ever learned ; snatches of holy melody, — echoes awakened by what voice you cannot tell come floating back upon you, or rise at the bidding of the will. Often have I said to myself, " Alas ! even memory is in bondage to sin." Nature, through her refining and spiritualizing agencies, emancipates it ; and sweet is it to think that, by and by, when our grossness is entirely purged away, all pure things passed by or forgotten will come back to us, and the past, in reference to whatever of goodness and truth it had in it, will be, to the holy, an eternal present. Such has been my experience, in reference to religious impressions, felt amid the solitude of forests. It takes more than one season to analyze your emotions. The mind, for a while deprived of the customary restraints and incitements of forms and ceremonies, is in a chaotic state. Thoughts come and go without order. Emotions are irregular and inconstant. The Occidental cast of intellect which conceives of God largely through the reason, changes slowly into the Oriental. It analyzes less, but it adores far more. The religion of the forest is emotional and poetic. No mathematician was ever born amid the pines. The Psalms could never have been written by one not inspired by the breath of the hills. The soul, when it spreads its wings for flight upward, must start from the summit of mountains. It must have the help of altitude, or no movement of wings will lift it. And I dare to say that he who has never passed a Sabbath amid the solemn loneliness of an uninhabited region, has never knelt in prayer at the base of overhanging mountains, has never fallen asleep with no roof above him but that of the heavens, and no protection from the dangers which lurk amid the darkness of the night season save the watchful care of God, can realize little the significance of these two words, — Adoration and Faith.

The day wore on as I mused. The sun passed
the meridian line, and soon the shadows of the pines
and hills began to stretch their cone-like formations out toward the east. As I gazed upon the
landscape, with a hundred mountains within sweep
of my eye, at whose feet lake after lake lay in peaceful repose, and between which numberless streams
flowed, gleaming amid the forests of pine and fir
as threads of silver woven into a robe of Lincoln-
green, I thought of the words of Isaiah : "I will
open rivers in high places, and fountains in the
midst of the valleys. I will make the wilderness
a pool of water, and the dry land springs of water."
"The beast of the field shall honor me, and the owls,
because I give waters in the wilderness and rivers
in the desert." And I said to myself, "Surely He
sendeth the springs into the valleys, which run
among the hills.'" About three o'clock in the afternoon, as I sat looking out upon the lake, a heavy
jar shook the earth, and simultaneously the air vibrated with the sound of thunder. Turning my
eyes toward the west, I perceived a whitish mist
gathering along the mountains, while a few ragged
scuds came racing up from behind it, and I knew
that in the valleys westward columns of storm
were moving to the onset.

Amid this mountainous region tempests give
brief warning of their approach. Walled in as
these lakes are by mountains, behind which the

cloud gathers unseen, the coming of a storm is like the spring of a tiger. A sudden peal of thunder, a keen shaft of lightning which cuts through the atmosphere in front of your startled vision, a puff of air, or the spinning of a whirlwind across the lake, and the tempest is upon you. So was it now. Even as I gazed into the white mist, a heavy bank of jet-black cloud rose up through its feathery depths, unrolled itself as a battery unlimbers for battle, and the next instant a sheet of flame darted out of its very centre, and the air seemed rent into fragments by the concussion. Here was an exhibition of grandeur and power such as one seldom beholds; and yet it did not seem out of harmony with the day. Behold, I said to myself, the symbol of the old dispensation. Here is Sinai, the terror, and the cloud; here is law and judgment, vengeance and wrath. And there, I said, turning to the eastern ridge, upon whose crest the sun, not yet obscured, shone warmly, is the symbol of the new, — of Calvary, its light and love. Warned by the scattering drops which, plunging through the air, smote like shot upon the beach and water, I hastened to the lodge; and as, seated in the door, I gazed into the dark masses now rolled in wild convolutions together, — through whose gloomy folds the winds roared and rushed, tearing the darkness into shreds, and scattering black patches on every side, — I thought of Him who "clothes the

heavens with blackness, and makes sackcloth
their covering."

The storm passed. The cloud toward the west
grew thinner, and broke into rifts and ridges,
through which the sun sent its radiance in diverg-
ing columns. As the beams deepened and spread
across the cloud, an arch of purple and gold began
to creep over it. Beginning at the southern and
northern extremities, the colors clomb upward until they joined themselves together at the centre,
and there, with two mountains for its pedestals,
the magnificent arch stood spanning the inky mass
from north to south; and as I sat silently gazing
upon the resplendent symbols of God's abiding
mercy, which stood out in bold relief against the
sombre cloud, in whose bosom might still be heard
the roll of thunder, I remembered the language of
Ezekiel, where he says, "I fell upon my face, and
I heard a voice of one that spake; for the appearance was of the likeness of the glory of the Lord."
Suddenly the colors faded away. The sun had
called home his beams, and the glory of their reflection deserted the cloud. I turned my eyes to
the west, and up to the summit of the mountain
overhanging our camp. For a moment the glowing
orb stood as though balanced on the top of the pines;
for a moment lake and forest and mountain were
ablaze with its radiance; the next it dropped from
sight. The dark trees gloomily outlined themselves

against the clear blue of the sky; and, as the shadows deepened, I thought of the day foretold in the Apocalypse, when "our sun shall no more go down, neither shall the moon withdraw herself. For the Lord shall be our everlasting light, and the days of our mourning shall be ended."

The day was over. Night spread her sable wings over the camp, and the lake darkened under the shadow. On the sky and highest peaks a few patches of crimson were still visible. For a few moments an aureole lingered around the head of Blue Mountain. The pines which adorn its crest gleamed like the rich plume of a king when he rideth at noonday to battle. One instant the beams lingered lovingly about the summit, and then, obedient to a summons from the west, flew to join their companions in another hemisphere. And now began the marvellous transformations from day to night. The clouds were rolled together and lifted from sight. Unseen hands flung out new tapestry for the skies, and lighted lamps innumerable around the circling galleries, as though the Sabbath had passed from earth, and the heavens were being made ready for service. If the day had been suggestive, much more so was the night. To the north the Dipper hung suspended in bold relief against the blue of the sky, journeying in silent revolution around the polar-star. Farther eastward, and higher up, the mourn-

9*

ful Pleiades began their nightly search for their lost sister. In the zenith a meteor wavered and trembled for a moment, then fell and faded away. "A wandering star," I said, "to which is reserved the blackness of darkness forever." The balsams felt the dew, and from their pendant spears dropped odors. I rolled myself in my blanket, and lay gazing upward. A thousand recollections thronged upon me; a thousand hopes rose up within me. The heavens elicited confidence, and unto them I breathed my aspirations. I felt that He who telleth the number of the stars took note of me. The Spirit which garnished the heavens would grant me audience. I approached Him reverently, and yet with confidence, for I remembered that it is written, "the heavens shall vanish away like smoke, and the earth shall wax old like a garment, but my salvation shall be forever, and my righteousness shall not be abolished."

Then, without help of book or spoken word, I committed myself to Him, in whose sight the night is as the day; and, alone in that vast wilderness, far from home and friends, I closed my eyes and slept as one who sleeps on a guarded bed.

XI.

A RIDE WITH A MAD HORSE IN A FREIGHT-CAR.

SHOULD the reader ever visit the south inlet of Racquette Lake, — one of the loveliest bits of water in the Adirondack Wilderness, — at the lower end of the pool, below the falls, on the left-hand side going up, he will see the charred remnants of a camp-fire. It was there that the following story was first told, — told, too, so graphically, with such vividness, that I found little difficulty, when writing it out from memory, two months later, in recalling the exact words of the narrator in almost every instance.

It was in the month of July, 1868, that John and I, having located our permanent camp on Constable's Point, were lying off and on, as sailors say, about the lake, pushing our explorations on all sides out of sheer love of novelty and abhorrence of idleness. We were returning, late one afternoon of a hot, sultry day, from a trip to Shedd Lake, — a lonely, out-of-the-way spot which few sportsmen have ever visited, — and had reached the falls on South Inlet just after sunset. As we were getting short of venison, we decided to lie by awhile, and float down the river on our way to camp, in hope of meeting a deer. To this end we had gone ashore at this point, and, kindling a small fire, were waiting for denser darkness. We had barely started the blaze, when the tap of a carelessly handled paddle against the side of a boat warned us that we should soon have company, and in a moment two boats glided around the curve below, and were headed directly toward our bivouac. The boats contained two gentlemen and their guides. We gave them a cordial, hunter-like greeting, and, lighting our pipes, were soon engaged in cheerful conversation, spiced with story-telling. It might have been some twenty minutes or more, when another boat, smaller than you ordinarily see even on those waters, containing only the paddler, came noiselessly around the bend below, and stood revealed in the reflection of the firelight. I chanced to be sitting in such a position as to command a full view of the curve in the river, or I should not have known of any approach, for the boat was so sharp and light, and he who urged it along so skilled at the paddle, that not a ripple, no, nor the sound of a drop of water falling from blade or shaft, betrayed the paddler's presence. If there is anything over which I become enthusiastic, it is such a boat and such paddling. To see a boat of bark or cedar move through the water noiselessly as a cloud-shadow drifts across a meadow, no jar or creak above, no gurgling of displaced water below, no whirling and rippling wake astern, is something bordering so nearly on the weird and ghostly, that custom can never make it seem other than marvellous to me. Thus, as I sat, half reclining, and saw that little shell come floating airily out of the darkness into the projection of the firelight, as a feather might come, blown by the night-wind, I thought I had never seen a prettier or more fairy-like sight. None of the party save myself were so seated as to look down stream, and I wondered which of the three guides would first discover the presence of the approaching boat. Straight on it came. Light as a piece of finest cork it sat upon and glided over the surface of the river; no dip and roll, no drop of falling water as the paddle-shaft gently rose and sank. The paddler, whoever he might be, knew his art thoroughly. He sat erect and motionless, the turn of the wrists, and the easy elevation of his arms as he feathered his paddle, were the only movements visible. But for these, the gazer might deem him a statue carved from the material of the boat, a mere inanimate part of it. I have boated much in bark canoe and cedar shell alike, and John and I have stolen on many a camp that never knew our coming or our going, with paddles which touched the water as snow-flakes touch the earth; and well I knew, as I sat gazing at this man, that not one boatman, red man or white, in a hundred could handle a paddle like that. The quick ear of John, when the stranger was within thirty feet of the landing, detected the lightest possible touch of a lily-pad against the side of the boat as it just grazed it glancing by, and his "Hist!" and sudden motion toward the river drew the attention of the whole surprised group thither. The boat glided to the sand so gently as barely to disturb a grain, and the paddler, noiseless in all his movements, stepped ashore and entered our circle.

"Well, stranger," said John, "I don't know how long your fingers have polished a paddle-shaft, but it is n't every man who can push a boat up ten rods of open water within twenty feet of my back without my knowing it."

The stranger laughed pleasantly, and, without making any direct reply, lighted his pipe and joined in the conversation. He was tall in stature, wiry, and bronzed. An ugly cicatrice stretched on the left side of his face, from temple almost down to chin. His eyes were dark gray, frank, and genial. I concluded at once that he was a gentleman, and had seen service. Before he joined us, we had been whiling away the time by story-telling, and John was at the very crisis of an adventure with a panther, when his quick ear detected the stranger's approach. Explaining this to him, I told John to resume his story, which he did. Thus

half an hour passed quickly, all of us relating some
" experience."   At last I proposed that Mr. Roberts
— for so we will call him — should entertain us;
" and," continued I, " if I am right in my surmise
that you have seen service and been under fire, give
us some adventure or incident which may have
befallen you during the war."   He complied, and
then and there, gentle reader, I heard from his
lips the story which, for the entertainment of
friends, I afterward wrote out.   It left a deep impression upon all who heard it around our camp-
fire under the pines that night ; and from the mind
of one I know has never been erased the impression made by the story, which I have named

A RIDE WITH A MAD HORSE IN A FREIGHT-CAR.

" Well," said the stranger, as he loosened his belt
and stretched himself in an easy, recumbent position, " it is not more than fair that I should throw
something into the stock of common entertainment ; but the story I am to tell you is a sad one,
and, I fear, will not add to the pleasure of the
evening.   As you desire it, however, and it comes
in the line of the request that I would narrate
some personal episode of the war, I will tell it, and
trust the impression will not be altogether unpleasant.

"It was at the battle of Malvern Hill, — a battle where the carnage was more frightful, as it seems to me, than in any this side of the Alleghanies during the whole war, — that my story must begin. I was then serving as Major in the —th Massachusetts Regiment, — the old —th, as we used to call it, — and a bloody time the boys had of it too. About 2 P. M., we had been sent out to skirmish along the edge of the wood in which, as our generals suspected, the Rebs lay massing for a charge across the slope, upon the crest of which our army was posted. We had barely entered the underbrush when we met the heavy formations of Magruder in the very act of charging. Of course, our thin line of skirmishers was no impediment to those onrushing masses. They were on us and over us before we could get out of the way. I do not think that half of those running, screaming masses of men ever knew that they had passed over the remnants of as plucky a regiment as ever came out of the old Bay State. But many of the boys had good reason to remember that afternoon at the base of Malvern Hill, and I among the number ; for when the last line of Rebs had passed over me, I was left amid the bushes with the breath nearly trampled out of me, and an ugly bayonet-gash through my thigh ; and mighty little consolation was it for me at that moment to see the fellow who run me through lying stark dead at my side,

with a bullet-hole in his head, his shock of coarse
black hair matted with blood, and his stony eyes
looking into mine.   Well, I bandaged up my limb
the best I might, and started to crawl away, for
our batteries had opened, and the grape and canis-
ter that came hurtling down the slope passed but
a few feet over my head.   It was slow and painful
work, as you can imagine, but at last, by dint of
perseverance, I had dragged myself away to the
left of the direct range of the batteries, and, creep-
ing to the verge of the wood, looked off over the
green slope.   I understood by the crash and roar
of the guns, the yells and cheers of the men, and
that hoarse murmur which those who have been
in battle know, but which I cannot describe in
words, that there was hot work going on out there ;
but never have I seen, no, not in that three days'
desperate _mélée_ at the Wilderness, nor at that terrific repulse we had at Cold Harbor, such absolute
slaughter as I saw that afternoon on the green
slope of Malvern Hill.   The guns of the entire
army were massed on the crest, and thirty thousand
of our infantry lay, musket in hand, in front.   For
eight hundred yards the hill sank in easy declen-
sion to the wood, and across the smooth expanse
the Rebs must charge to reach our lines.   It was
nothing short of downright insanity to order men
to charge that hill ; and so his generals told Lee,
but he would not listen to reason that day, and so

N

he sent regiment after regiment, and brigade after brigade, and division after division, to certain death. Talk about Grant's disregard of human life, his effort at Cold Harbor — and I ought to know, for I got a minie in my shoulder that day — was hopeful and easy work to what Lee laid on Hill's and Magruder's divisions at Malvern. It was at the close of the second charge, when the yelling mass reeled back from before the blaze of those sixty guns and thirty thousand rifles, even as they began to break and fly backward toward the woods, that I saw from the spot where I lay a riderless horse break out of the confused and flying mass, and, with mane and tail erect and spreading nostril, come dashing obliquely down the slope. Over fallen steeds and heaps of the dead she leaped with a motion as airy as that of the flying fox, when, fresh and unjaded, he leads away from the hounds, whose sudden cry has broken him off from hunting mice amid the bogs of the meadow. So this riderless horse came vaulting along. Now from my earliest boyhood I have had what horsemen call a 'weakness' for horses. Only give me a colt of wild, irregular temper and fierce blood to tame, and I am perfectly happy. Never did lash of mine, singing with cruel sound through the air, fall on such a colt's soft hide. Never did yell or kick send his hot blood from heart to head deluging his sensitive brain with fiery currents, driving

him to frenzy or blinding him with fear; but
touches, soft and gentle as a woman's, caressing
words, and oats given from the open palm, and
unfailing kindness, were the means I used to 'sub-
jugate' him. Sweet subjugation, both to him
who subdues and to him who yields! The wild,
unmannerly, and unmanageable colt, the fear of
horsemen the country round, finding in you, not
an enemy but a friend, receiving his daily food
from you, and all those little 'nothings' which go
as far with a horse as a woman, to win and retain
affection, grows to look upon you as his protector
and friend, and testifies in countless ways his fondness for you. So when I saw this horse, with
action so free and motion so graceful, amid that
storm of bullets, my heart involuntarily went out
to her, and my feelings rose higher and higher at
every leap she took from amid the whirlwind of
fire and lead. And as she plunged at last over
a little hillock out of range and came careering
toward me as only a riderless horse might come,
her head flung wildly from side to side, her nostrils
widely spread, her flank and shoulders flecked with
foam, her eye dilating, I forgot my wound and all
the wild roar of battle, and, lifting myself involuntarily to a sitting posture as she swept grandly
by, gave her a ringing cheer.

"Perhaps in the sound of a human voice of
happy mood amid the awful din she recognized a

resemblance to the voice of him whose blood moistened her shoulders and was even yet dripping from saddle and housings. Be that as it may, no sooner had my voice sounded than she flung her head with a proud upward movement into the air, swerved sharply to the left, neighed as she might to a master at morning from her stall, and came trotting directly up to where I lay, and pausing, looked down upon me as it were in compassion. I spoke again, and stretched out my hand caressingly. She pricked her ears, took a step forward and lowered her nose until it came in contact with my palm. Never did I fondle anything more tenderly, never did I see an animal which seemed to so court and appreciate human tenderness as that beautiful mare. I say ' beautiful.' No other word might describe her. Never will her image fade from my memory while memory lasts.

" In weight she might have turned, when well conditioned, nine hundred and fifty pounds. In color she was a dark chestnut, with a velvety depth and soft look about the hair indescribably rich and elegant. Many a time have I heard ladies dispute the shade and hue of her plush-like coat as they ran their white, jewelled fingers through her silken hair. Her body was round in the barrel, and perfectly symmetrical. She was wide in the haunches, without projection of the hip-bones, upon which the shorter ribs seemed to

lap.   High in the withers as she was, the line of
her back and neck perfectly curved, while her
deep, oblique shoulders and long thick fore-arm,
ridgy with swelling sinews, suggesting the perfec-
tion of stride and power.   Her knees across the
pan were wide, the cannon-bone below them short
and thin; the pasterns long and sloping; her hoofs
round, dark, shiny, and well set on.   Her mane
was a shade darker than her coat, fine and thin,
as a thoroughbred's always is whose blood is without taint or cross.   Her ear was thin, sharply
pointed, delicately curved, nearly black around the
borders, and as tremulous as the leaves of an
aspen.   Her neck rose from the withers to the
head in perfect curvature, hard, devoid of fat, and
well cut up under the chops.   Her nostrils were full,
very full, and thin almost as parchment.   The eyes,
from which tears might fall or fire flash, were well
brought out, soft as a gazelle's, almost human in
their intelligence, while over the small bony head,
over neck and shoulders, yea, over the whole body
and clean down to the hoofs, the veins stood out as
if the skin were but tissue-paper against which the
warm blood pressed, and which it might at any
moment burst asunder.   'A perfect animal,' I said
to myself, as I lay looking her over, — 'an animal
which might have been born from the wind and
the sunshine, so cheerful and so swift she seems;
an animal which a man would present as his

choicest gift to the woman he loved, and yet one which that woman, wife or lady-love, would give him to ride when honor and life depended on bottom and speed.'

"All that afternoon the beautiful mare stood over me, while away to the right of us the hoarse tide of battle flowed and ebbed. What charm, what delusion of memory, held her there? Was my face to her as the face of her dead .master, sleeping a sleep from which not even the wildest roar of battle, no, nor her cheerful neigh at morning, would ever wake him? Or is there in animals some instinct, answering to our intuition, only more potent, which tells them whom to trust and whom to avoid? I know not, and yet some such sense they may have, they must have; or else why should this mare so fearlessly attach herself to me? By what process of reason or instinct I know not, but there she chose me for her master; for when some of my men at dusk came searching, and found me, and, laying me on a stretcher, started toward our lines, the mare, uncompelled, of her own free will, followed at my side; and all through that stormy night of wind and rain, as my men struggled along through the mud and mire toward Harrison's Landing, the mare followed, and ever after, until she died, was with me, and was mine, and I, so far as man might be, was hers. I named her Gulnare.

"As quickly as my wound permitted, I was transported to Washington, whither I took the mare with me. Her fondness for me grew daily, and soon became so marked as to cause universal comment. I had her boarded, while in Washington, at the corner of — Street and —— Avenue. The groom had instructions to lead her round to the window against which was my bed, at the hospital, twice every day, so that by opening the sash I might reach out my hand and pet her. But the second day, no sooner had she reached the street than she broke suddenly from the groom and dashed away at full speed. I was lying, bolstered up in bed, reading, when I heard the rush of flying feet, and in an instant, with a joyful neigh, she checked herself in front of my window. And when the nurse lifted the sash, the beautiful creature thrust her head through the aperture, and rubbed her nose against my shoulder like a dog. I am not ashamed to say that I put both my arms around her neck, and, burying my face in her silken mane, kissed her again and again. Wounded, weak, and away from home, with only strangers to wait upon me, and scant service at that, the affection of this lovely creature for me, so tender and touching, seemed almost human, and my heart went out to her beyond any power of expression, as to the only being, of all the thousands around me, who thought of me and loved me. Shortly after her appearance at my window, the groom, who had divined where he should find her, came into the yard. But she would not allow him to come near her, much less touch her. If he tried to approach she would lash out at him with her heels most spitefully, and then, laying back her ears and opening her mouth savagely, would make a short dash at him, and, as the terrified African disappeared around the corner of the hospital, she would wheel, and, with a face bright as a happy child's, come trotting to the window for me to pet her. I shouted to the groom to go back to the stable, for I had no doubt but that she would return to her stall when I closed the window. Rejoiced at the permission, he departed. After some thirty minutes, the last ten of which she was standing with her slim, delicate head in my lap, while I braided her foretop and combed out her silken mane, I lifted her head, and, patting her softly on either cheek, told her that she must 'go.' I gently pushed her head out of the window and closed it, and then, holding up my hand, with the palm turned toward her, charged her, making the appropriate motion, to 'go away right straight back to her stable.' For a moment she stood looking steadily at me with an indescribable expression of hesitation and surprise in her clear, liquid eyes, and then, turning lingeringly, walked slowly out of the yard.

"Twice a day, for nearly a month, while I lay in

the hospital, did Gulnare visit me. At the appointed hour the groom would slip her headstall, and, without a word of command, she would dart out of the stable, and, with her long, leopard-like lope, go sweeping down the street and come dashing into the hospital yard, checking herself with the same glad neigh at my window ; nor did she ever once fail, at the closing of the sash, to return directly to her stall. The groom informed me that every morning and evening, when the hour of her visit drew near, she would begin to chafe and worry, and, by pawing and pulling at the halter, advertise him that it was time for her to be released.

"But of all exhibitions of happiness, either by beast or man, hers was the most positive on that afternoon when, racing into the yard, she found me leaning on a crutch outside the hospital building. The whole corps of nurses came to the doors, and all the poor fellows that could move themselves, — for Gulnare had become an universal favorite, and the boys looked for her daily visits nearly, if not quite, as ardently as I did, — crawled to the windows to see her. What gladness was expressed in every movement ! She would come prancing toward me, head and tail erect, and, pausing, rub her head against my shoulder while I patted her glossy neck; then, suddenly, with a sidewise spring, she would break away, and, with her long tail elevated until her magnificent brush, fine and silken

10

as the golden hair of a blonde, fell in a great spray on either flank, and her head curved to its proudest arch, pace around me with that high action and springing step peculiar to the thoroughbred. Then like a flash, dropping her brush and laying back her ears, and stretching her nose straight out, she would speed away with that quick, nervous, low-lying action which marks the rush of racers, when, side by side, and nose to nose, lapping each other, with the roar of cheers on either hand and along the seats above them, they come straining up the home stretch. Returning from one of these arrowy flights, she would come curvetting back, now pacing sidewise, as on parade, now dashing her hind feet high into the air, and anon vaulting up and springing through the air, with legs well under her, as if in the act of taking a five-barred gate, and, finally, would approach and stand happy in her reward, — my caress.

"The war, at last, was over. Gulnare and I were in at the death with Sheridan at the Five Forks. Together we had shared the pageant at Richmond and Washington, and never had I seen her in better spirits than on that day at the capital. It was a sight, indeed, to see her as she came down Pennsylvania Avenue. If the triumphant procession had been all in her honor and mine, she could not have moved with greater grace and pride. With dilating eye and tremulous ear, cease-

"And finally approach and stand happy in her reward, — my caress."

lessly champing her bit, her heated blood bringing
out the magnificent lace-work of veins over her entire body, now and then pausing, and, with a snort,
gathering herself back upon her haunches, as for a
mighty leap, while she shook the froth from her
bits, she moved with a high, prancing step down
the magnificent street, the admired of all beholders,
cheer after cheer was given, huzza after huzza rang
out over her head from roofs and balcony, bouquet
after bouquet was launched by fair and enthusiastic admirers before her ; and yet, amid the crash
and swell of music, the cheering and tumult, so
gentle and manageable was she, that, though I
could feel her frame creep and tremble under me
as she moved through that whirlwind of excitement, no check or curb was needed, and the bridle-
lines — the same she wore when she came to me
at Malvern Hill — lay unlifted on the pommel
of the saddle.　Never before had I seen her so
grandly herself.　Never before had the fire and
energy, the grace and gentleness, of her blood so
revealed themselves.　This was the day and the
event she needed.　And all the royalty of her ancestral breed, — a race of equine kings, — flowing
as without taint or cross from him that was the
pride and wealth of the whole tribe of desert
rangers, expressed itself in her.　I need not say
that I shared her mood.　I sympathized in her
every step.　I entered into all her royal humors.

I patted her neck, and spoke loving and cheerful words to her. I called her my beauty, my pride, my pet. And did she not understand me? Every word! Else why that listening ear turned back to catch my softest whisper? why the responsive quiver through the frame, and the low, happy neigh? "Well," I exclaimed, as I leaped from her back at the close of the review, — alas! that words spoken in lightest mood should portend so much! — 'well, Gulnare, if you should die, your life has had its triumph. The nation itself, through its admiring capital, has paid tribute to your beauty, and death can never rob you of your fame.' And I patted her moist neck and foam-flecked shoulders, while the grooms were busy with head and loins.

"That night our brigade made its bivouac just over Long Bridge, almost on the identical spot where, four years before, I had camped my company of three months' volunteers. With what experiences of march and battle were those four years filled! For three of these years Gulnare had been my constant companion. With me she had shared my tent, and not rarely my rations, for in appetite she was truly human, and my steward always counted her as one of our 'mess.' Twice had she been wounded, — once at Fredericksburg, through the thigh; and once at Cold Harbor, where a piece of shell tore away a part of her scalp. So completely did it stun her, that for some moments

I thought her dead, but to my great joy she shortly recovered her senses. I had the wound carefully
dressed by our brigade surgeon, from whose care
she came in a month, with the edges of the wound
so nicely united that the eye could with difficulty
detect the scar. This night, as usual, she lay at
my side, her head almost touching mine. Never
before, unless when on a raid, and in face of
the enemy, had I seen her so uneasy. Her
movements during the night compelled wakeful-
ness on my part. The sky was cloudless, and in
the dim light I lay and watched her. Now she
would stretch herself at full length, and rub her
head on the ground. Then she would start up,
and, sitting on her haunches, like a dog, lift one
fore leg and paw her neck and ears. Anon she
would rise to her feet and shake herself, walk off
a few rods, return, and lie down again by my side.
I did not know what to make of it, unless the
excitement of the day had been too much for her
sensitive nerves. I spoke to her kindly, and petted
her. In response she would rub her nose against
me, and lick my hand with her tongue — a peculiar habit of hers — like a dog. As I was passing
my hand over her head, I discovered that it was
hot, and the thought of the old wound flashed into
my mind, with a momentary fear that something
might be wrong about her brain, but, after thinking it over, I dismissed it as incredible. Still I

was alarmed.   I knew that something was amiss, and I rejoiced at the thought that I should soon be at home, where she could have quiet, and, if need be, the best of nursing. At length the morning dawned, and the mare and I took our last meal together on Southern soil, — the last we ever took together.   The brigade was formed in line for the last time, and, as I rode down the front to review the boys, she moved with all her old battle grace and power.   Only now and then, by a shake of the head, was I reminded of her actions during the night.   I said a few words of farewell to the men whom I had led so often to battle, with whom I had shared perils not a few, and by whom, as I had reason to think, I was loved, and then gave, with a voice slightly unsteady, the last order they would ever receive from me : ' Brigade, attention ! Ready to break ranks, *Break ranks !'*   The order was obeyed.   But ere they scattered, moved by a common impulse, they gave first three cheers for me, and then, with the same heartiness and even more power, three cheers for Gulnare.   And she, standing there, looking with her bright, cheerful countenance full at the men, pawing with her fore feet, alternately, the ground, seemed to understand the compliment ; for no sooner had the cheering died away than she arched her neck to its proudest curve, lifted her thin, delicate head into the air, and gave a short, joyful neigh.

"My arrangements for transporting her had been made by a friend the day before. A large, roomy car had been secured, its floor strewn with bright, clean straw, a bucket, and a bag of oats provided, and everything done for her comfort. The car was to be attached to the through express, in consideration of fifty dollars extra, which I gladly paid, because of the greater rapidity with which it enabled me to make my journey. As the brigade broke up into groups, I glanced at my watch and saw that I had barely time to reach the cars before they started. I shook the reins upon her neck, and with a plunge, startled at the energy of my signal, away she flew. What a stride she had! What an elastic spring! She touched and left the earth as if her limbs were of spiral wire. When I reached the car my friend was standing in front of it, the gang-plank was ready, I leaped from the saddle, and, running up the plank into the car, whistled to her; and she, timid and hesitating, yet unwilling to be separated from me, crept slowly and cautiously up the steep incline, and stood beside me. Inside I found a complete suit of flannel clothes, with a blanket, and, better than all, a lunch-basket. My friend explained that he had bought the clothes as he came down to the depot, thinking, as he said, 'that they would be much better than your regimentals,' and suggested that I doff the one and don the other. To this I assented

the more readily as I reflected that I would have
to pass one night, at least, in the car, with no better bed than the straw under my feet. I had
barely time to undress before the cars were coupled
and started. I tossed the clothes to my friend
with the injunction to pack them in my trunk and
express them on to me, and waived him my adieu.
I arrayed myself in the nice, cool flannel, and
looked around. The thoughtfulness of my friend
had anticipated every want. An old cane-seated
chair stood in one corner. The lunch-basket was
large, and well supplied. Amid the oats I found
a dozen oranges, some bananas, and a package of
real Havana cigars. How I called down blessings
on his thoughtful head as I took the chair, and,
lighting one of the fine-flavored *figaros*, gazed out
on the fields past which we were gliding, yet wet
with morning dew. As I sat dreamily admiring
the beauty before me, Gulnare came and, resting her
head upon my shoulder, seemed to share my mood.
As I stroked her fine-haired, satin-like nose, recollection quickened, and memories of our compan-
ionship in perils thronged into my mind. I rode
again that midnight ride to Knoxville, when Burn-
side lay intrenched, desperately holding his own,
waiting for news from Chattanooga, of which I
was the bearer, chosen by Grant himself because
of the reputation of my mare. What riding that
was ! We started, ten riders of us in all, each

with the same message. I parted company the
first hour out with all save one, an iron-gray stallion of Messenger blood. Jack Murdock rode
him, who learned his horsemanship from buffalo
and Indian hunting on the Plains, — not a bad
school to graduate from. Ten miles out of Knoxville the gray, his flanks dripping with blood,
plunged up abreast the mare's shoulders and fell
dead; and Gulnare and I passed through the lines
alone. *I had ridden the terrible race without whip
or spur.* With what scenes of blood and flight
she would ever be associated! And then I thought
of home, unvisited for four long years, — that
home I left a stripling, but to which I was returning a bronzed and brawny man. I thought of
mother and Bob, — how they would admire her! —
of old Ben, the family groom, and of that one who
shall be nameless, whose picture I had so often
shown to Gulnare as the likeness of her future
mistress; — had they not all heard of her, my
beautiful mare, she who came to me from the
smoke and whirlwind, my battle-gift? How they
would pat her soft, smooth sides, and tie her mane
with ribbons, and feed her with all sweet things
from open and caressing palm! And then I thought
of one who might come after her to bear her name
and repeat at least some portion of her beauty, —
a horse honored and renowned the country through,
because of the transmission of the mother's fame.

10 *   o

"About three o'clock in the afternoon a change came over Gulnare. I had fallen asleep upon the straw, and she had come and awakened me with a touch of her nose. The moment I started up I saw that something was the matter. Her eyes were dull and heavy. Never before had I seen the light go out of them. The rocking of the car as it went jumping and vibrating along seemed to irritate her. She began to rub her head against the side of the car. Touching it, I found that the skin over the brain was hot as fire. Her breathing grew rapidly louder and louder. Each breath was drawn with a kind of gasping effort. The lids with their silken fringe drooped wearily over the lustreless eyes. The head sank lower and lower, until the nose almost touched the floor. The ears, naturally so lively and erect, hung limp and widely apart. The body was cold and senseless. A pinch elicited no motion. Even my voice was at last unheeded. To word and touch there came, for the first time in all our intercourse, no response. I knew as the symptoms spread what was the matter. The signs bore all one way. She was in the first stages of phrenitis, or inflammation of the brain. In other words, *my beautiful mare was going mad.*

"I was well versed in the anatomy of the horse. Loving horses from my very childhood, there was little in veterinary practice with which I was not familiar. Instinctively, as soon as the symptoms had developed themselves, and I saw under what frightful disorder Gulnare was laboring, I put my hand into my pocket for my knife, in order to open a vein. *There was no knife there.* Friends, I have met with many surprises. More than once, in battle and scout, have I been nigh death; but never did my blood desert my veins and settle so around the heart, never did such a sickening sensation possess me as when, standing in that car with my beautiful mare before me, marked with those horrible symptoms, I made that discovery. My knife, my sword, my pistols even, were with my suit in the care of my friend, two hundred miles away. Hastily, and with trembling fingers, I searched my clothes, the lunch-basket, my linen; not even a pin could I find. I shoved open the sliding door, and swung my hat and shouted, hoping to attract some brakeman's attention. The train was thundering along at full speed, and none saw or heard me. I knew her stupor would not last long. A slight quivering of the lip, an occasional spasm running through the frame, told me too plainly that the stage of frenzy would soon begin. 'My God!' I exclaimed, in despair, as I shut the door and turned toward her, 'must I see you die, Gulnare, when the opening of a vein would save you? Have you borne me, my pet, through all these years of peril, the icy chill of winter, the heat and torment of summer, and all the thronging dangers of a hundred bloody battles, only to die torn by fierce agonies, when so near a peaceful home ?

But little time was given me to mourn. My life was soon to be in peril, and I must summon up the utmost power of eye and limb to escape the violence of my frenzied mare. Did you ever see a mad horse when his madness is on him ? Take your stand with me in that car, and you shall see what suffering a dumb creature can endure before it dies. In no malady does a horse suffer more than in phrenitis, or inflammation of the brain. Possibly in severe cases of colic, probably in rabies in its fiercest form, the pain is equally intense. These three are the most agonizing of all the diseases to which the noblest of animals is exposed. Had my pistols been with me, I should then and there, with whatever strength Heaven granted, have taken my companion's life, that she might be spared the suffering which was so soon to rack and wring her sensitive frame. A horse laboring under an attack of phrenitis is as violent as a horse can be. He is not ferocious as is one in a fit of rabies. He may kill his master, but he does it without design. There is in him no desire of mischief for its own sake, no cruel cunning, no stratagem and malice. A rabid horse is conscious in every act and motion. He recognizes the man he destroys. There is in him an insane *desire* to *kill*. Not so with the phrenetic horse. He is unconscious in his violence. He sees and 'recognizes no one. There is no method or purpose in his madness. He kills without knowing it.

" I knew what was coming. I could not jump out ; that would be certain death. I must abide in the car and take my chance of life. The car was fortunately high, long, and roomy. I took my position in front of my horse, watchful and ready to spring. Suddenly her lids, which had been closed, came open with a snap, as if an electric shock had passed through her, and the eyes, wild in their brightness, stared directly at me. And what eyes they were ! The membrane grew red and redder, until it was of the color of blood, standing out in frightful contrast with the transparency of the cornea. The pupil gradually dilated until it seemed about to burst out of the socket. The nostrils, which had been sunken and motionless, quivered, swelled, and glowed. The respiration became short, quick, and gasping. The limp and drooping ears stiffened and stood erect, pricked sharply forward, as if to catch the slightest sound. Spasms, as the car swerved and vibrated, ran through her frame. More horrid than all, the lips slowly contracted, and the white, sharp-edged teeth stood uncovered, giving an indescribable look of ferocity to the partially opened mouth ! The car suddenly reeled as it dashed around a curve, swaying her almost off her feet, and, as a contortion shook her, she recovered herself, and, rearing upward as high as the car permitted, plunged directly at me. I was expecting the movement, and dodged. Then followed exhibitions of pain which I pray God I may never see again. Time and again did she dash herself upon the floor, and roll over and over, lashing out with her feet in all directions. Pausing a moment, she would stretch her body to its extreme length, and, lying upon her side, pound the floor with her head as if it were a maul. Then, like a flash, she would leap to her feet, and whirl round and round, until, from very giddiness, she would stagger and fall. She would lay hold of the straw with her teeth, and shake it as a dog shakes a struggling woodchuck; then dashing it from her mouth, she would seize hold of her own sides, and rend herself. Springing up, she would rush against the end of the car, falling all in a heap from the violence of the concussion. For some fifteen minutes, without intermission, the frenzy lasted. I was nearly exhausted. My efforts to avoid her mad rushes, the terrible tension of my nervous system produced by the spectacle of such exquisite and prolonged suffering, were weakening me beyond what I should have thought it possible an hour before for anything to weaken me. In fact, I felt my strength leaving me. A terror, such as I had never yet felt, was taking possession of my mind. I sickened at the

sight before me, and at the thought of agonies yet
to come. ' My God,' I exclaimed, ' must I be killed
by my own horse in this miserable car !'   Even as
I spoke, the end came.   The mare raised herself
until her shoulders touched the roof, then dashed
her body upon the floor with a violence which
threatened the stout frame beneath her.   I leaned,
panting and exhausted, against the side of the car.
Gulnare did not stir.   She lay motionless, her
breath coming and going in lessening respirations.
I tottered toward her, and, as I stood above her,
my ear detected a low, gurgling sound.   I cannot
describe the feeling that followed.   Joy and grief
contended within me.   I knew the meaning of
that sound.   Gulnare, in her frenzied violence,
had broken a blood-vessel, and was bleeding inter-
nally.   Pain and life were passing away together.
I knelt down by her side.   I laid my head upon
her shoulders, and sobbed aloud.   Her body moved
a little beneath me.   I crawled forward and lifted
her beautiful head into my lap.   O, for one more
sign of recognition before she died !   I smoothed
the tangled masses of her mane.   I wiped, with
a fragment of my coat, torn in the struggle, the
blood which oozed from her nostril.   I called her
by name.   My desire was granted.   In a moment
Gulnare opened her eyes.   The redness of frenzy
had passed out of them.   She saw and recognized
me.   I spoke again.   Her eye lighted a moment

with the old and intelligent look of love.   Her ear
moved; her nostril quivered gently as she strove
to neigh.   The effort was in vain.   Her love was
greater than her strength.   She moved her head a
little, as if she would be nearer me, looked once
more with her clear eyes into my face, breathed
a long breath, straightened her shapely limbs, and
died.   And there, holding the head of my dead
mare in my lap, while the great warm tears fell
one after another down my cheeks, I sat until the
sun went down, the shadows darkened in the car,
and night drew her mantle, colored like my grief,
over the world."

APPENDIX.

———◆———

BEACH'S SIGHT.

I FEEL that I cannot do my brother sportsmen who may read this book a greater service than by bringing this invention to their notice.

The great desideratum and problem with rifle-makers and sportsmen, as all are aware, has been to invent a sight that would combine all the merits of "bead" and "open" sight, so that the hunter would be able at will, and without a moment's delay, to use the globe or open sight, according as the game might be in motion or stationary, amid the shadows of the forest or in the sunlight of the fields, or as the color of the object might be dark or bright.

All sportsmen know how vexatious it is to have to "rap" out one sight to insert another, necessitating as it does tedious delay and the wearisome process of "sighting," when there may be neither time nor powder to spare, and no appliances at hand to effect an accurate adjustment.

In this invention this desideratum is met, and the solution found.

By a glance at the following cuts, every man acquainted with the rifle will see how completely Mr.

Beach's ingenuity has furnished what every rifleman has so long desired. He will see that this sight combines, in a cheap and simple form, the merits of the "bead" and "open" sights, so that without any removal, without an instant of delay, by a single movement of the finger, the hunter can use either, as his judgment decides is best, *when he stands looking at his game.*

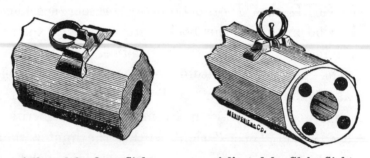

Adjusted for Open Sight.   Adjusted for Globe Sight.

The writer of this has had for nearly a year this sight upon his favorite rifle, where it has had months of actual trial; and, whether upon the target-grounds of our best clubs or amid the Adirondack wilderness, it has met every want, and remains to-day, where it always will remain, on his rifle, an indisputable witness to the value of the invention.

If space would allow, we might quote the enthusiastic indorsement of such men as Lewis of Troy, W. P. McFarland, Superintendent of the Massachusetts Arms Company; the celebrated veteran sportsman Edward Stabler, Esq., of Maryland; F. G. Gunn, Esq., President of the Hawk Eye Rifle Club of Connecticut, and of scores of hunters and trappers in Northern New York, where the sight was taken for trial last summer.

Without a single exception, the verdict has been unanimous for its adoption.

A hunter in Canada writes : " I would not part with Beach's sight, after four months' trial, for twenty mink-skins." Another, from Connecticut, writes : " Fifty dollars would not purchase my sight." Yet another, from the North Woods, declares : " The best thing I ever saw. I have hunted and trapped for thirty years, and I can kill *one third more game* with this sight than with any other I ever had." An amateur in New York City writes : " The moment I *saw* the sight, my heart leapt for joy. Here is what I have always been looking for. I would have bought it at ten times its price. No rifle is fit for use without it."

The following note is from Mr. Stabler.

SANDY SPRING, November 30, 1867.

To E. B. BEACH, *Patentee of Beach's Combination Sight, West Meriden, Connecticut :* —

I duly received, by mail, the patent bead or globe rifle sight. In principle it is by far the most complete and perfect affair of the kind I have ever seen. In thus combining the two sights, the hunter has all the advantage of both, by a mere touch of the finger, — a perfect *bead* sight for hunting, and a *globe* for close and long range shooting.

Very respectfully,

EDWARD STABLER.

The two illustrations will serve to give you an idea of how the sight operates, but to fairly appreciate it you must have it on your own rifle a few days, and see how admirably and completely it meets every want of the practical sportsman, in wood and field service. The sights are made with bases of different sizes, so as to fit any rifle, whether the slot is wide or narrow. In ten minutes, any man with a file can fit one to his rifle. Every sight is *warranted*. If it does not give *perfect* satisfaction, upon trial, you can return it and the money will be *refunded*.

Unfortunately, the firm which contracted with Mr. Beach to manufacture the sights failed before introducing them to the public, and the affairs of the company still being in litigation, the demand for these sights is left unsupplied. I understand that arrangements are making by which Mr. Beach will proceed to manufacture them himself; and I advise every one who owns a rifle to write him on the receipt of the information herein given, which, without the solicitation or knowledge of Mr. Beach, I gladly and freely impart.

Address, E. B. BEACH, Esq., *West* Meriden, Conn.

THE END.

Cambridge : Electrotyped and Printed by Welch, Bigelow, & Co.

J. C. CONROY & CO.,

IMPORTERS AND MANUFACTURERS OF

Fish - Hooks, Fishing Tackle, &c.,

No. 65 FULTON STREET,

NEW YORK.

J. C. CONROY & CO. (late J. & J. C. CONROY), 35 years manufacturers and importers of Fish-Hooks and Fishing Tackle, in all its branches, inform their friends, amateurs, and the trade generally, that they have usually on hand, and are continually making, to supply deficiency, a very complete assortment of

THE BEST ANGLING MATERIALS,

as well as a desirable stock for the Wholesale Trade.

————

In competition, J. C. C. & Co. have been

AWARDED THE ONLY GOLD MEDAL

EVER GIVEN IN THE UNITED STATES,

AND NINE SILVER MEDALS

FOR

THE BEST ARTICLES OF AMERICAN MANUFACTURED
FISHING TACKLE.

WILLIAM READ & SONS,

13 Faneuil Hall Square, Boston,

DEALERS IN

FINE FISHING-RODS AND TACKLE,

KEEP CONSTANTLY ON HAND

The celebrated "Tout" make fine-spliced Bamboo Trout and Salmon Rods, for fly and bait fishing, of very best quality.

Medium Quality Fly Rods of Hornbeam, with spliced bamboo tips, in great variety.

Medium and Common Fly-bait, and General Rods of all prices and kinds.

ALSO, REELS, FLY-BOOKS, BASKETS, HOOKS, FLIES, in great variety, and every article in the line.

ALSO, A LARGE STOCK OF FINE

MUZZLE AND BREECH LOADING GUNS,

Comprising all the best English and other makes, —

WESTLEY RICHARDS, SCOTT, GREENER, DOUGALL, POPE, PURDEY, ELLIS, AND OTHERS,

With every article in the line of Shooting-Tackle,

As ELEY'S CAPS, WADS, and WIRE CARTRIDGES, DIXON & SONS' FINE FLASKS, POUCHES, &c.

ALL THE DIFFERENT AMERICAN RIFLES AND REVOLVERS.

ALSO, FINE

"BRONZE YACHT GUNS,"

ONE-POUNDERS, MOUNTED ON BEST MAHOGANY CARRIAGES.

ON THE WING.

A BOOK FOR YOUNG SPORTSMEN.

By JOHN BUMSTEAD.

Richly Illustrated. . . **One Vol. 16mo. $2.50.**

This book, prepared by one of the most experienced sportsmen of New England, treats of all the principal subjects that engage the attention of a sportsman; and the author's ideas respecting the elementary matters connected with the use of the gun are not only practicable, but they are imbued with much common sense. The book is eminently a practical one. It contains much valuable information respecting the various styles of weapons now in use, — how they are made, and what constitutes the superiority of one weapon over another.

The author's long experience has enabled him to gather much that is necessary for every sportsman to know, respecting the habits and haunts of the many varieties of game-birds found in our Northern States, — the Woodcock, the Quail, and the Partridge, as well as the game-birds and water-fowl of New England. The observations of the author, however, apply to sporting everywhere, as, to use words of the Preface, " to be a good shot in New England is to be one the world over."

The volume is fully and appropriately illustrated.

APPENDIX

THE ADIRONDACKS.

Murray on Murray's Fools.

His Reply to His Calumniators—The Fools' Experience—True and
False Chroniclers—The Guide Question—Sport for Sportsmen—A
Free and Healthy Wilderness.

To the Editor of The Tribune.

Sir: Since my return from the Wilderness, I have received many
letters, earnestly requesting me to give to the public a paper upon
the subject of this article. This request comes, as I judge, chiefly
from two classes. The first consists of persons who, in this or some
former season, have visited the mountains and lakes of Northern
New-York, and who are justly incensed at the unfair and false representations which have been given to the public through the press
of the country. It seems to them greatly to be regretted that one of
the loveliest and most romantic sections of our country should,
even for a brief season, suffer from the aspersions of people incapable of appreciating its beauty and grandeur. The other class is
made up of such as have not as yet visited the region, and who are
in a state of doubt and bewilderment concerning even the existence of a wilderness, owing to the contradictory reports which
have gone out in reference to it, so conflicting, indeed, that no wit
or device can harmonize the diverse statements.

The correspondents of either class insist that it is due to the Wilderness itself, and also to a confused and bewildered public, that
an intelligent and candid statement of the facts in the case should
be published, in order that the public may be able to get a right
understanding of the whole matter. They also do me the honor to
suggest, that owing to my familiarity with the subject, I should
prepare such a paper. Upon reflection, I have concluded to accede
to this request. I do not conceive that it would be becoming,
should any pride of reticence restrain me from doing what appears
to be so honestly desired. Nor do I in complying with this reqquest
[*sic*] break over that rule, which, on my entrance into public life, I

77

made for my guidance, *i.e.*, never by words printed or spoken, to reply to criticisms and abuse which might fall to my lot. And in this paper I do not propose to allude to the animadversions, which from certain questionable sources, publicly and privately, have been made against me, beyond what may be necessary for a full and clear explanation of the subject.

THE WILDERNESS.

In the first place, then, let me say, that I do not retract a single word which I published in my book, entitled "Adventures in the Wilderness." A wilderness of about the size of the State of Connecticut does exist in the northern part of New-York State. It is a wilderness in the true and broadest sense of the word; and, with the exception of one or two small settlements, or clearings, it is entirely uninhabited, save by hunters and trappers, or by sportsmen and tourists who make excursions into it. A very small portion of this wilderness has been lumbered; but seventeen-twentieths of its entire area is covered with a forest, as yet untouched by the woodman's axe. This forest is composed of pine, spruce, balsam, and hemlock, with a fair sprinkling in certain sections, of beech, birch, and maple. In respect to its geography, it is mountainous. The high peaks of the Adirondack range, from which the Wilderness takes its name, wall it from observation on its eastern side, and from 5,000 feet in hight [*sic*] they slope down in lesser parallel ranges and isolated cones, until they lose themselves in the valley of the St. Lawrence and the Mohawk.

The novel and romantic peculiarity of this wilderness, and that which distinguishes it from all others in this country, or the world, is its marvelous water communication. On Mr. Colton's late map, over 500 lakes are set down. From my own knowledge of the Wilderness, and from computations made with some of the best guides —men familiar with it from life-long residence—I have no hesitation in saying that not half the number existing are sketched on the map. It is safe to assert that there are, at least, 1,200 lakes and ponds, detached and isolated pieces of water, included in the area mentioned. These lakes vary in size from Racquette Lake, with a shore line of, perhaps, fifty miles, to ponds half a mile across in their widest part. Hundreds of these lakes are connected by creeks and rivers, so that by an occasional "carry" around a fall, or stretch of rapids, or over a spur of intervening land, one can travel in a canoe or light boat for hundreds of miles in all directions through the forest. Such, in brief, is the Adirondack Wilderness.

MR. MURRAY'S BOOK.

Up to within a few years, this region was comparatively unknown to the public. A few scores of sportsmen monopolized it for their own profit and amusement. By a selfish instinct, they have concealed its charms from general knowledge—shrouded it in mystery, or made ingress thereto and life therein, appear to such as heard rumors of its loveliness and grandeur, extremely difficult and irksome. Nevertheless, of late years its fame has so far spread, that many tourists and invalids have visited it; the one class to revel in its enchanting scenery, and the other to be benefited by its health-giving atmosphere.

This was the condition of things when my little book was published. The book was well received by the reading public, and a cordial greeting given it by the press of the country. Its descriptive articles were pronounced readable; and the directions to tourists contained in the first ninety pages, were full and complete. Old Adirondackers welcomed it as something they had desired for years; and in private correspondence, and through the public journals, expressed their approbation of it. During the Summer, however, certain charges of exaggeration have been brought against the author, which deserve no notice, except so far as the fact of their remaining uncontradicted might mislead the public touching the Wilderness itself. I propose, therefore, to call attention to several of the more prominent of these, and to show the character of the sources from which they sprang.

THE FOOLS.

Early in July, a swarm of people rushed into the Adirondacks. It was a motley crowd, indeed. There were fashionables of the Long-Branch order, and exquisite swells with light kids [gloves] and

rattan canes, fresh from the Broadway. There were mechanics and
puddlers from the iron-founderies [*sic*] of Troy; gentlemen sportsmen, with their English suits, and eye-glasses; together with row-
dies from all quarters. One young lady came in with baggage
amounting to seven large trunks. One gentleman, who brought his
wife, had ten trunks—the gentleman three, and the lady seven—an
evidently unfair arrangement, in that it gave the gentleman at least
one too many, leaving his wife short.

Several hundred people of this character rushed to the woods in
the first half of July. They took Martin by storm; and introduced
the habits of Newport and Whitehall, Broadway and the Bowery,
to the hitherto retired and peaceful region of Lower Saranac. The
character and breeding of these classes are best ascertained from
their inscriptions on the hotel register. Coarse expressions, vulgar
quotations, some of them in feminine hand, and not a little profan-
ity testify to their character and position at home. A certain lady
(*sic*) who afterward became a correspondent of a Cincinnati paper,
but whose name I withhold, lest some of her most distant relations
might be pained, went into the burlesque business against a person
who was quietly enjoying himself sixty miles away in the Wilderness, and passed most of the entire night before she started to return to her accustomed haunts, in screaming anathemas against
him, with guides, tavern hangers-on, and stable boys for her audience. I understand that they appreciated her manner and vocabu-
lary, and cheered her to the echo. It is seldom that speaker and audience, so kindred in nature and breeding, are permitted to meet.

Such, in brief, were many of the parties who rushed early in the
season to the Wilderness. It is the best vindication of the Wilderness to say, that they did not long remain. Disgusted they undoubtedly were; and they started pell-mell for Lake Champlain;
some paying their bills; many, in their haste to get their epistles
into the newspapers, forgetting to do so. From such visitors as
these the outcry against the Adirondacks was started; and the
amount of deliberate and persistent falsifying which has been in-
dulged in by them is something marvelous. I give only a few illustrations. One says, in speaking of the guests at Martin's, "Nor do
the sick get well—some of them in fact have died without even
Murray to bury them." When, "in fact," not a person died at Martin's this Summer. Another, in alluding to what I say in my book to
sportsmen, touching the rifle and shot-gun, says "that Mr. Murray
sent 17 miles for a shot-gun and used it all the season." The truth

being that in my eight years of camping I never had a shot-gun in camp for an hour, and have never taken one in my hands during all that time. Again, the number of wives I have had and the multitude of my children, if these correspondents are to be believed, is absolutely fearful for an heirless man of my years to contemplate. The wave of misrepresentation was thus started; and was kept rolling for some weeks, by certain interested parties, chiefly sportsmen, who selfishly wish to appropriate the Wilderness to their own uses, until the country was flooded with false reports and mischievous exaggerations.

CORRESPONDENTS.

In alluding to the ignorance of many of the correspondents, who, without entering beyond "Root's," or Martin's or Bartlett's, oracularly rendered their verdict *pro* and *con*, a few exceptions should be made. Miss Kate Field penetrated some 80 miles into the Wilderness, along the main water-course leading southerly from Martin's, and wrote, considering her brief stay in the woods, a very intelligent and appreciative account of the region. Her letters to THE NEW-YORK TRIBUNE were candid and truthful; and as far as her limited experience enabled her to do so, she did ample justice to the region. "Wachusett," in *The Boston Advertiser*, in a series of letters, also gave the public an accurate conception of the peculiarities of the region he visited. The letters of both these correspondents are marked with great neatness of expression, and fine appreciation of the beauties of the Wilderness. With certain minor corrections, they would make a valuable contribution to the Tourist's Handbook, and take a valued place among the literature of the Adirondacks. It is a great pity that two writers so well adapted to the work could not have spent as many months as they did weeks in the Wilderness, and penetrated its depths, seen its resources for sport and health, and given to the public in a more extended and permanent form their impressions of the region.

It should be kept in mind, that the "hotels" for the most part are not *in* the Wilderness but along the margin of it, and hence people who go no farther than Paul Smith's, Martin's or Bartlett's know nothing whatever of the Wilderness. The Saranac and St. Regis regions are those sections which have been lumbered, and give one no adequate idea of the forest which stretches for a hundred miles to the South. The lakes around these public houses have been fished for years to supply the table with food; and for the same purpose the mountains and streams for miles around have been scoured for deer. Now it has been, as all can see, the interest of the proprietors of these hotels to keep sportsmen as boarders at their tables or in such proximity to their houses as to be weekly purchasers of supplies; and so it has come about that many had been deceived as to the extent, peculiarities, and sporting facilities of the Wilderness. People who have spent a month or so at some of these houses, and had little or no success in hunting or fishing, have gone out and spread the report, "We have been in the Adirondacks, and there is no game there."

I met a gentleman, a clerical brother, who gravely informed me that "Mr. Murray had grossly exaggerated the size of the Wilderness, for he himself had been all over it and knew." Upon inquiry I ascertained that he had been from Martin's to Cold River on the Racquette River; and as his guide had assured him he was then at the southern end of the woods, he had returned to Martin's to take up testimony against me. The fact is I go every year 30 or 40 miles directly South from where he turned back, before I even make my central camp. Yet within two weeks this gentleman has publicly repeated his charge of exaggeration, and honestly believes it to be true.

Now so far as I have seen, a vast deal of the correspondence purporting to come from the "Adirondack Wilderness," during the past Summer, has not been from the "Adirondack Wilderness" at all, but from localities along the margin of it which have been cleared and settled for 30 or 40 years. Take for illustration an extract from a letter to a Chicago paper—*The Evening Journal,* I think. It is written from "Root's Hotel, Adirondack Mountains," &c. In this letter, our special correspondent says:

"In my last letter from New-York City, I stated my determination of going to the Adirondacks, and discovering for myself whether or not there was any foundation for all the hue and cry raised against Mr. Murray and his volume on these regions. After a week of discovery, I am forced to the conclusion that the said book is about evenly divided between fact and fiction. The author states a good many matters of interest, and at the same time sandwiches them between stories which do not possess a particle of foundation. For example, when he says that the bracing air here is most invigorating he tells the truth, and when he affirms that it is impossible to take cold he tells a 'whopper.' All in all, I should say that for a Minister of the Gospel, the said Murray has a decided faculty for exaggeration, and Fields, Osgood & Co., would do well to compel him to 'take in sail' a little in a new edition of his Adirondack volume."

Now this gentleman states his "determination of going to the Adirondacks, and of discovering for himself whether or not there was any foundation for all the hue and cry against Mr. Murray and his volume upon these regions," and he leaves the reader to infer that he was then writing from the Adirondacks, with every facility for correct judgment. But where, in point of fact, was he? "At Root's Hotel." And where is Root's Hotel, pray? Why, only some thirty miles west of Fort William Henry Hotel, on Lake George, and forty miles east of Long Lake, which is itself a settlement on the eastern boundary of the Wilderness. Writing from a section which has had a Post-Office and church for half a century, with no woods worthy of the name within forty miles of him—never having boated a single day on one of the thousand lakes that lie to the west—he undertakes to pronounce whether my description of the Wilderness is "fact or fiction." From his abundant data for correct judgment, found at "Root's Hotel," he comes to the grave conclusion that "the said book is about evenly divided between fact and fiction." It is also at "Root's Hotel," that this writer discovers that when I expressed my belief that it is impossible for one to catch cold in the Wilderness, I tell a "whopper."

Now it is not for the sake of retorting upon this gentleman, but in order to reiterate to the public my belief that I say, being acquainted with hundreds who have camped in the woods, having seen both ladies and gentlemen of delicate constitutions and feeble health, persons exposed to all the contingencies of camp life, heat and frost, snow and rain—having seen them, who were guarded from even the least current of air at home, drenched to the skin, and lifted from boats one-third full of water, I have never heard or known of an instance where such a person camping in the Wilderness has "caught cold." In journeying by night, ladies, members of my own family, have slept for hours, and slept soundly, upon the balsam-boughs and lilies with which they had filled their boat; and with no covering but the heavens, and with their faces moist with the dew or descending mists. It may be that the atmosphere at Root's Hotel is different, and that our oracular friend "saw through a glass darkly."

GUIDES.

One of the principal causes of the embarrassment and disappointment experienced by tourists this season has been owing to many of the guides employed. Some persons, foreseeing the rush which would be made to the Wilderness during the Summer, wisely engaged their guides in early Spring, but others neglected to do this until all the trusty and capable guides were engaged. When the rush, therefore, occurred in July the number of the guides was by no means equal to the demand. Few guides being available, and many of these inclined to profit by the public necessities, prices suddenly jumped up from $2 50 [*sic*] to $4 and $5 per diem, with such additional bonus as was offered, often amounting to $20 or $30.

The news of the advance in the wages and the scarcity of guides, led men, and even boys, to offer their services, who, in point of fact, knew no more about guiding, nor about the Wilderness, than a farm-hand in Massachusetts. Log-drivers and canal men even, from Whitehall, attracted by the rumors of fabulous prices which guides commanded, flocked to the hotels on the edge of the Wilderness and were hired by parties for the most difficult of duties without one question as to their character or fitness. Many parties discovered, when it was too late, that they were duped, and repented with much vexation of heart, over what the exercise of ordinary prudence would have guarded against.

A man who will hire a guide without informing himself as to his knowledge and habits, and start out with him on an intricate and lonely voyage through a wilderness justly deserves what he is sure to experience, failure and mortification. Yet this was done in numberless instances. Men who had never paddled a mile on those lakes, men who had never seen even a map of the region—brutal, drinking, swearing ruffians, were eagerly engaged, without being questioned, at double the rates at which old and trusty guides were laboring, by men and women green enough, nay imprudent enough, to risk their honor and their lives in such poor keeping. All this, too, when information could have been had for the asking. In the chapter of directions to tourists, in my book, I called special attention to the matter of selection of guides, warned the public against certain classes, and made the success or failure of the trip depend upon the party's choice of guides.

Under the head of "Guides," in my directions to sportsmen and tourists, (see Adventures, pp. 32 and 33,) I say—and it sums up the whole matter:

> "An ignorant, low-bred guide is a nuisance in camp and useless everywhere else. A skillful, active, well-mannered guide, on the other hand, is a joy and consolation, a source of constant pleasure to the whole party. With an ignorant guide you will starve; with a lazy one, you will lose your temper; with a low-bred fellow, you can have no comfort. Fortunate in the selection of your guide, you will be fortunate in everything you undertake clean through the trip."

It is not because I "exaggerated," but because I told simple truth, that many have found wood life so disagreeable this Summer. Warned, and that too in the plainest language, they certainly were, but they did not heed the warning, and found by bitter experience that it would have been far wiser if they had. No amount of care and caution could have prevented all from being deceived, but in their hurry and eagerness to obtain a guide, parties threw caution and prudence to the winds, and put a premium upon deception by the ease with which they permitted themselves to be duped. It is safe to say such a condition of things will not be seen again, because of the better arrangements which are being made for the public's convenience; and because, also, of the lesson which the public have already been taught.

In some cases, I am convinced, blame has unjustly, and unreasonably been laid to the guides. Hundreds visited the region expecting to "do the Wilderness" in a week, or ten days at the most. The pace at which parties, composed of both sexes, have been pushed through the woods, was appalling to old Adirondackers. Ladies, fresh from Saratoga, school girls delicate and fragile, and even invalids were hurried from Martin's up to Blue Mountain Lake and back at a rate which would have endangered a divorce in my family had I attempted it, and all this at the request and entreaties of the tourists themselves. Parties had only so many days to devote to the excursion, and their chief desire seemed to be to go as far and suffer as much as possible. Guides were charged by such people, with "laziness" if they did not make their 30 or 40 miles a day regardless of wind and weather; and abused because they had not arranged a better camp at night, which might have been done could the guide have had two or three hours of daylight to devote to that purpose.

A guide is a very convenient scapegoat upon which to visit the sins of a party; and many a good guide has had his reputation injured this season by the abuse of parties whom he had faithfully served, but whose ignorance and temper were such that no skill or effort could secure them game or happiness. I heard a certain gentleman (I am tempted to give his name and make an example of him) abusing his guide before a company of twenty people, and anathematizing a certain other person in "our special correspondent's" style, with which the public are somewhat familiar, saying that he had been "fooled," "humbugged," *et cetera*. He said that his guide was a "lazy lout," that there were no deer in the woods, and that when he reached home he "would show the whole thing up in the papers." Now to my certain knowledge the guide referred to is one of the best in the Wilderness, skillful and energetic; and during the gentleman's stay, of a week, in the woods, he had paddled him up within easy range of five deer, none of which he had killed, and the last of which he shot at three times, at about ten rods distance, before the buck condescended to move, and even then, the deer walked away so deliberately that "Sportsman" had time to fire three more shots from his Ballard before he disappeared in the woods. Yet this renowned hunter had a room full of auditors, many of whom believed every word implicitly.

Much has been said about the ignorance of the guides in respect to the prominent localities of the Wilderness, and their lack of familiarity with the names of the mountains, and lakes, and rivers, and creeks—and many a chapter has been written this Summer concerning their "stupidity." All this reads very well to those who know nothing about the matter, but to those who know the facts of the case it sounds rather oddly. What, then, are the facts? They are, in brief, these. It is only within a year or two that any reliable map of the Wilderness has been published, and large portions of it to-day are not accurately surveyed; hundreds of its lakes are unnamed and its rivers untraced. On the other hand, many are overnamed. There is the Indian name, the local name given by the guides, and the geographical name—and this multiplicity of names begets confusion and embarrassment. The tourist of this season came in with Colton's latest map; a map which the guides had never seen, and which, when they saw, served more to bewilder than assist, owing to the names of the mountains and lakes being different from the local ones. The tourist was thus surprised to find that the guides were less informed in respect to names and the position of certain localities than he was himself. Many a time, after consulting the map, have I asked "John" where "Lake———" was, and received in reply, "There is no such lake." When calling his attention to its locality on the map, he would exclaim, "Pshaw, that is not the name of that lake—it is Lake so-and-so."

It should moreover be considered, that the Wilderness is too large and difficult of access for the majority of the guides to visit it all. The St. Regis guides and the Saranac guides are acquainted with the northern portion; the Potsdam and St. Lawrence guides with the western; the Brown's Tract guides with the southern; and the Long Lake guides with the central part of the Wilderness. A few men there are who have traversed the region in its length and breadth, and know it thoroughly, but you can number them on the fingers of one hand. Generally speaking, you hire a guide for a certain locality, and should be content if you find him familiar with it. Nothing is more unreasonable than to expect your guide to know the names of mountains and lakes that the latest maps do not mention, and for which no names exist. It should be remembered that even to the Indians this was a region so remote, so wild and savage, that they named it the "Dismal Wilderness." To them a large portion of it was *terra incognita*—through which they hurried in going to or returning from battle-fields further to the north or south. When all these considerations are taken into account, it will not seem a matter of surprise that many guides, and good ones too, should not be very familiar with all parts of the Wilderness, or occasionally at fault amid the intricate network of lakes and creeks with which it is threaded.

GAME.

A great deal has been said concerning the absence of game in the Adirondacks, and the ill success of sportsmen this season has been pointed at as a proof of the fact, and many inquiries have been addressed to me touching the truth or falsity of the assertions. My reply is this: There is good, fair sporting for *sportsmen*—men who know how to shoot and fish in the wilderness. But game in the woods is not game in camp, and this season it has taken a practical hand at the rifle and rod, and a good guide to feed a camp. There are two reasons why it has been so difficult to get game this season. The first is, because of the peculiar and unusual character of the season itself. It has been a very rainy Summer. The frequent, almost daily, showers and storms have kept the rivers and creeks full, and the water cold, and deer dislike to enter the water under such circumstances. The lily pads, and roots, and river grasses on which they love to feed, were for the most part covered; and hence there was no temptation for them to come down from the mountains. The frequent showers also kept the grass and shrubs in the woods green and juicy, and the deer found succulent feeding without coming to the streams. This unusual state of things would of itself have made the season a dull one for the sportsman. In addition to this, other things have contributed to make hunting in the water-courses and around the larger lakes a difficult matter.

IGNORANT SPORTSMEN.

Hundreds of sportsmen (?) visited the Wilderness this Summer, absolutely ignorant of the first principles of shooting. Some guides found, after making camp, on some lovely point or island, that these "gentlemen couldn't hit a barn door at twenty paces." The first thing for the guides to do, therefore, was to teach these gaily equipped sportsmen how to shoot. A target was arranged, and the novice, for two or three days, was put through a course of rifle practice, at the rate of some 200 shots per day. I lay in my camp on the Racquette this Summer, and for hours together listened to the echoes chasing each other across the lake and along the mountain sides as the rifles of these amateur sportsmen cracked and rung in preparation for the morrow's hunt. From morning till night the guns exploded. In the evening, bonfires and rejoicing enlivened the darkness, in anticipation of coming sport. Now, it is undoubtedly true that such a method has its advantages. It lightens the baggage of surplus lead, and gets the sportsman familiar with his piece. But deer will not stand any such bombardment. After a few days devoted to such preparation for deer-hunting, you have nothing but hunting left. From these two reasons the hunting was poor this Summer on the larger lakes. By striking off from these, and camping on uufrequented [sic] lakes and ponds, many parties had good sport and fair success.

The fishing this season, so far as my experience and observation went, was good. Lake trout were freely taken at the buoys, and with set lines; spotted trout took the fly finely, and the average catch was heavier than usual. For weeks together, a friend of mine, who had never handled a fly rod before this season, kept the camp, numbering with our guides twelve persons, abundantly, indeed lavishly supplied. Some of his catches averaged as high as 15 pounds at a single fishing. I accompanied a certain lady to Nameless Creek—which some persons, who fail to find it, say does not exist—in order that she might enjoy what I experienced when John and I first entered it, and in two hours of fishing, she captured 46 trout, some of which balanced two pounds. Our united catch was 107. We made our first cast at eight a. m., and our last at ten; the rises being as rapid when we unjointed our rods as when we began and the fish being heavier. I did not meet a person, nor have I heard of one at all skilled, who did not have good success with the rod.

I wish to reiterate to sportsmen the opinion I expressed in my book concerning the size and kind of flies best adapted to the Adirondack waters. I tested, with a care and thoroughness few could excel, as great a variety of flies as was ever, as I have reason to believe, taken into the Wilderness; and the suggestions I gave to the public last Spring, were fully verified. I am well aware that many sportsmen ridicule my recommendation of large-sized flies; but another season of honest and painstaking experiment, has served to confirm me in my opinion. My guide is known to many of the sportsmen who visit the woods, as not only a good fly-fisher himself, but as having served for years with some of the very best fishermen in the country; and he coincides entirely with me in this conclusion. If I should ever visit those waters again, and the matter might be pleasantly arranged, I should be pleased, in order that the correctness or incorrectness of my views might be shown, to fish for any number of days side by side with any fisherman who advocates the use of small flies—he using his selection, and I choosing from the list published last Spring.

THE BLACK FLY.

In reference to the "black-fly" question of which so many lugubrious accounts have been given, this should be said. In ordinary seasons the black-fly disappears early in July. June is its legitimate month and with June it disappears. But this year the Spring opened unusually late and the weather continued cold. In fact July was what June commonly is, and the black-fly continued in full force up to August. In my direction to tourists I especially warned not to go in during the month of June, but to delay until the Wilderness has become dry and the black-fly has gone. This season has proved an exception, such as may not occur again for twenty years, and which could not by any prophetic power given to man at the present day, have been foreseen. Visitors have experienced this Summer what those who justly called themselves old Adirondackers never saw before—the black-fly holding on until August, and musketoes and insects, owing to the continual rains, ten fold thicker than was ever known.

On the other hand it is simply just to state that many parties came into the Wilderness wholly unprepared for the excursion. Ladies were dressed as for a promenade along Broadway, or a day's pic-nic in some frequented grove. Many, provided with gloves and nets, refused to don them until the musketoes and flies had set the skin aflame, and then by a free and unrestrained use of their finger-nails upon the inflamed parts soon succeeded in giving an expression to their countenances anything but lovely. Many parties had guides so ignorant of the rivers and the lakes, that they could exercise no discretion in the selection of a camp ground; but pitched their tents in localities where no experienced guide would ever run his boat ashore for ten minutes. In my voyaging around the Wilderness during the last two weeks of my stay, I found scores of camps, some occupied, others deserted, pitched on the margin of sloughs, or within a few rods of a low marsh, where I would not stay over night for all the deer that are in the woods. Here parties had been "dumped down" as John expressed it, by guides too ignorant or lazy to select a proper site, and here they had stayed, men, women and children, tormented by musketoes and gnats, when a few miles further a good guide would have found a camp ground rarely if ever visited by the pests.

HARDSHIPS OF CAMP-LIFE.

Not a little has been written the past Summer concerning the hardships incidental to a visit to the wilderness, and the impossibility of any but very robust persons enduring the necessary fatigue. It has also been asserted in many ways and styles of expression, that the author of the "Adventures in the Wilderness" underrated the difficulty of entering and sojourning in the woods. Now I do not think that many "correspondents" can enlighten me much concerning the amount of effort required to pass from Martin's to almost any accessible point within 60 miles of Lower Saranac, for I have traversed not only once, but many times, most of the water-courses, and backed my boat over nearly every carry across which any intelligent guide would think of taking a party, or indeed of going himself, and now I repeat what I have before said, that ladies, even invalids, granted that they are not in dying condition, can penetrate the wilderness for scores of miles without making any exertion which a healthy child of five years cannot safely and easily put forth; and I will now prove it. I will suggest certain excursions, with the distances noted, so that any intelligent reader can judge for himself as to the correctness of my assertion.

Starting from Martin's, in their boats, a party can pass through the Lower Saranac and Round Lakes to Bartlett's, a distance of some 12 miles. In making those 12 miles, they will only have to walk some 15 rods. From Bartlett's to the Upper Saranac, they must walk from 80 to 100 rods more. Crossing the Upper Saranac to Corry's Landing they come to a carry of a mile, the walking being as good as on a country road. Crossing this they take to their boats again, pass through two small lakes, and down Ramshorn Creek, which brings them to Racquette River. Down this river, which for loveliness of scenery is unsurpassed, without interruption, they journey for 20 miles, which brings them to Big Tupper Lake, six miles in length. On the shores of this lake are many delightful sites for a camp. Here then is an excursion of over 40 miles, with less than a mile and a half's walking in it all. Will any one please point out where the "exaggeration" is here?

Or if they wish to visit the St. Regis Region, they can, when they take their boats at Barlett's carry, on Upper Saranac, pass up that lake to Fish Creek Bay, thence to Big Square Pond—thence to Little Square—thence to Floodwood Lake, without a single carry, a distance, I should judge, from Martin's, of some 30 miles, with only half a mile of walking. Or again, instead of turning down stream, where Ramshorn Creek enters the Racquette, they can turn up stream, and journey, with only a mile and a half of carry, to the southern end of Long Lake, one of the most beautiful lakes in the whole Wilderness, on the shores of which a hundred camps might be pitched, without interfering with each other. Here then they have voyaged southward from Martin's some 50 miles, walking less than two! I might instance further, but the above will serve to show the public, and such as may be in want of information, the real facts in the case, as well as the ease with which the Wilderness can be entered, and rest and health secured.

THE WILDERNESS HEALTH.

Upon no point has more misrepresentation gone forth than concerning the fate of those who visited the Adirondacks in search of health and strength. If "our correspondent" were to be believed, the Wilderness was full of the dead and dying, Martin's was a vast hospital, and the region filled with lamentation. But unfortunately for these sympathetic and indignant writers, facts do not justify the picture. Of the hundreds of invalids who went into the Wilderness, many of them far gone with consumption and kindred diseases, only three died, and one of these, a gentleman in charge of his physician, never lived to reach Martin's. This surely cannot be called a great rate of mortality, considering the circumstances.

Scores of testimonials are before me, from invalids who went into the woods, some of them as a last resort, and who write, expressing their gratitude to me for having directed them to the Wilderness, and their indignation at the false and wicked rumors which have been put in circulation. Physicians, also, who visited the woods to observe the effect of the change upon their patients, add their testimony to that of the convalescent. That the climate is wonderfully adapted to benefit those suffering from dyspepsia, consumption, and kindred complaints, cannot, with the least regard to facts, be denied, and I trust that none of this class will be deterred from testing its strengthening and healing properties, because of the ignorant and grossly exaggerated statements which have been sent out to the contrary. It is not in my power to say who will be benefited, or who should undertake the journey. Upon this point the family physician is the better judge. I mention what I have seen and know, and feel that, with the statement of facts, I have done all that belongs to me to do. I predict that the Wilderness will be more and more frequented by invalids, as accommodations are provided for their reception and comfort, and that the region will become the resort of thousands each year seeking restoration to health.

THE WILDERNESS TREE.°

I know that a certain class of sportsmen are indignant because their sporting has been spoiled and the "woods filled with people." To such I have only to reply that I am glad if the woods are filled with people, and I trust that thousands will visit them yearly. With all legitimate sport I sympathize, both by nature and habit, and would be as quick as any to resent improper interference with it; but I have no sympathy at all with those two or three hundred gentlemen who would selfishly monopolize the Adirondack Wilderness for their own exclusive amusement and benefit. Indeed I do not look at the Wilderness as belonging to sportsmen or any other class; it belongs to the country at large. Its magnificent mountains, its thousand lakes, many of them perfect gems of scenery set in their dark green framework of pine and cedar; the pure, health-giving quality of its atmosphere, the refreshing coolness of its Summer winds, the odor of its lilies, are for all.

Its true worth does not consist in the game that is now there. Every deer may be killed and every trout disappear from its waters, and yet all its intrinsic excellence would remain, and its value to the country be undiminished. We sportsmen can go elsewhere for game; we can go East to the Provinces, or North to the Canadas, or West to the Rocky Mountains. But this wilderness, lying as it does within two days' ride of our great cities, is not for us to selfishly appropriate. It is, and is to be regarded in the future, a place to which not only the artist, and the lover of nature in her grandest aspects; but the business man and the professional man, weary and jaded by months and years of over work, can go and find in its recesses, rest and recuperation for body and mind. There are thou-

° FREE. A typographical error in the original.

sands of men in our cities, clergymen, lawyers, physicians, merchants and bankers—men whose lives are too valuable to the country to be shortened by a day—to whom a month's annual sojourn in this wilderness would bring a renewal of their powers and a vast increase of all their energies. The over-worked student and professor in our colleges, the clerks in our stores, and every young man whose habits or occupation put a heavy strain upon his body and mind, should visit this region; not to sit down in idleness at the hotels along the margin of the Wilderness, but to take a guide and penetrate into its recesses, and by steady, daily work at the oar, and by paddling, build up his body in muscular power, and add to the strength and vigor of his brain. This, as it seems to me, is the true use of the Wilderness, and its value to the country at large.

In this I do not wish to be understood as saying that the sporting facilities of the Wilderness are now, or soon will be exhausted. No matter how many thousands visit the North Woods, years must pass before a good sportsman with a capable guide will find it difficult to feed his camp with venison, while its trout-producing capacity is practically inexhaustible. It sounds queerly to one who knows from actual experience the extent of the Wilderness, to hear people talk about the "Wilderness being overrun," and "crowded with visitors." Why, I know of scores of lakes within two days' journey of my camp on the Racquette (and the Racquette this season was the most frequented of any lake), where a boat never penetrated, and a fly, so far as the best guides know, was never cast. You may put 10,000 people into the Wilderness, and localities can be found where, for the entire Summer through, no face save your guide's shall be seen, and where deer and trout shall be found in lavish abundance. But so long as the public seem inclined to take the assertions of men and women who never saw even the margin of the Wilderness until this year, and who visited only a dozen of its thousand lakes, spending merely two or three weeks in the woods, they must blame no one if they are imposed upon. It is easy for ignorance and selfishness to prefer the charge of exaggeration against a writer, and for a time, by reiteration and persistent defamation of well-informed authority, to cause his testimony to be discredited. But time justifies that which is true, and there are thousands in the country who know that instead of exaggerating the extent, beauty, and health-giving properties of the Wilderness, I have, in no passage of what I have given to the public, painted up to the reality. The more the region is visited, the more will this be acknowledged.

I have now complied with what seemed to be a very general desire on the part of the reading and travelling public, and given as fair and candid a statement as I am able to make of the causes which led to the defamation of the Adirondack Wilderness. The best argument against such as have misrepresented the beauty and health-giving qualities of the region, is found in the fact, that every prominent hotel has already all its rooms engaged for next season by the visitors of this; and other and larger hotels are being rapidly built to meet the demand for accommodation. I predict that the Wilderness is to be the great Summer resort for the class of men I have designated in this letter. Hotels will multiply, cottages will be built along the shores of its lakes, white tents will gleam amid the pines which cover its islands, and hundreds of weary and over-worked men will penetrate the Wilderness to its innermost recesses, and find amid its solitude health and repose. Let no lover of the Wilderness fear that selfishness or ignorance can so blind the eyes of the American people by false and injurious reports that they will not visit and behold for themselves one of the most charming and picturesque sections of our beloved country.

W. H. H. Murray.